BELOW THE SURFACE

BELOW THE SURFACE

The History of Competitive Swimming

JOHN LOHN

ROWMAN & LITTLEFIELD

Lanham • Boulder • New York • London

Published by Rowman & Littlefield
An imprint of The Rowman & Littlefield Publishing Group, Inc.
4501 Forbes Boulevard, Suite 200, Lanham, Maryland 20706
www.rowman.com

6 Tinworth Street, London, SE11 5AL, United Kingdom

British Library Cataloguing in Publication Information Available

Library of Congress Cataloging-in-Publication Data

Names: Lohn, John, 1976– author.
Title: Below the surface : the history of competitive swimming / John Lohn.
Description: Lanham : Rowman & Littlefield, [2021] | Includes
    bibliographical references and index. | Summary: "This book is the first
    complete history of swimming that looks at multiple aspects of the sport,
    including the top swimmers, major moments, controversies, developments,
    innovations, and more. Leading up to the 2020/2021 Olympic Games,
    it is the most up-to-date resource on competitive swimming"— Provided by
    publisher.
Identifiers: LCCN 2020043423 (print) | LCCN 2020043424 (ebook) |
    ISBN 9781538142929 (cloth) | ISBN 9781538142936 (ebook)
Subjects: LCSH: Swimming—History.
Classification: LCC GV836.4 .L63 2021 (print) | LCC GV836.4 (ebook) |
    DDC 797.2/1—dc23
LC record available at https://lccn.loc.gov/2020043423
LC ebook record available at https://lccn.loc.gov/2020043424

CONTENTS

ACKNOWLEDGMENTS

Throughout the process of researching, writing, and editing this book, my family and friends have been endlessly supportive. Then again, endless support is all I have ever known, which makes me an extremely fortunate person.

My wife, Dana, might know the number of hours I sat in the corner of the couch, sifting through my notes, and pecking away at the keyboard. She understood the personal importance of this project and enabled me to focus. Meanwhile, our kids—Taylor, Tiernan, and Tenley—knew dad had work to do, and kindly postponed using me as a jungle gym to a later time.

For as long as I can remember, my mom and dad have been my biggest supporters. No matter my age, they expressed their pride, and regardless if we were speaking in person or chatting on the phone, they always asked how this book was coming along. That interest in my life has always been evident and has meant so much.

The wonderful photographs in this book are courtesy of Peter Bick, a friend who has so generously provided images for each of my books on the sport of swimming. Peter has an innate ability to capture emotion and excitement at such a high level, and to have him contribute his talent to this book is much appreciated.

Finally, thankyou to Tom Robinson and Craig Lord. Tom is a longtime friend who helped educate me about competitive swimming when I was first introduced to it. He patiently answered questions and alerted me to nuances as I grew to understand the finer details of the sport. Meanwhile, it is an honor to call Craig a friend and colleague. Whether at SwimVortex or Swimming World, Craig has valued my opinion and work, and has continued my education of the sport, especially from a historical perspective.

INTRODUCTION

A race to the end of the block. A duel to reach the top of the stairs first. A challenge to see who can jump the farthest. From a young age, life is full of competition and people possess an innate instinct to complete a task faster or more proficiently than an opponent. Competitive swimming can be traced to the simplest of these contests: Who can get to the other side of the pool first?

Really, the hastily organized backyard race isn't too different from what unfolds in an Olympic final. The goal is to beat the guy on the right or the girl on the left. Obviously, the hoopla and pressure of chasing a gold medal on the biggest stage in the world mark vast differences, but the crux of each situation is shared.

Competitive swimming, on an internationally organized level, has been around for more than a century, a part of every Olympiad since the Modern Games debuted in Athens in 1896. Since the sport features more than 100 years of history, it seemed appropriate to generate a book that looked at the various aspects of the past: Legends, historic moments, controversies, and breakthroughs, to name a few of the areas that are examined in the ensuing pages.

Over the course of more than a year, meticulous research was conducted to create an exhaustive cache of content for consideration. It was important to view the sport through a wide lens and place consideration on all generations and angles. Eventually, categories for inclusion were identified and chapters were written, edited, rewritten, and reviewed again.

Given that this book focuses on the history of competitive swimming, certain sections were easy to select. It was a no-brainer for the book to include a section on the sport's legends and some of the most historic moments. Still, wielding an axe was necessary to fit the word-count parameters that were provided. While some categories were eliminated before writing even began, several chapters were written that simply did not make the final cut—at least for this work.

There is no frustration with the fact that some chapters hit the cutting-room floor. Rather, the inability to fit all that was drafted was a reminder of the historical depth of the sport and the sensational stories that have arisen decade after decade. More, the opportunity to conduct the research and further learn from the writing of these eliminated chapters was a bonus, an endeavor that will prove beneficial at another point in time.

Ultimately, there is a deep satisfaction with the content that was chosen, as it covers the most significant athletes, moments, and issues. The chapters that follow celebrate the contributions of men and women, measure the cultural impact, and examine both the brightest and the darkest days.

If this project seems like it places a heavy emphasis on the Olympic Games, that would be an accurate assessment. Although the World Championships have taken on greater significance through the years and the global competition schedule is busier than ever before, the Olympics remain the sport's focal point. If an athlete claims a medal at the quadrennial event, it is a spectacular achievement. If that medal is gold, membership to an ultra-exclusive club is earned. More than one? Consider legendary status attained.

Beyond the Olympic Games' ability to define careers, the four-year buildup and global emphasis on the event generates an abundance of stories. Some are feel-good tales. Others are stories of redemption. Whatever their composition, they attract attention, are frequently retold, and have become part of swimming's historic fabric—far beyond what is produced in non-Olympic years. So, with the Olympics carrying such weight, it only makes sense for this book to feature a high percentage of Olympic-related content.

In presenting the material contained in this book, it is necessary to provide an overview of the sections and an explanation as to why the categories were selected. By taking this approach, clarity can be provided to the process that unfolded. Additionally, smaller introductions can be utilized to set the stage for what will be encountered.

THE LEGENDS

In any sport, the athletes are the most important element. Without them, there would be no competition. And in any sport, a few names—current and from a historical perspective—always stand above the rest. They attract greater attention to their field or court, and swimming is no different. The pool has been home to numerous stars through the years, but a select few are identified as the finest of all time.

For this venture, ten athletes—five men and five women—received their own chapters and had their career accomplishments highlighted. Michael Phelps and Mark Spitz headlined the men's choices, with Johnny Weissmuller, Ian Thorpe, and Matt Biondi rounding out the top five. For the women, current star Katie Ledecky and Tracy Caulkins occupied the top two slots, followed by Krisztina Egerszegi, Janet Evans, and Dawn Fraser.

On the men's side, the first four names were locks. For Biondi, his choice was more complicated, but the three-time Olympian ultimately earned his placement over Hungarian medley star Tamas Darnyi. The nod was based on Biondi's seven-medal showing at the 1988 Olympics in Seoul, a feat that still ranks highly in Games lore.

For the women, the process was more difficult, as Australian legend Shane Gould was left on the outside. Gould received her own chapter in the Historic Moments section for her individual exploits at the 1972 Olympics, but it was the brevity of her career (she retired at 16) that left her sixth in The Legends section.

HISTORIC MOMENTS

Oh, how it was a challenge to choose and exclude for this section! When working with 100-plus years of achievements and barrier-breaking performances, selecting the moments that make the printed pages can be overwhelming. Truthfully, there were times when a chapter was cut and replaced by another, only to have that decision reversed a few hours, days, weeks, or months later. Yes, there was plenty of juggling that took place with this section.

When selecting which moments to include, it was important to weigh several factors. Was there cultural significance, such as Fanny Durack becoming the first female Olympic gold medalist in 1912? Did the moment play a role in a bigger storyline, such as Jason Lezak saving Michael Phelps' eight-gold pursuit at the 2008 Olympics in Beijing?

The moments included are all significant, span more than 100 years, and will not be forgotten. Of the 7 chapters in the section, 4 focus on events that unfolded 40 or more years ago, evidence that this exercise was not limited to what is most fresh in the mind but also included what is most deserving and impactful.

GREATEST RIVALRIES

Rivalries come in varied forms. Some are bitter. Some are cordial. They can endure. They can be short-lived. Some are domestic in nature. Others cross oceans. They can be individual. They can be team oriented. Despite the different versions, all rivalries share something in common: They bring a certain level of excitement.

The clock might be the ultimate dictator in the sport. What it says goes. There is no argument. But the digits that flash onto the scoreboard at the conclusion of a race, indicating the placement of the participants, only tell part of the tale. The story includes a deeper layer, and that is where rivalries play an integral role.

Rivalries are not born. They are made. It is this organic development—built over time—that allows them to lure attention. Fans and journalists alike enjoy down-to-the-wire finishes in which the combatants have previously exchanged barbs and are not on good terms. They appreciate a long-standing duel in which the results have gone back and forth. They love showdowns between countries—especially when political differences add to the drama.

The profiled rivalries certainly possess the characteristics that define the best duels. From the cold nature of the faceoffs between Russian Alexander Popov and American Gary Hall Jr. to the respectful showdowns between Michael Phelps and Ryan Lochte, there is something special about athletes squaring off for bragging rights.

CONTROVERSY REIGNS

Controversy is part of life, disagreements regularly arising between individuals or groups. Sometimes, settlements are reached, and those involved are provided with a sense of satisfaction and closure. Other times, there is no amicable solution to the debate or divisive situation, and one or all parties in the dispute walk away displeased.

Through the years, there have been more than a few controversies in the swimming world, ranging from clashes over races to equipment use to political influence. The common thread among these disputes is their impact on athletes and their pursuits to reach the pinnacle of the sport.

Again, when dealing with more than a century's worth of options, a few fitting entries will not have the opportunity to be included. Nonetheless, the controversies selected are significant to the history of the sport. Examination is given to how local politics affected Rick DeMont and how governmental influence changed the sport—and other sports—in 1980. More, a deep look is taken at the 2008–2009 introduction of tech suits, which fundamentally changed the sport for those two years, and into the future.

BIGGEST UPSETS

The term "freeroll" is used in the poker world to describe a situation in which a player is given a complimentary entry into a tournament and, therefore, has nothing to lose. In this scenario, the player can be more aggressive than usual and take a few risks. If the player is knocked out, there is little concern. Simply, a chance was taken, and it didn't work out.

For decades, underdog stories have been part of the sports world. Fans tend to love a tale in which a longshot, someone who is not expected to emerge victorious, finds a way to knock off the prerace favorite. It is the athletic version of a freeroll. More, an upset is a relatable occurrence that allows Joe Everyone to feel he can compete with—and defeat—the best of the best.

The beauty of upsets is their once-in-a-while frequency. They cannot be predicted or anticipated, and it is this surprising nature that intensifies the excitement level when one is registered. The upset winner is usually shocked, leading to either a raucous or a muted celebration—nothing in between. Meanwhile, the crowd almost always buys into the moment, elevating its noise level and celebrating with enthusiasm.

In this brief section, two of the biggest upsets in Olympic history are reviewed. The first features the U.S. women's improbable defeat of East Germany in the 400 freestyle relay at the 1976 Olympics in Montreal. It was a win that was impossible to foretell, given East Germany's victories in 11 of the first 12 events at those Games.

The second upset that is dissected is Duncan Armstrong's triumph in the 200 freestyle at the 1988 Olympics in Seoul. Ranked 46th in the world, Armstrong beat three world-record holders on the way to gold, an effort that made Armstrong one of the greatest upset stories in Olympic history.

DARK DAYS OF DOPING

The urge to win can be so great in the sports world that cheating is viewed as an acceptable decision—in the eyes of the athletes who choose to cut corners. Corked bats, doctored balls, and sign-stealing have long been dishonest methods utilized in baseball. On the football field, the New England Patriots have been cited for illegally videotaping their opponents, in addition to deflating balls to improve grip and catching ability. The Boston Marathon once had a woman emerge from the crowd, just shy of the finish line, and win the event without having truly completed the race.

But the most familiar form of cheating—regardless of sport—has been the use of performance-enhancing drugs, most notably steroids. They have been detected in the bodies of NFL players. They played a major role in baseball's home-run chases of the 1990s, Mark McGwire, Sammy Sosa, and Barry Bonds all displaying major changes in their physiques on the way to putting up historic statistical seasons. In the pool, doping has been a common practice, sometimes undertaken on an individual basis and sometimes orchestrated on a more widespread basis.

In this section, emphasis is placed on the biggest doping scandals in history. None is more prevalent than the program orchestrated by East Germany from the early 1970s through the late 1980s, when a systematic approach was put in place at the governmental level and enabled East German athletes to dominate. Meanwhile, the sudden emergence of Ireland's Michelle Smith as a robust force in the mid-1990s is examined, along with two stories related to China—the first the sudden rise of the Chinese women in the 1990s and the recent escapades of distance-freestyle star Sun Yang.

A RARITY IN THE SPORT

Look around a pool and a few differences will emerge in the swimmers stroking through the water. Some are taking it easy, moving slowly through their laps. Others are moving at a moderate pace, perhaps as part of a workout program. A handful are moving at a high rate of speed, testing themselves at race pace. The sport offers something for everyone, serving as an enjoyable activity for children and the elderly, as well as all ages in between.

However, the same pool that features variety in the aquatic experience being sought is anything but diverse when it comes to the demographic of the individuals in the water. With a few exceptions, the population of most pools—and most swim teams—is white. It goes hand-in-hand, then, that history reflects few African American swimmers finding international success in a sport that has been part of the Olympic Games since their modern inception in 1896.

This section serves as a celebration of the handful of individuals who have proven that race is not an impediment to swimming success. Enith Brigitha, Anthony Nesty, Anthony Ervin, Cullen Jones, and Simone Manuel have all shown that black swimmers can excel, and they all have done their part to promote change and encourage others from their background to achieve excellence.

GREATEST COACHES

Just as certain athletes are revered, admiration is equally paid to the finest coaches in the sport's history. And just as swimmers excel in different events and distances, coaches find success through a variety of training approaches. The common thread between the elite coaches, however, is the production of Olympic champions and world-record setters, the characteristics that separate good from great.

Of the ten coaches featured in this work, eight hail from the United States, while two are products of Australia. If the breakdown seems uneven from a global perspective, it is worth noting that the United States and Australia sit first and second on the all-time Olympic medals chart by a substantial margin. More, the 553 medals of the United States far outdistance the 188 medals of Australia.

The careers of the coaches who made the Top-10 span more than 100 years, Robert J.H. Kiphuth, the eldest statesman with a debut year of 1918, and the likes of Eddie Reese, Mark Schubert, and Bob Bowman active into the 2021 season. Add up the gold medals won by these coaches' athletes and the number easily ventures into triple digits.

Beyond the number of gold medals collected under the guidance of these men, it would take hours to read out their combined achievements. They all have been head coaches at the Olympic Games and have steered their swimmers to the likes of World Championships, NCAA titles, national championships, and Commonwealth crowns. Except for Bowman, the youngest member of the group and whose day is coming, each of these coaches is a member of the International Swimming Hall of Fame.

Some of the most important innovations in the sport have been contributions from the coaches profiled in this section, including interval training, dryland training, and tapering. Simply, they make up a special group and have made the sport what it is today.

ENJOY

Putting this book together has been a daunting task, requiring countless hours of dedication to provide a comprehensive look at the history of competitive swimming. Yet, it has also been an enjoyable and educational process, and to be able to share dozens of stories with you, the reader, is meaningful.

As you peruse the various chapters and themes that appear in the following chapters, it is hoped that you will enjoy the stories told, that your knowledge of this great sport is expanded, and that your appreciation for the athletes is heightened.

Chapter 1

THE LEGENDS (MEN)

Through the years, only a handful of men have accomplished enough to earn status among the finest the sport has seen. Although Michael Phelps and Mark Spitz top the list, the careers of Johnny Weissmuller, Ian Thorpe and Matt Biondi were spectacular in their own ways.

MICHAEL PHELPS

On the surface, it seemed like a conversation that was glaringly inappropriate. How could a coach, regardless of the talent he has seen, ask for a meeting with an athlete's parents and suggest their 12-year-old son was on a path to the next Olympiad? It made no sense. Based on historical records, it was insanity unleashed.

Had this chat taken place with the parents of a female swimmer, it would have been within the boundaries of sound judgment. It is not uncommon for early-teenage girls to qualify for the Olympic Games and even earn a place on the podium. Hungary's Krisztina Egerszegi won gold as a 14-year-old. Katie Ledecky topped the world as a 15-year-old.

The conversation Bob Bowman scheduled was with the parents of a boy who would be only 15 during the 2000 Olympic Games in Sydney, Australia. And as much potential as Michael Phelps exhibited at a young age, the notion of an Olympic berth was lunacy. Heck, the last time the United States placed a boy as young as Phelps on the Olympic swim team was 1932, when 13-year-old Ralph Flanagan qualified to contest the 1,500-meter freestyle.

Coach Bob Bowman was the man responsible for guiding Michael Phelps to his immense success. Peter H. Bick.

But Bowman saw something special in this phenom that tripped the legend-in-making alarm and, as risky as it may have been, he wisely called for a gathering with Debbie and Fred Phelps. There are several reasons Bowman will one day receive induction into the International Swimming Hall of Fame. One of them is intuition.

"I told them that things are going to change, and they'll never be the same," Bowman said. "I wanted everyone to be ready for 2000. Debbie (Phelps' mom) said, 'Oh, no, not Michael. He's too young.' But I told her, 'What are we going to do to stop it? When he's ready to go, he's got to let it go.'"

There was a good reason why Debbie Phelps flinched at Bowman's forecast. Entering the 1996 United States Olympic Trials, Phelps' sister, Whitney, was a favorite to qualify for the Olympics in the 200 butterfly.

But back injuries hampered her and a sixth-place finish left Phelps unable to qualify for the Atlanta Games.

Although his sister's bad luck caused family heartache, less than two years after the Bowman-initiated summit, the youngest Phelps indeed let go, and for nearly two decades he displayed powers in the water rivaled only by Poseidon. He collected Olympic and world titles by the armful, established world records on four continents, and produced some of the most unbelievable finishes in history.

At the time Bowman held his conference with Phelps' parents, he knew Indianapolis would be the site of his pupil's breakthrough performance. Working with the youngster at the prestigious North Baltimore Aquatic Club, known for its production of Olympic athletes, Bowman witnessed rapid progressions from his charge. The question: Was there enough time to punch a ticket to the Sydney Games?

As Phelps and Bowman arrived at the Indiana University Natatorium, at the time the hub of major competition in the United States, they faced no pressure at a meet recognized as the most pressure-filled on the planet. The United States Olympic Trials are as cutthroat as it gets. Finish first or second in an event and dreams are fulfilled. Finish third or worse and they are crushed. Every quadrennial, in more than one event, the third-place finisher at Trials, and sometimes beyond, has the potential to medal at the Olympic Games, only to be forced to watch from a living-room sofa—if he or she can even stomach watching.

So, as Phelps walked the deck free of stress and largely unknown, the likes of Jenny Thompson and Gary Hall Jr., among other veterans, tried to handle the weight upon their shoulders. Phelps was in the proverbial nothing-to-lose position. If he somehow earned a spot on the Team USA roster for Sydney in the 200-meter butterfly, the Olympic experience would be a bonus for his fledgling career. If he came up short, there was much to look forward to, including the next year's World Championships in Japan and the 2004 Olympics in Athens, where Phelps would still be a teenager.

It turned out Sydney became part of the grand plan.

After advancing through the preliminaries and semifinals of the 200 butterfly, Phelps entered the final chasing what was basically one bid to Sydney. As the world-record holder and silver medalist in the event from the Atlanta Games four years earlier, Tom Malchow had a firm grip on the top spot. Phelps believed that second position belonged to him.

Remaining in touch with the field through the opening three laps, Phelps turned to his exquisite finishing power down the last lap. The ability to close with a flourish would become a Phelps trademark over the years, and Indy served as its debut. Splitting 30.02 for the last 50 meters, Phelps overhauled Jeff Somensatto and finished second to Malchow. The results showed Malchow touching in 1:56.87, with Phelps at 1:57.48 and Somensatto at 1:58.07. So dominant was Phelps over the last lap that he outsplit Malchow and Somensatto by more than a second and a half.

As he prepared to chase gold in Sydney, Malchow was well aware of this up-and-comer and eventual challenger.

"Phelps is awesome," Malchow said. "I might have retired a little sooner with someone like that coming up. He didn't get caught up in the hype, which is a credit to him. He stuck to his game plan. He doesn't know what it means to go to the Olympics and how it's going to change his life. He's going to find out soon."

In Sydney, Phelps wasn't close to the most-discussed teenage male on deck. That role was filled by Australian Ian Thorpe, the 17-year-old freestyle star who won the 400 freestyle and helped his country unseat the United States in the 400 freestyle relay for the first time in Olympic competition. Really, Phelps was able to quietly go about his business Down Under.

As was the case at Trials, Phelps had little trouble qualifying for the final of the 200 butterfly, and his finishing prowess was again on display. As Malchow captured gold, fulfilling his goal of improving a podium step from the prior Olympiad, Phelps finished fifth, a mere .33 out of the bronze-medal position. Given another few meters or even another two weeks of development, the 15-year-old likely would have had a medal draped around his neck.

Despite his narrow medal miss, Phelps put his experience in perspective. He knew bigger days awaited.

"That was a dream," he said. "A medal would have been nice, but I wanted to race at the Olympics, and I did. It was pretty amazing."

Although Phelps enjoyed the moment and his initial Olympic experience, Bowman was busy designing the next steps for his protégé. Never one to plan in small increments, Bowman had a vision for the next quad, or the four-year timeframe leading to the 2004 Olympics in Athens. As far as the 200 fly was concerned, the coach earmarked a major opportunity in early 2001.

Meanwhile, Bowman was also planning the expansion of Phelps' program to include multiple individual events, and for Phelps to become a regular cog on American relays. What this kid showed in Indianapolis and Sydney was just the beginning of a grander spectacle.

"Michael and I left Sydney hungry for more success," Bowman said.

While a fifth-place showing at 15 was respectable, we both knew he was capable of much more. I remember giving him his training set the day after his 200 final, and on the corner of the page, I wrote: "WR Austin." I didn't have to explain it. He already knew it meant world record. His next chance to do it would be in Austin the next (March) at the World Championship Trials. It was a way of refocusing and resetting our goals. Of course, he came through that April with his first world record in the 200 fly. Sydney inspired us to keep working and to really ask what was possible in the sport of swimming.

Confirming his dual role as a clairvoyant and coach, Bowman perfectly predicted Phelps' first world record in Austin. En route to securing a berth to the World Championships, Phelps clocked a time of 1:54.92 to remove Malchow's name from the record book. The effort made Phelps, at 15 years and nine months, the youngest male world-record setter in the sport's history.

A few months later, at the World Championships in Fukuoka, Japan, Phelps took the standard to 1:54.58 and corralled his first world title. What unfolded over the next two years was the complete unveiling of a swimming savant, as Phelps displayed his vast arsenal and set in motion a countdown to Athens.

Between the 2002 and 2003 seasons, Phelps established himself as his sport's Great White Shark, supplanting Thorpe in that role. He was a predator in several events, his 200 fly excellence complemented by world records in the 200 individual medley and 400 individual medley. At the 2003 World Championships, he earned gold medals and set world records in his three prime events and added a silver medal in the 100 butterfly.

Now, with the Athens Games a year away, talk of Phelps matching the seven gold medals of Mark Spitz from the 1972 Olympics intensified. The last time this discussion surfaced was in 1988, when American Matt Biondi contested seven events at the Seoul Olympics. When the meet was over, Biondi had five gold medals, a silver and a bronze, and his effort—at least by some—was considered a failure.

For Phelps, chasing Spitz's seven golds was not going to be an easy challenge, and he also risked the possibility of anything less than seven titles being viewed as a disappointment. Forget the fact that he had additional races to contest and global depth was more impressive than three decades earlier. When someone chases a goal and does not achieve it, the immediate reaction is to judge the pursuit not for what it was but for what it wasn't.

Still, Phelps embraced the challenge—and then some. At the United States Trials in Long Beach, California, Phelps qualified for Athens in six individual events—the 200 freestyle, both butterfly events, both medley disciplines and the 200 backstroke. With duty on three relays, that meant Phelps would attack a nine-event schedule. Ultimately, the 200 backstroke was dropped from the program, setting the stage for eight events in the home of the Olympic Games.

Obviously, Phelps' pursuit garnered significant attention. His sponsor, Speedo, offered a $1 million bonus if he could match Spitz. Meanwhile, former and current legends weighed in on Phelps' odds. Thorpe, for one, doubted whether the feat was doable in the modern age of event specialists and enhanced depth. As for Spitz, he straddled the fence.

"I think Michael is capable of winning seven, just like I was capable of winning seven," Spitz said prior to Athens. "But a lot of things had to happen just right for me. And the U.S. relays were unquestionably stronger in 1972, relative to the competition. I hope he does it. It would be great for the sport and great for Michael. And it's already been great press for me that he's trying."

Although Phelps started strongly in Athens with a world record in the 400 individual medley, it became immediately apparent just how perfectly the stars must align to achieve history. In his next two events, Phelps earned bronze medals. First came the 400 freestyle relay, where the United States was hindered by a poor opening leg by Ian Crocker and never recovered while finishing behind South Africa and the Netherlands.

The second bronze arrived in the 200 freestyle and was far less startling than the relay. By adding the 200 freestyle to his schedule, Phelps made himself vulnerable to defeat. New to Phelps' international program, the 200 freestyle meant dueling with Thorpe and the Netherlands' Pieter van den Hoogenband, and placed Phelps in the unusual role of underdog.

Despite Phelps setting an American record, the 200 freestyle went according to the script, Thorpe getting to the wall ahead of van den Hoogenband to avenge his loss to the Dutchman from the Sydney Games. In winning bronze, Phelps looked at the outcome and the race with wisdom and a sense of history.

"I swam in a field with the two fastest freestylers of all-time and I was right there with them," Phelps said. "I'm extremely happy with that. It's a (personal) best time. It's a new American record. I wanted to race those guys and that's what I did. It was fun."

Through the rest of Athens, Phelps was perfect. He notched solo Olympic crowns in the 200 individual medley, 100 butterfly and 200 butterfly and added relay golds for his contributions in the 800 freestyle relay and 400 medley relay. The eight medals—six of them gold—set an

Olympic record for a single Games, and although some mainstream newspapers and magazines focused on Phelps coming up short of Spitz, knowledgeable fans knew they had witnessed something spectacular.

There was a humanitarian element to the week, too. By winning the 100 butterfly over countryman Ian Crocker with a late rally, Phelps earned the right to handle the fly leg on the U.S. medley relay. But in an act of sportsmanship, Phelps yielded that honor to Crocker and watched the relay unfold from the stands. Because Phelps raced in the prelims of the relay, he was awarded a gold medal after the United States prevailed in the final.

"I feel like it is a huge gift that is difficult to accept, but it makes me want to go out and tear up the pool," Crocker said of Phelps' gracious act. "I'm kind of tearing up, too".

With Athens in the rearview mirror, Phelps returned to training and won world titles in the 200 medley and 200 freestyle in Montreal in 2005. But that year was also marked by Phelps' first public embarrassment, a DUI charge in his native Baltimore. Phelps completed community service for the act, vowed it was a singular mistake, and resumed training under Bowman. In time, the DUI was forgotten, and Phelps was cruising toward his next chance at Spitz's record.

As well prepared as Phelps was for Athens, he revealed himself to be better positioned for Beijing. At the 2007 World Championships in Melbourne, which served as a test run for the 2008 Games, Phelps was untouchable. He won all five of his individual events in convincing fashion,

The ability to focus was one of Michael Phelps's strongest attributes. Peter H. Bick.

four of them producing world records. With two relay victories, his seven gold medals reignited discussion of matching or beating Spitz's standard. The only reason he didn't win eight golds in Melbourne was the disqualification of the United States in the prelims of the 400 medley relay.

It was difficult to pick which event was the standout performance of the week, such was Phelps' dominance. An argument can be made for the 200 freestyle, where Phelps broke Thorpe's world record and became the first man to break the 1:44 barrier. The 200 butterfly deserves a look based on Phelps obliterating the field by three seconds. And a case can be made for the 400 individual medley, in which Phelps broke the world record by more than two seconds despite the event being held on the final day of the meet, and on the heels of 15 races.

"There has been nobody that's been not just as dominant, but as versatile," said USA Swimming National Team director Mark Schubert of Phelps. "His performance this week was the greatest performance of all-time. I don't really look at it by (the five individual) medals, but by the dominance and by the records and the way he handled it from event to event to event. I just didn't notice any weak points. He can do it from behind. He can do it from the front. He can do it when it's close. He can do it when it's not close."

Phelps' achievements in Athens and his showing in Melbourne assured that the road to Beijing would be filled with hype. His face graced magazine and newspaper covers around the world and NBC, the network that owned the Olympic rights in the United States, convinced the International Olympic Committee to hold morning finals in China so Phelps' events could be broadcast in primetime in the United States.

Once in Beijing, Phelps did not disappoint. Over eight days of action, he won eight gold medals and set seven world records. Really, the week had it all. There were a few dominant victories. There were a couple of nail-biters. But in the end, it was everything Phelps and Bowman envisioned, and it went down as one of the greatest performances in sports history.

On two occasions, Phelps' pursuit of the Great Eight appeared sunk. In the 400 freestyle relay, the United States faced a massive deficit against France until anchor Jason Lezak improbably rallied Team USA to victory behind the fastest relay split of all time. A few nights later, Phelps looked beaten by Serbia's Milorad Cavic at the finish of the 100 butterfly, only for the scoreboard to show the American won by the slimmest of margins, 50.58 to 50.59.

As he approached the wall and was clearly trailing Cavic, Phelps opted to take an extra half-stroke, instead of gliding to the finish. The innate decision proved to be a stroke of good fortune, as Cavic's glide left him beaten and in shock. The victory marked the second straight Olympiad in which Phelps pulled off a late rally in the 100 fly and, coupled with Lezak's heroics in the relay, proved that everything had to go right—and did. Phelps was perfect, 8-for-8.

"Everything was accomplished," Phelps said after his Beijing program wrapped up. "I will have the medals forever. Nothing is impossible. With so many people saying it couldn't be done, all it takes is an imagination, and that's something I learned and something that helped me."

Following the Beijing Games, motivation was hard to come by for Phelps. Truthfully, who could blame him? He had delivered the greatest Olympic showing in history and there was nothing left to accomplish. Still, he was sharp enough to set a pair of world records in the butterfly events at the 2009 World Championships and doubled in the fly events at the World Champs in 2011.

At the same time, a few kinks started to show. At the 2011 World Championships, longtime rival Ryan Lochte got the best of Phelps in the 200 freestyle and 200 individual medley. Additionally, Phelps wasn't treating his training with the same dedication he had from Sydney through Beijing. When Phelps didn't want to attend practice, he didn't. Bowman was simply pleased when his pupil walked through the door.

With less-than-optimal training logged as the 2012 Olympic Games in London opened, Phelps and Bowman didn't know what kind of results would be posted. What they did know was the performances would be produced using smoke and mirrors. And after Phelps opened the week with a fourth-place finish in the 400 individual medley, an event won by Lochte, there were questions whether this farewell Olympiad would be a disaster.

As London progressed, Phelps improved, evident in his wins in the 200 individual medley and 100 butterfly. Those victories handed Phelps three-peats in both events, granting him inclusion in a unique club. Prior to Phelps, only Australian Dawn Fraser (100 freestyle; 1956–1964) and Hungarian Krisztina Egerszegi (200 backstroke; 1988–1996) had won an event at three consecutive Olympiads.

However, in the event that jumpstarted Phelps' career, South Africa's Chad Le Clos pulled off a major upset. In a reversal of normalcy, it was Le Clos who picked up the pace in the final strokes and ran down Phelps to win the gold medal in the 200 butterfly. Nonetheless, Phelps was satisfied with six more Olympic medals and the chance to enter retirement.

"I wanted to change the sport and take it to a new level," Phelps said. "That was a goal of mine. If I can say I've done that, then I can say I've done everything I've wanted to do in my career. This sport has done so much for me, and I'll continue to give back as much as I can."

It turned out that Phelps' hiatus would be short-lived, as he made his return to competition in the spring of 2014. But by the fall of that year, Phelps had more important things to worry about than training for the 2016 Olympic Games in Rio de Janeiro. For the second time, Phelps was arrested for DUI, the second charge following a night of drinking and poker at a local casino. During his drive home, Phelps was caught speeding and crossing a double yellow line in Baltimore's Fort McHenry Tunnel. A blood-alcohol test showed Phelps was twice the legal limit to operate a vehicle.

In the days following his second drunk-driving incident, Phelps cut himself off from his family and friends and experienced a handful of moments in which he contemplated suicide. Eventually, those close to him contacted Phelps and convinced him to enter a 45-day treatment program at The Meadows, a rehabilitation facility in Arizona. During his stay, Phelps was forced to confront his struggles, including his addiction to alcohol and his long-strained relationship with his father.

When Phelps left the rehab center, he had a greater appreciation for life and who he was as a person, not just an athlete who captivated the world. Phelps also yearned to compete at the 2016 Olympics and finish his career the proper way, and not via the half-hearted dedication that led him to the 2012 Games in London.

"I wound up uncovering a lot of things about myself that I probably knew, but I didn't want to approach," he said of his time in rehab. "One of them was that for a long time, I saw myself as the athlete that I was, but not as a human being. I would be in sessions with complete strangers who know exactly who I am, but they don't respect me for things I've done, but instead for who I am as a human being. I found myself feeling happier and happier. And in my group, we formed a family. We all wanted to see each other succeed. It was a new experience for me. It was tough. But it was great."

Phelps returned to training with an invigorated love for the sport. But due to his DUI charge, his preparation for Rio had to be adjusted by Bowman. While most of the world's top swimmers used the 2015 World Championships as their final major tune-up for the Olympics, Phelps couldn't compete at Worlds. A suspension by USA Swimming left him ineligible for the qualifying meet, which meant Phelps had to compete in a watered-down version of the United States National Championships during the summer.

Throughout his career, Phelps never had difficulty finding motivation. He would hold onto quotes from his rivals and use them as fuel leading into major competitions. For Nationals, Phelps knew the fastest times in the world in a variety of events and viewed the clock as his primary foe. As he left the meet, Phelps had three world-leading times and was gearing up for Rio.

In Rio, Phelps wasted no time showing he was in peak form. Handling the second leg of the U.S. 400 freestyle relay, Phelps delivered a scintillating split that dictated a special week was on the way. Specifically, it was Phelps' turn at the midway point of his swim that showed he was the Phelps of old. Pushing off the wall, Phelps utilized several powerful dolphin kicks to comfortably pull ahead of the field. With Phelps lifting the relay into first place, the United States went on to capture the gold medal.

In the days that followed, and in front of his wife, Nicole, and son, Boomer, Phelps added gold medals in the 200 individual medley and 200 butterfly and shared the silver medal in the 100 butterfly. There were also triumphs in the 800 freestyle relay and 400 medley relay. Without question, his victory in the 200 butterfly meant the most.

Not only did the 200 fly put Phelps on the international map, the way he was beaten by Le Clos in 2012 had left a sour taste. It didn't help, either, that Le Clos had questioned Phelps' ability to rekindle his past success and tried to intimidate Phelps prior to the semifinals with a shadow-boxing routine. Phelps used the combination of incidents to push him to the top of the medals stand.

"That was the race I really wanted back," Phelps said. "This was the cherry on top that I wanted. I couldn't be any happier with the end of my career."

As Phelps left Rio, there were some—athletes, coaches, and fans—who thought Phelps would come out of retirement a second time and make a run at the 2020 Olympics in Tokyo. But the most decorated Olympian in history made it clear that was not his intention, and even with the Tokyo Games delayed by a year due to the coronavirus, Phelps had no intention to change his mind.

Instead, he placed his emphasis elsewhere. In addition to growing his family to three sons, Phelps has been an advocate for mental health and eliminating the stigma that is sometimes associated with depression. In promoting mental health, Phelps can be seen in television commercials and performing public-speaking engagements around the country.

"When I was in my room and not wanting to talk to anybody for a number of days and not wanting to be alive, I wanted to see what other roads I could take to see if there was help," Phelps said.

Michael Phelps claimed twenty-eight Olympic medals during his career, including twenty-three gold. Peter H. Bick.

> I know (support) is something that changed my life and saved my life and allowed me to be able to be where I am today, enjoying the platform of talking about something that's so important. When I first really opened up about the struggles that I had, obviously I dreamed of being able to get more publicity to this and to really share my journey and have other people share their journeys with me as well. Honestly, I never thought it would be as big as this, but it's been a true dream to be able to watch the growth that mental health has taken, almost being at center stage.

The numbers that define Phelps' career are staggering: Twenty-eight Olympic medals, including twenty-three of the golden variety. Thirty-nine world records, including twenty-nine individual. Eighty-three medals won in international competition, including a record twenty-six World Championships.

The number that cannot be measured is the impact that Phelps had on the sport and its growth, particularly in the United States. As he was setting records and winning gold medals around the world, how many youngsters turned to their parents and said, "I want to be the next Michael Phelps." There will never be a concrete figure, but he surely encouraged growth and sparked dreams.

As the cliché goes, records are made to be broken. But the prospect of another man or woman winning 28 Olympic medals is difficult to fathom.

"This all started and began with one little dream as a kid," Phelps said. "I wanted to try to change the sport of swimming and do something no one else has ever done—and it turned out pretty cool."

MARK SPITZ

He had it all. An eye-catching physique. A calling-card mustache. Bravado. Motivation. Top-tier coaching. And, most important, talent that spanned multiple strokes and distances and had never been previously witnessed. Really, it was simply a matter of when—not if—Mark Spitz would take the throne as the greatest swimmer in history.

It's normal in the sports world for a prodigious youngster to be labeled as a can't-miss star, and Spitz fit that category perfectly. As a 15-year-old, he was a four-time champion at the Maccabiah Games, known as the Jewish Olympics. And as a 17-year-old, world records started to fall to the native of Northern California.

Although Spitz had much to prove on the global stage before he would be awarded icon status, there were plenty of signs that designation was within reach. Perhaps the most telling indicator of what was to come was the analysis of his first coach, Sherm Chavoor. The founder of the Arden Hills Swim Club, Chavoor had an eye for talent, as he pegged not only Spitz but also future gold medalists Debbie Meyer and Mike Burton for stardom.

"He almost lifted himself out of the pool to pass his opponents," Chavoor said of Spitz's impressive skill set. "He has had the ability to do that all his life. It's a natural, inborn talent to extend himself beyond all physical endurance when the time comes. When I saw him do it in that obscure little meet for little kids back in 1960, there was no longer any doubt in my mind. I knew even then that I had a great one."

The ability recognized by Chavoor carried Spitz to national age-group records by the time he was ten, but Spitz's father, Arnold, sought greater guidance as his son entered his teens. During much of Spitz's career, his father was a meddler, regularly making his presence and opinions known during practices and competitions.

When Spitz was 14, his family moved to Santa Clara, California, so he could join the Santa Clara Swim Club and begin working with George Haines. Despite Chavoor's excellent reputation, Arnold Spitz wanted the best coach possible for Mark, and that meant relocating to join the squad of Haines. At Santa Clara, Haines had built the world's finest club, one that was churning out Olympic medalists with regularity. Gold medalists guided by Haines included Don Schollander, Chris von Saltza, Donna de Varona, and Claudia Kolb, among others, and Spitz's father saw Haines as the next critical piece in his son's Olympic puzzle.

The move to Santa Clara brought together two of the greats in the sport. While Spitz was the emerging star, Schollander was the best American to come along since the legendary Johnny Weissmuller, having won four gold medals at the 1964 Olympics in Tokyo. Still going strong on the way to the 1968 Games in Mexico City, Schollander had to practice in an adjacent lane to his heir apparent. Making the setup even more intriguing was the fact that Spitz contested the 100 freestyle and 200 freestyle, Schollander's primary events.

If there was any belief Schollander would become a mentor to Spitz, that possibility was squashed in their early days of being teammates. Privately, Schollander didn't speak kindly of his challenger and, while he was beaten frequently in practice sets by the upstart, he fought furiously to maintain his perch. Publicly, Schollander took the high road.

"I don't associate with Mark because he's 17 and I'm 21," Schollander said. "I generally hang around with guys more my own age. Mark is immature in a lot of ways, but basically he's a pretty good kid."

The shift from Chavoor to Haines paid quick dividends. In June of 1967, Spitz broke the first of his 23 career world records, clocking 4:10.6 in the 400 freestyle to shave a half-second off the previous record, held by East Germany's Frank Wiegand. Prior to Wiegand, Schollander was the world-record holder. Clearly, Spitz had increased the heat on his teammate, but there was still enough of a separation that both excelled at the 1967 edition of the Pan American Games in Winnipeg.

In what was his biggest international meet to date, Spitz won five gold medals at the Pan American Games, his individual crowns in the 100 butterfly and 200 butterfly punctuated by world-record performances. Meanwhile, Schollander emerged on top in the 200 freestyle, which Spitz did not contest. Together, Spitz and Schollander helped the United States to victories in the 400 freestyle relay and 800 freestyle relay.

"I've got my life tied up in this kid," Arnold Spitz said. "There is nothing wrong with parents giving to their children. If people don't like it, the hell with them. There was a point when I pushed him, I guess, but if I hadn't pushed my son he would never have been at Santa Clara. Swimming isn't everything, winning is. Who plays to lose? I'm not out to lose. I never said to him, 'You're second. That's great.' I told him I didn't care about winning age groups. I care for world records."

The effort at the Pan American Games appeared to establish a strong foundation for Spitz heading into the 1968 Olympic campaign. He set another world record in the 100 butterfly on the path to Mexico City and was touted to win as many as six gold medals—three as an individual and three in relay duty. But Spitz's first Olympiad was largely a flop, which is an unusual way to describe a meet in which he exited with four medals.

While Spitz helped both American freestyle relays to the top of the podium, he failed to capture any gold medals in individual action. A bronze medal in the 100 freestyle was a solid result, as it was a developing event on Spitz's slate, but his efforts in the butterfly disciplines were disastrous. In the 100 butterfly, Spitz was beaten by U.S. teammate Doug Russell and forced to settle for the silver medal. In the 200 butterfly, Spitz's world-record status meant nothing as he finished last in the final, nearly eight seconds off his global standard.

There are stories that during the 100 butterfly, Team USA members cheered raucously as Russell defeated Spitz, evidence of their disdain for Spitz's cockiness. Before Mexico City, friction was evident during Santa Clara practices, where Spitz was an outcast and primarily operated in his own circle. From a mental standpoint, he went to Mexico City without the supportive boost that teammates can provide.

"He talked a little too much, but so did some of the other kids," Haines said. "He got a lot of his talking ability from his father. He was fairly cocky, and a lot of the older boys didn't like the idea of being beaten by a young upstart. I think they were at fault, a lot of the older boys on the team, for him not swimming well in the 1968 Olympics."

Arnold Spitz blamed his son's struggles solely on Haines, and for two reasons. In addition to accusing Haines of not controlling the training environment and protecting his son from inside-club negativity, the father suggested his son's schedule was too demanding, his events not spaced out enough to optimize his performances.

In the aftermath of the 1968 Games, the friction with Haines and the Spitz family had grown irreparable. When Spitz refused to compete at the AAU Nationals after returning from a six-gold showing at the 1969 Maccabiah Games, Haines booted Spitz and his younger sister, Nancy, off the Santa Clara team. Spitz's absence from Nationals likely cost Santa Clara the team title and Haines had tired of Spitz's selfishness.

With their ties to the Santa Clara Swim Club severed, the Spitz family moved to Sacramento, where Chavoor was tabbed to coach Spitz's sisters. For Mark, it was off to Indiana University and a collegiate career under Doc Counsilman, like Haines, one of the greatest coaches in the world. As

Spitz prepared to arrive in Bloomington, Counsilman conducted a meeting with his swimmers to make them aware of expectations.

"Mark Spitz is coming to school and I know he has a reputation, but I personally like him, and I want you to give him a chance," Counsilman said. "You know how I feel about guys belittling, browbeating, and picking on an individual. I'm not going to have any of that crap on this team. Not with Mark Spitz, or anybody. I don't tolerate that."

At Indiana, Spitz immediately became the premier performer on the college scene, winning NCAA championships while helping the Hoosiers to four team titles. He also added to his world-record collection, complementing his world marks in the butterfly events with global standards in the 100 freestyle and 200 freestyle. Any hangover from Mexico City had disappeared and the march toward the 1972 Olympic Games in Munich was underway.

Fine-tuning Spitz's strokes and providing him with effective training regimens was the secondary objective of Counsilman, who recognized the need to enhance Spitz's psyche. Counsilman helped Spitz become more confident in who he was as a person, not as a swimmer, and assisted in Spitz's emergence from his former cocoon to become a friendlier person who welcomed more interpersonal connections.

"I've always had a soft spot in my heart for Mark because he's gotten a raw deal," Counsilman said. "When he came to me, his self-image was pretty low, and I felt he didn't have a true picture of himself. He felt very competent athletically, but he didn't think he was very smart because some people had told him he wasn't—and he didn't feel competent socially. Here, though, everybody likes him, and he's gained confidence intellectually and socially."

During his days at Santa Clara, Spitz knew what it was like to walk into practice and be surrounded by Olympic-level athletes. It was the same scenario in Indiana, where Counsilman recruited many of the best prospects in the country. Every day, Spitz could look to the lanes to his left and right and find someone capable of pushing him, Gary Hall and John Kinsella among them.

Spitz had something else fueling his push toward Munich. Although he didn't let the events of Mexico City hinder his progression, he refused to leave that week to history. Rather, Spitz generated motivation from not meeting expectations and used his initial Olympic foray as a learning experience. He wouldn't fold under pressure a second time and would approach the meet in compartmental fashion, going day by day.

"I had a difficult time from the 1968 Olympic Games in Mexico City where I was expected to win a lot of gold medals," Spitz said.

> And if I just look at my performance of winning two gold, a silver and a bronze, I mean that is pretty remarkable. But the problem was, is that I didn't win a gold medal in two events I held a world record in. And that was just the reason that I basically had this fire in my system to be able to want to actually go for another four years. I found it kind of difficult to work out and train. But I had a focus and the focus was to do the best I could.

The Munich Olympics will be remembered for multiple storylines, a mix of uplifting tales and heartache. The tragic deaths of 11 Israeli athletes and team officials at the hands of the terrorist group Black September will forever stain the Olympiad. Yet, what Spitz and Australian teenager Shane Gould pulled off in the pool will stand out from an athletic standpoint.

As Spitz chased seven medals, the 15-year-old Gould set a record for the most individual medals earned in a single games. Winning three gold medals, a silver and a bronze, Gould established a mark that stood until Michael Phelps matched it in 2004 and 2008. Shockingly, it was Gould's only Olympics, as she retired in early 1973 due to the pressure and expectations placed on her.

Spitz wasted little time mining gold in Munich. On the opening day of action, he doubled in the 200 butterfly and 400 freestyle relay, both victories in world-record time. The 200 fly was an emphatic redemption swim for his last-place finish four years earlier. Spitz won the event by more than two seconds over Hall and left no doubt that he was in the finest form of his career.

Triumphs and world records in the 200 freestyle and 100 butterfly followed and put Spitz more than halfway through his demanding program. With each win, Spitz's shoulders relaxed and his confidence grew. Barring a swim for the ages from an opponent, coupled with a subpar performance from Spitz, there was no way he was going to lose.

Spitz's medal ceremony following the 200 freestyle brought controversy. As Spitz stood on the top step of the podium, a pair of Adidas sneakers sat behind him. As Spitz prepared to step down, he picked up the shoes and extended his arms to acknowledge the crowd's applause. The Soviet Union claimed Spitz was advertising for Adidas by raising the shoes and, therefore, violated amateurism bylaws. The International Olympic Committee reviewed the incident and cleared Spitz of any wrongdoing. If he couldn't be beaten in the water, maybe he could be taken down outside of it.

"Each day that I swam and I won a gold medal, it was like one brick shy of a load getting off of the cart," Spitz said. "And so, I felt that I was actually having a better go of it."

An anticipated rout by the United States in the 800 freestyle relay handed Spitz his fifth gold and world record and, for all intents and purposes, left only the 100 freestyle between him and a record seven golds. Although the 100 freestyle was his sixth event of the week, the 400 medley relay on the last day of the meet was a mere formality. So, if Spitz could win the 100 freestyle, he was guaranteed to be perfect—provided Team USA didn't suffer a disqualification.

However, the 100 freestyle was the one time during the week in which Spitz felt a measure of pressure. Having already contested five events, the grind of his program was taking a toll. Additionally, American teammate Jerry Heidenreich was a legitimate threat. For a brief moment, Spitz thought about dropping the event, surmising that going 6-for-6 would be better than capturing six golds and a silver.

Chavoor, who was on the American coaching staff and was coaching Spitz again when he was not at Indiana, let his protégé know he would be deemed a "chicken" if he backed out of the showdown with Heidenreich. Consequently, Spitz forged ahead and used a quick start to build a lead, ultimately holding on for a world record of 51.22, comfortably clear of the 51.65 of Heidenreich. A day later, Spitz handled the butterfly leg on the world-record-setting 400 medley relay.

There it was, seven golds in seven events, and as many world records. It was Olympic history.

"I was exhausted by the time it came to my last individual event," Spitz said. "And I have to say that the last stroke that I took at the Olympic Games, I don't think I could have taken another stroke. I was 100 percent up until the last stroke, and I literally had one drop of gas in my tank at the end of that. So thank goodness it ended."

Spitz's record week in Munich had him splashed on magazine and newspaper covers all over the world, with television giving him equal play. Because professionalism did not exist in the sport, the Olympics marked Spitz's competitive farewell. However, he used his standing to earn money as a motivational speaker.

One must wonder, though, if Spitz could have continued his record-setting ways at the next year's inaugural World Championships, and beyond. If nothing else, he set a bar for others to chase. At the 1988

Nearly a half-century after winning seven gold medals at the 1972 Olympics, Mark Spitz is still revered in the sport. Peter H. Bick.

Olympics, American Matt Biondi raced in seven events and repeatedly heard the comparisons to Spitz. He walked away with five gold medals, a silver, and a bronze.

Sixteen years after Biondi, Phelps made his first run at eight gold medals in a single Olympiad, leaving the 2004 Athens Games with six golds and two bronze. While he set a record for most medals in a single Games, his week was called a failure in some circles because Phelps did not match Spitz's seven wins.

The possibility of Phelps first eclipsing Spitz entered the mind of Phelps' coach, Bob Bowman, during the 2002 United States National Championships. During that meet, where Phelps won both butterfly events and both medley disciplines, the numbers started to add up. It didn't hurt that Phelps was quickly rising in the 200 freestyle, too.

"I thought that Michael could do a lot of stuff, but it was then that I thought about Spitz's record and told myself, 'Wow, he can really do this,' " Bowman said of the 2002 National Championships. "That was in the back of my mind, but I still didn't want to think about seven medals. The way to think about seven medals isn't to talk about it; it's to train. When we left that meet, we knew at the least, that Michael was going to be our Ian Thorpe."

Whether Spitz wanted to see Phelps succeed, or believe he could win seven or more gold medals, was always a question mark. At times, Spitz was gracious and complimentary toward Phelps and his pursuit. Other times, Spitz questioned Phelps' chances to win seven gold medals—or more.

At the 2008 Olympic Games in Beijing, Spitz learned that Phelps indeed was capable. In what has gone down as one of the greatest performances in sports history, and the finest in Olympic lore, Phelps won eight gold medals and set seven world records. The effort is the iconic chapter of a career that saw Phelps win a record 28 Olympic medals, 23 of them of the gold variety.

"Records are always made to be broken no matter what they are," Phelps said.

> Anybody can do anything they set their mind to. I've said it all along. I want to be the first Michael Phelps, not the second Mark Spitz. Never once will I ever downplay his accomplishment and what he did. It's still an amazing feat and will always be an amazing accomplishment in the swimming world and the Olympics. To have something like that to shoot for, it made those days when you were tired and didn't want to be (at practice) and just wanted to go home and sleep, it made those days easier to be able to look at him and say, "I want to do this." It's something that I've wanted to do, and I'm thankful for having him do what he did.

Mark Spitz's name will forever be revered in the sport. For more than 30 years, he held the pinnacle Olympic record, a mark that was—until Phelps' emergence—considered untouchable. While that standard has since been surpassed, Spitz remains a legend, an athlete who wowed millions and never believed there was a limit on what he could accomplish.

At times, Spitz was cocky and didn't connect well with his teammates. But those personality traits are forgotten when his portfolio is revealed. A perfect Olympiad. Twenty-three individual world records. Hall of Fame induction in 1977.

"I set a record that lasted 36 years until Michael Phelps broke it," Spitz said. "It's amazing that I was an inspiration to someone not even born yet to achieve and excel in my sport. That's the greatest accolade I could leave for my sport and the Olympic movement. What is a higher regard?"

JOHNNY WEISSMULLER

The way he is remembered varies from person to person. For as many people who know him as one of the greatest swimmers in history, an equal number remember him for playing the prominent Hollywood role of Tarzan. Either way, Johnny Weissmuller—granted a star on the Hollywood Walk of Fame and induction into the International Swimming Hall of Fame—was revered as one of the twentieth century's most iconic figures.

Many recollections of Weissmuller paint a man running around bare-chested and wearing nothing more than a loin cloth. A cinematic star during the first half of the twentieth century, Weissmuller was the human King of the Jungle, perfecting the Tarzan scream while becoming the most-famed actor to handle the role on the big screen.

Yet, before he went to Tinsel Town, Weissmuller etched his name in the annals of swimming, becoming the biggest star of his time and an Olympic champion. Even today, nearly a century after Weissmuller rode his freestyle stroke to multiple gold medals and numerous world-record performances, he is an easy choice as one of the top-10 swimmers of all time.

Ask anyone with a vast knowledge of swimming about the greatest American men to ever hit the pool and chances are you'll get a six-name list that spans 100 years. The list will include Duke Kahanamoku and Weissmuller as stars of the early years, setting the table for Don Schollander and Mark Spitz and, eventually, Matt Biondi and Michael Phelps.

How Weissmuller came to stardom is a unique story. Like most swim-mers, he was in the water at a young age, instructed by a doctor to start building muscle after dealing with a bout of polio. While Weissmuller was a member of a YMCA team in Chicago, the extent of his talent was not immediately realized.

Coached by William Bachrach, Weissmuller was kept out of the pub-lic eye by his mentor until the finer details of the sport were enhanced. It wasn't until Bachrach was satisfied with Weissmuller's skill and all-around ability that he allowed him to reveal his talent to a wider audience.

"Bachrach kept young Weissmuller under wraps for a year, refining his start and stroke," a *Chicago Tribune* article once stated. "In August 1921, he turned his protege loose to win national championships in the 50-yard and 220-yard distances. He never lost a swimming competition after that."

The unchaining of Weissmuller set in motion what proved to be the most-illustrious career of any swimmer at the time, as Weissmuller went on to set more than 50 world records and win more than 50 national champi-onships. More impressive, his excellence spanned several distances and was not confined to just the freestyle stroke.

Rather than focus on the shortest distances contested at the time, Weissmuller set world records—at one point or another—in the 100, 200,

400, and 800 distances. For good measure, he was a stellar backstroker, even setting a world record in that stroke. Further setting Weissmuller apart was the fact that he was far ahead of his time.

The future film star didn't just establish world records. His global standards endured for years, most notably his marks in the 100 freestyle and 200 freestyle. In the 100 free, Weissmuller was the first man to break the one-minute barrier and held the world record from 1922 to 1934. In the 200 free, he stood as the world-record holder from 1922 to 1935, shaving 11 seconds off the global standard between the first and the last time he set the record.

It was in Olympic competition, however, where Weissmuller excelled greatest and forever made himself a household name. To attain that Olympic glory, Weissmuller first had to pull off one of the greatest bits of deception in sports.

As the 1924 Olympic Games in Paris neared, questions surrounding Weissmuller's American citizenship began to surface, and with good reason. Weissmuller was actually born—according to official records—on June 2, 1904, in the small town of Freidorf, part of Romania. Although he moved to the United States with his parents seven months later, he was not an American citizen.

This fact became an issue leading up to the Paris Games because Weissmuller needed official documentation of his citizenship to secure an American passport, which would enable his travel to the Olympics. For this reason, Weissmuller put into motion a major ruse, one which proved to be successful.

While his father once insisted Weissmuller was born in Chicago, it was later changed to state Weissmuller was born in Windber, a small town in Southwestern Pennsylvania. Indeed, a Weissmuller was born in this town, but it was Johnny's younger brother, Peter. Using this familial connection to his advantage, Weissmuller got hold of baptismal records from St. John Cantius Catholic Church for his brother, Petrus Weissmuller. Inserted between the first and the last name, and in different ink and penmanship, was "John." Weissmuller asserted that this official record was his and it met the needs to allow Weissmuller participation in the 1924 Olympics.

"After satisfying Olympic and government officials of his American citizenship, Weissmuller joined the U.S. team and swam in Paris," stated a 1984 *Sports Illustrated* article on the doubts concerning Weissmuller's citizenship. "He became an instant national hero. It seemed nobody now wanted to raise questions about his citizenship. Claiming Windber as his birthplace not only gave Weissmuller the opportunity to produce 'proof' of his American birth but also provided him with a new hometown, which in later years would welcome him back as its most famous native son."

Weissmuller ran with the deceit for years, even celebrating a day in his honor in Windber in 1950, years after his Olympic exploits. On that day, Weissmuller went as far as to say, "I have always wanted a hometown, and now I have one. This is the biggest thrill I ever had in my life and this includes the events when I won the Olympic titles in 1924 and 1928 and was presented medals by the queen of the Netherlands."

Throughout his life, Weissmuller ensured his secret was well protected. He never told his family of his true birthplace, including his five wives and only son, Johnny Jr., and he told his biographer that he was born in Windber, Pennsylvania. According to the *Sports Illustrated* article, those in Romania who knew the true story of his birth in their homeland did not want to ruin his success, for they were proud of what he achieved.

After Weissmuller died in 1984, his son learned the truth when interviewed about the topic. After the initial shock, he toasted his father to Arlene Mueller of *Sports Illustrated*, "To the old man. He sure could keep a secret."

If there were ever concerns about Weissmuller's accomplishments being stricken due to his trickery, it seems those days have passed. Instead, Weissmuller is revered for his excellence in the pool. With his citizenship issues resolved, Weissmuller went to the 1924 Olympics and won three gold medals. He won individual titles in the 100 freestyle and 400 freestyle and helped the 800 freestyle relay to victory. He added a bronze medal as a member of the American water polo team.

By setting world records in the 100 freestyle, 200 freestyle, and 400 freestyle in 1922, Weissmuller set himself up for Olympic success and headed to Paris with high expectations. His triumph in the 100 freestyle was the marquee win, as Weissmuller prevailed by more than two seconds over Kahanamoku, the Olympic champion in the event in 1912 and 1920, and, had it not been for the cancellation of the 1916 Games due to World War I, a likely three-time Olympic champion. Although Weissmuller had already set world records, his win over Kahanamoku marked the official changing of the guard.

Despite having to unseat the legendary Kahanamoku, who went on to become the "Father of Surfing" by spreading the popularity of that sport, Weissmuller's win in the 100 freestyle proved to be his easiest individual event. In the 400 freestyle, which didn't suit Weissmuller as well as the shorter events, the American engaged in a tight duel with Sweden's Arne

Borg and Australia's Andrew "Boy" Charlton, considered two of the finest distance swimmers in history.

Weissmuller and Borg battled for the lead throughout the race, the Swede in front with 50 meters remaining. Over the last lap, Weissmuller summoned every ounce of his energy to regain the lead from Borg, and to fend off Charlton, who was surging at the finish.

"Much was expected of the meeting of three great champions in this Olympic competition: Johnny Weissmuller, Australia's Boy Charlton and Sweden's Arne Borg," wrote Emile-Georges Drigny, who was responsible for the swimming reports at the 1924 Games. "And indeed, from start to finish, the contest between these true mermen produced an aquatic battle the likes of which we have seldom seen and might never see again."

The winning ways continued for Weissmuller through the 1928 Olympics in Amsterdam, where he repeated as champion of the 100 freestyle and again led the United States to gold in the 800 freestyle relay. When his amateur career ended, Weissmuller was known to have lost only two races, both to Olympic medalist Ludy Langer in the early 1920s.

The dominance exhibited by Weissmuller in Paris and Amsterdam was nothing short of phenomenal and placed him on a pedestal with other sports stars of his era, including Babe Ruth, Bobby Jones, Red Grange, and Bill Tilden. He clearly showed himself to be in another realm than the competition, leaving his foes to compete for the minor medals. A vote of 250 sports journalists named Weissmuller the greatest swimmer of the first half of the twentieth century. It was no surprise when he was inducted as a member of the inaugural class of the International Swimming Hall of Fame in 1965.

Still swimming and working for a bathing suit company two years after the Amsterdam Games, Weissmuller was approached about taking a screen test while in Los Angeles for the upcoming movie, *Tarzan the Ape Man*. He went to MGM Studios for the shoot, along with 150 other men, but never thought the test would work out.

"I had to climb a tree and then run past the camera carrying a girl," he said. "There were 150 actors trying for the part, so after lunch, I took off for Oregon on my next stop for the swimsuit outfit. Somebody called me on the phone and said 'Johnny, you got it.' 'Got what?' 'You're Tarzan.' 'What happened to those other 150 guys?' 'They picked you.'

"So the producer asked me my name and he said it would never go. 'We'll have to shorten it,' he said. 'Weissmuller is too long. It will never go on a marquee.' The director butted in. 'Don't you ever read the papers? This guy is the world's greatest swimmer.' The producer said he only read the trade papers, but okay, I could keep my name and he told the writers, 'put a lot of swimming in the movie, because this guy can swim.' "

"So you see why I owe everything to swimming," Weissmuller said. "It not only made my name, it saved my name. Without swimming, I'd be a nobody. Who ever heard of Jon Weis, marquee or no marquee?"

Weissmuller starred in 12 Tarzan films and enjoyed other roles in movies and television. He was a high-paid star and affirmed himself as that unique person who could close one career and excel at an equally successful level in another.

Still, it was swimming—namely what he achieved in the Olympic Games—which made his vast success a possibility.

"Johnny Weissmuller was the first swimmer to bring the sport into the mainstream with his popularity, especially with his subsequent Tarzan roles," said Bill Mallon, one of the world's foremost Olympic experts.

> He was not just a public persona, however, as he was perhaps the most dominant swimmer of all-time, shattering barriers in several events. The rumors that he was never defeated from the early 1920s onward are not quite true, but his losses to other swimmers were exceedingly rare. In today's era, with many more events and professional swimming, he likely would have competed into the 1930s and maybe approached Michael Phelps' later marks in terms of medals and gold medals won.

IAN THORPE

Two Olympiads. Three World Championships. Sixteen titles and 22 medals earned in global competitions. Thirteen world records. Ian Thorpe accomplished all there was to achieve during his reign as one of the sport's greats, and yet a question persists, as unfair as it might be: How much did the Australian leave on the table?

Athletes owe no explanation on their chosen timeframe to walk away. When they want to go, it is their prerogative, years of grinding—at a level unfathomable to the Average Joe—enough of a payment to make the decision without judgment. Still, when a guy exits at the top of his profession, questions are expected. Why now? Isn't there a little more gas in the tank? Couldn't a little more be added to the legacy?

Few in the sport had a more recognizable profile than Thorpe. Always clad in his black, wrist-to-ankle bodysuit, Thorpe couldn't be missed. His physique wasn't as muscular as some of his foes, but his 6-foot-3 frame and size-17 feet stood out. And then there was his stroke. It was unmistakable beauty, exactly what should go on how-to-swim videos. Every arm movement and kick encompassed the perfect combination of power and grace.

In the rich lore of Australian swimming, it's hard to argue anyone but Thorpe as the No. 1 male performer. Yes, supplemental votes might be cast for distance aces Murray Rose and Kieren Perkins, along with Grant Hackett. But Thorpe is the undisputed Aussie King, and his global standing is somewhere between third and fifth, depending on opinion. While Michael Phelps and Mark Spitz convincingly hold the top spots, Thorpe battles Americans Johnny Weissmuller and Matt Biondi for the third position.

"He's a phenomenon," legendary Aussie coach Don Talbot once said of Thorpe. "I've been around swimming ever since I was a kid, and I have never come across a swimmer like him. We treat him as a normal athlete, but he is different."

It was quickly evident that Thorpe was going to be special. Setting national age-group records from an early age, Thorpe won five events as a 13-year-old at the prestigious Australian Age-Group Championships. He followed a year later by securing a berth at the 1997 Pan Pacific Championships, where he claimed a silver medal in the 400 freestyle.

It was at the 1998 World Championships in Perth, though, where Thorpe launched himself to global fame and embarked on an international career of Hall of Fame status.

Just three months beyond his 15th birthday, Thorpe became the youngest world champion in history by reeling in Hackett, who had beaten him comfortably at the preceding year's Pan Pacific Champs. More than a body length behind Hackett at one point, Thorpe still trailed his mate significantly heading into the final lap. But with each stroke, Thorpe narrowed the gap, until he pulled ahead in the final few meters to prevail in 3:46.29, Hackett touching in 3:46.44.

Thorpe's triumph marked a shift in power with Hackett, whose own Hall of Fame career would be frequently overshadowed by the exploits of his countryman. Although Hackett undoubtedly had his shining moments in the sport, particularly as a repeat Olympic champion in the 1,500 freestyle, Perth officially defined him as Thorpe's sidekick.

"I wasn't too sure if I would be able to do it," Thorpe said of his breakthrough. "I can't get over this. I thought I might have had a chance, but to win a world championship is unbelievable. It's only second to the Olympics. I don't think I'll believe this for a while."

The events of Perth were merely a starting point for Thorpe, who was handed the catchy nickname "The Thorpedo." Considering the way his career launched from his inaugural World Championships, the moniker was more than appropriate. From that point forward, Thorpe sunk holes in the opposition.

As exciting as it was for Thorpe to establish himself as a world champion in his home country, the 1999 Pan Pacific Championships in Sydney provided greater moments. Raised in a suburb of Sydney, Thorpe had the chance to compete in front of a hometown crowd and made the most of the opportunity with gold medals in the 200 freestyle and 400 freestyle, and world records on three successive days.

On the opening day of competition, Thorpe obliterated the world record in the 400 freestyle, clocking 3:41.83 to shave nearly two seconds off the previous standard, set by Aussie legend Kieren Perkins five years earlier. Illustrating how far he had developed in the span of a year, Thorpe beat Hackett by more than four seconds.

There was more to come.

On the second and third days of the meet, Thorpe set world records in the 200 freestyle, first in the semifinals and then in the final, his gold-medal outing a mark of 1:46.00. Simultaneously, Thorpe proved himself a key cog of Australia's relays, as he helped his country to gold in the 400 freestyle relay and 800 freestyle relay.

With the 2000 Olympic Games returning to the Sydney Aquatic Centre the next summer, the hype surrounding Thorpe exploded after Pan Pacs. In addition to becoming one of the faces of a home Olympiad, along with aboriginal track star Cathy Freeman, Thorpe attracted coverage from points all around the globe. Even *Sports Illustrated*, which rarely dabbles in the sport, sent feature-writer extraordinaire Gary Smith to produce an extended piece on the Aussie teen.

If the spotlight seemed bright after Pan Pacs, the bulbs were only going to intensify as the months to the Games passed. And when Thorpe blasted three more world records at the Australian Olympic Trials in May of 2000, the host country—and Sydney in particular—was abuzz.

"I've never seen a better swimmer than him," Talbot said of Thorpe. "He's got a great feel for the water. He makes it look easy. His maturity, that's what you notice. He's 17, but he seems like he's someone in his 30s or 40s. It's almost spooky."

It didn't take long for Thorpe to star at the Sydney Games, thanks to an opening-night schedule that offered up the 17-year-old as the focal point in two events. Jumpstarting his evening was the 400 freestyle and his race against the clock. It's rare in Olympic competition for an outcome to be determined ahead of the race, but the 400 freestyle was a coronation of sorts, and Thorpe indeed thrilled the adoring crowd, which repeatedly chanted his name.

Touching the wall in 3:40.59, good for a world record, Thorpe thumped Italy's Massimiliano Rosolino, the silver medalist, by almost three seconds. Thorpe was subdued in his celebration, as he slowly pumped his fists before sheepishly extending his arm to acknowledge a raucous ovation. The victory was expected for Thorpe, but his reaction was also a combination of relief and the knowledge that additional work remained that evening.

"I was so confused," Thorpe said of his Olympic debut.

> Before the race, it didn't feel like the Olympics. It felt no different. But as soon as I walked out (to the starting blocks), it all hit me. All this emotion inside of me came out when the crowd cheered. To be able to perform in front of my home crowd, in my home country and in my hometown, it was incredible. Thank you, Australia. Thank you, Sydney. Thank you to everyone who had a part in this.

About an hour later, Thorpe was back in the water for an equally important endeavor. In the previous seven Olympiads in which the event was contested, the United States had never lost the 400 freestyle relay. But with Michael Klim and Thorpe bookending the relay for the home country, Australia believed it could end the streak. Meanwhile, the United States had sprint star Gary Hall Jr. serving as its anchor. It was a much-ballyhooed event that lived up to expectations.

Fueled by Klim's world record on the leadoff leg, Australia ended the Americans' reign. While Chris Fydler and Ashley Callus handled the middle legs for the Aussies, Thorpe had to deliver on the anchor leg, and opposite Hall. After Hall built a half-body-length advantage on the first lap of the anchor leg, Thorpe came roaring back over the final 50 meters. Grabbing his second gold of the night, and setting off a national party for the host nation, Thorpe pulled ahead in the final few meters and touched for a world record of 3:13.67, the United States also under the former world record in 3:13.86.

Reacting to a prerace claim by Hall that the United States would "smash them like guitars," the Aussies celebrated by performing an air-guitar riff behind the blocks. For Thorpe, the night cemented his standing as one of his country's greatest athletes of all time.

"It's pretty amazing to be in front of your home crowd," Thorpe said. "I'm so glad I performed well in front of them. It's really a dream come true. I'm on such a high. I really wanted to bring it home for the crowd.

I just had all this emotion inside of me when the crowd cheered when we all walked out."

A pair of titles secured, Thorpe cruised through the next night, comfortably advancing out of the preliminaries and semifinals of the 200 freestyle. But if Thorpe was a lock in the 400 freestyle, that scenario did not apply to the shorter distance. In the semifinal before Thorpe, the Netherlands' Pieter van den Hoogenband broke Thorpe's world record with a time of 1:45.35.

Indeed, the final produced an epic showdown, but instead of Thorpe adding a third gold medal to his collection, van den Hoogenband matched his world record and won by almost a half-second, as Thorpe touched the wall in 1:45.83. Thorpe was in the lead at the 150-meter mark, a position that seemed to assure victory given his finishing power. However, scripts are sometimes ripped to pieces, and that was the case down the last lap.

Van den Hoogenband's triumph was followed later in the week by a gold medal in the 100 freestyle and a bronze medal in the 50 freestyle. But it was the 200 freestyle that stood out from Sydney, the fact that he beat Thorpe on his home soil carrying incredible weight.

"The whole year, when he was down here setting all those world records, I was working hard back home and thinking about the Olympics," van den Hoogenband said. "I don't realize yet what I have achieved. I enjoyed every stroke of it. I wanted to get the best out of this body. I did not want to look at him. Only after I pushed off the last wall did I think, 'I really want the gold medal.' "

When Sydney wrapped up, Thorpe had five medals—three gold and two silver. After the 200 freestyle setback to van den Hoogenband, he helped Australia to gold and a world record in the 800 freestyle relay. He added a silver medal in the 400 medley relay, where he handled the free-style leg during prelims.

Often, the post–Olympic year leads to sabbaticals or scaled-back training, but Thorpe attacked the 2001 season with ferocity, that intensity rewarded at the World Championships. Racing in Fukuoka, Japan, Thorpe put together one the greatest meets in history. It might rank a notch below Phelps' eight gold medals at the 2008 Olympics in Beijing and Spitz's seven golds from the 1972 Munich Games, but Thorpe's week was epic.

Beating van den Hoogenband in the 200 freestyle and Hackett in the 400 freestyle and 800 freestyle, Thorpe set three world records. For good measure, he anchored three winning relays to go 6-for-6.

"This is the most successful meet I've been to. My achievements here have been far greater than anything else I've done," Thorpe said.

I didn't think, coming into the meet, that I'd win six gold medals. I didn't think I was ready at this stage of my career. I have no idea where I am now or where I will go in the future—up or down, faster or slower. I don't know when I'll hit my peak. I may have already reached it, but I really don't know. Nobody will know that until my career's over. I face a lot of challenges now just trying to stay at this level. I have to try and be as consistent as I can.

The path to the next Olympiad in Athens remained smooth for Thorpe, who won seven medals at the 2002 Commonwealth Games and six medals at that same year's Pan Pacific Champs. In both meets, Thorpe won gold in the 100 freestyle, an achievement that demonstrated his distance skills were complemented by sprinting prowess. At the Commonwealth Games, where Thorpe took down his own world record in the 400 freestyle, he also exhibited range to the 100 backstroke in the form of a silver medal.

In his final tune-up for the Athens Games, Thorpe managed his familiar 200 freestyle/400 freestyle double and won bronze in the 100 freestyle at the 2003 World Championships. In the 200 individual medley, the Aussie sought out a race against Phelps. While Thorpe couldn't keep pace as Phelps set a world record, his steadiness over all four strokes generated a silver medal.

Certainly, Thorpe was in good form when Athens rolled around, but it took a sacrifice by an Aussie teammate for Thorpe to defend his crown in the 400 freestyle. At the Australian Olympic Trials, Thorpe lost his balance before the start of the event and tumbled into the water for a false start. With Thorpe disqualified, Hackett and Craig Stevens earned the invitations to the Olympics. Stevens, however, eventually ceded his spot to Thorpe during an announcement that was broadcast on Australian television. Stevens' decision was controversial, as rumors swirled that he was lured by money. Additionally, there was major pressure on Stevens—from fans and journalists—to vacate his slot to a national hero.

"This would have to be the toughest moment of my life, whether to swim an event at an Olympic Games or to look after one of your best mates," Stevens said during his announcement.

There was a lot of stress, and there were a lot of assumptions without me even saying anything, which was very upsetting. There have been a lot of people helping me make the decision, but they've just been showing me the options of either way I go. In the end, it's all just been based on me. The decision I have made has come from the heart, which is always what I have done. That's me. I follow my heart and do what I think is best.

Given a reprieve, Thorpe took to the blocks in Athens and fought off Hackett in what was the best duel of their rivalry. Thorpe narrowly bested his countryman, 3:43.10 to 3:43.36, and repeated as champion of the 400 freestyle. Two nights later, he came out on top again, this time in the Race of the Century.

In the 200 freestyle, Thorpe didn't just face van den Hoogenband in a rematch from Sydney but also had to deal with Phelps, who added the 200 freestyle to his schedule. The race was highly anticipated in the weeks leading up to the Games, thus the nickname given to the event. Van den Hoogenband led at all three turns, but Thorpe—unlike four years earlier—powered away on the last lap and won in 1:44.71, with van den Hoogenband earning silver in 1:45.23 and Phelps claiming bronze in 1:45.32.

Thorpe thrust his arm in the air to celebrate, evidence of his desire for redemption. To that win, he added a bronze medal in the 100 freestyle and a silver medal in the 800 freestyle relay, where he unleashed a spectacular anchor leg, but could not run down the United States' Klete Keller.

"Well, I guess we're even. It was tough," Thorpe said of his win in the 200 freestyle. "But I was able to produce a pretty good performance and I'm ecstatic about the result. I knew (van den Hoogenband) would go out quick and I just wanted to stay with him. I stuck to my plan. It became something that was almost mathematical, where you have no emotion and let your body do what you have trained it to do."

The Athens Games moved Thorpe's Olympic medal count to nine, including five gold, and that is where it remains. It is the highest total among Australians and ranks Thorpe sixth among Olympic male swimmers.

The Thorpedo opted to take off during the 2005 season and while he returned in 2006 and qualified for the Commonwealth Games in the 100 freestyle and 200 freestyle, he swore off the 400 freestyle, which was his signature event.

Australian National Team Coach Alan Thompson tried to convince Thorpe to rethink his decision to give up the eight-lap event but to no avail. Meanwhile, Hackett mourned his rival's absence. Through years of head-to-head races, a deep appreciation for one another emerged.

"If he never swims another 400 again, so be it," Hackett said. "What he has done in that event is second to none. I think he can depart from that race and be totally content. I'd love to see him back there again, but whether we do or don't, we'll have to wait and see. But it's not a nice thought to think that I won't race him again (in the 400). I'll definitely miss that."

Thorpe's plan to focus on the 100 freestyle and 200 freestyle appeared wise when he qualified for the Commonwealth Games, but a bout of glandular fever forced his withdrawal prior to the competition. A move to the United States to train followed his recovery, but by the end of the year, Thorpe announced his retirement, which was not unexpected given his reported lack of focus on his training. Thorpe noted that retirement had been a consideration for some time, but its "safety blanket" sense pushed him to stay active—at least for a while.

Despite being out of the pool, Thorpe was thrust into the headlines during the 2007 World Championships when it was reported a 2006 doping test he gave before his retirement returned abnormal levels of natural-occurring hormones. The Australian Sports Anti-Doping Authority investigated the results and cleared Thorpe of any doping violations.

During the investigation, Thorpe fully cooperated with ASADA and FINA, the sport's international governing body. And while he was found innocent of any wrongdoing, having his name associated with a doping investigation was difficult to accept.

"When something like this happens, you get tarnished with a kind of black spot," Thorpe said. "I didn't know how to react. I was physically shaking. I didn't understand it. It's gut-wrenching. It was at the other end of the spectrum to winning a gold medal."

In his time out of the pool, Thorpe was still consulted for his thoughts. As Phelps prepared for the 2008 Games in Beijing and his second chase of Spitz's seven gold medals, Thorpe didn't hold back. He indicated he didn't believe Phelps could match Spitz's record, let alone win all eight of the events in which he was entered.

Thorpe didn't make his comments haphazardly. As he contemplated Phelps' odds, he considered the fact that Phelps was set to tackle a 17-race schedule and when he faced fresher athletes, he might come up short. He also referenced the greater depth that had developed through the years and the need for a few lucky breaks.

Always one to seek out doubts and use them as motivation, Phelps was keenly aware of Thorpe's comments. Bob Bowman, Phelps' coach, would make his pupil aware of the slights, and Phelps would use clippings as regular reminders of those questioning his prospects.

Of course, when the 2008 Games concluded, Phelps stood alone on the top of Mount Olympus. Behind a pair of stunning victories that preserved his quest, Phelps collected eight gold medals and set seven world records. Thorpe was forced to swallow his words.

"Every day when I'd open that locker, it was the first thing I'd see, that article, Ian's words, dangling there," Phelps said. "Every day when I'd close that locker door, that fluttering piece of paper served as a reminder of the many doubters."

Following a few years of retirement, Thorpe opted for a comeback in 2011, the ultimate goal to qualify for the 2012 Olympic Games in London. At the Olympic Trials, Thorpe advanced to the semifinals of the 200 freestyle before being ousted. The 100 freestyle was a bigger disaster, as Thorpe could not advance beyond the preliminaries.

Thorpe did not abandon his career after his Olympic miss, stating that he hoped to qualify for the 2013 World Championships. But a shoulder injury hindered those prospects and Thorpe faded into retirement for a second time. If nothing else, he was proud of his comeback attempt and willingness to test himself once again.

"Compared to how I have raced before and how I have competed, the success that I have had, this does look like doom compared to it," Thorpe said at the Olympic Trials. "But I'm glad that I was willing to put myself out there. I don't regret giving this a go. I think it's better to attempt something and fail than it is to not even attempt it, so I'm glad that I've been prepared to put myself on the line."

Throughout his career, Thorpe was known for the bodysuit he wore. In the Land Down Under, Speedo has long been the suit-maker of choice, but Thorpe went with Adidas and he made the bodysuit popular before it took off during the suit wars days of 2008 and 2009.

While the suits of the late 2000s were made of rubber and served as a flotation device of sorts, especially in the latter stages of races when fatigue was supposed to take a toll, Thorpe's bodysuit was made of textile fabric and not deemed to provide an advantage anywhere near that of the shiny suits. Still, one legendary coach would have liked to see Thorpe, and others of his era, race in a regular suit to eliminate any doubt concerning assistance.

"Ian Thorpe may be right in claiming that it is 'hard training' rather than (it being down to) high-tech fabrics and various other attached devices which have contributed most to the highest standard of swimming we have yet seen by Australians," said Forbes Carlile. "I shall be convinced that Ian is right when I see more of our top performers racing and setting their times in the attractive brief suits which saw our champions of the recent past make their records. The integrity of swimming as a 'pure sport' is at stake, where we can be sure the swimmer, not the equipment used, determines the winner."

Yes, questions will be framed concerning Thorpe's relatively short career. What if he didn't take that year off in 2005? What if the fire continued to burn? Could he have added to his Olympic medal collection? Obviously, those questions will never be answered.

The answer that is unequivocally known is that Ian Thorpe is a legend, one of the greatest swimmers in history and possibly the finest freestyler of all time. Not surprisingly, he relied on a mental approach that separated him from the rest.

"When I go out and race, I'm not trying to beat opponents," he once said.

> I'm trying to beat what I have done . . . to beat myself, basically. People find that hard to believe because we've had such a bias to always strive to win things. If you win something and you haven't put everything into it, you haven't actually achieved anything at all. When you've had to work hard for something and you've got the best you can out of yourself on that given day, that's where you get satisfaction from.

Surely, the sport got satisfaction from Thorpe.

MATT BIONDI

The scene was the 1984 United States Olympic Trials, held at the iconic Indiana University Natatorium. That year, a tradition was launched inside the Indianapolis venue that called for a calligrapher to script the names of all Olympic qualifiers on the wall behind the diving boards. After the 100-meter freestyle, Matt Biondi watched his name get etched—literally—in history.

Biondi's place on the immortal Indy Wall was the result of his fourth-place finish in the 100 free, a showing that earned the 18-year-old a position on the U.S. 400 freestyle relay. There would be no individual events at the Olympics for Biondi, and it was immediately clear he had to prove his worth to his American teammates.

After securing one of the two individual berths to the Los Angeles Games in the 100 freestyle, eventual Olympic champion Rowdy Gaines allowed his eyes to scan the remainder of the finishing order. When he got to the fourth-place name, he uttered two words that are now infamous in the sport: "Matt who?"

That moment was the last time Biondi was an unknown and able to traverse the aquatic landscape in under-the-radar fashion. By the time the 1984 Olympics were over, Biondi was an Olympic gold medalist, part of a relay triumph over Australia, and the years ahead saw the California native blossom into a superstar over several events.

"When I saw him at the Olympic Trials, I knew he was going to be this country's premier swimmer," legendary coach Mark Schubert said of Biondi in 1987. "I think he is probably the most talented male swimmer to come along since Mark Spitz. He not only has the speed, but he has the endurance."

It's never easy to select a sport's Mount Rushmore, but for American men's swimming, an argument can be made for Biondi to join three athletes who are locks: Michael Phelps, Mark Spitz, and Johnny Weissmuller. If some pundits prefer to include Don Schollander, they would be well within their rights, but Biondi certainly warrants a long, hard look for inclusion.

It didn't take long for Biondi to rise beyond a relay contributor and become one of the world's most-watched Olympic athletes. At the 1985 Pan Pacific Championships in Tokyo, the 6-foot-6 Biondi pulled in a seven-medal haul, headlined by victories in the 50 freestyle and 100 freestyle. From that point forward, he was tabbed as the next American sensation in the pool, and his career would never be the same.

Matt Biondi is best known for winning seven medals at the 1988 Olympics, including five gold. Peter H. Bick.

Generational comparisons have been part of the sports world for decades, fans and journalists always eager to identify the next . . . fill in the blank. Because he raced three of the same events, Biondi was inevitably dubbed the next Spitz, and given the not-so-enviable task of matching the achievements of a guy who produced perfection.

At the 1972 Olympics in Munich, Spitz not only won a record seven gold medals but captured each piece of hardware in world-record time. Never mind the growth in depth the sport had seen in the 16 years since Spitz's greatness. Because Biondi and Spitz shared the 100 freestyle, 200 freestyle, and 100 butterfly as common events, there would be no separating the two. Biondi was the latest American phenom and everything he did was going to be measured against the previous man to hold that title.

"I don't feel it's a fair comparison," said Nort Thornton, Biondi's coach at Cal.

> But people are going to do it. You can't stop them. It is unfortunate people get compared, but that's human nature. The rules have changed, and people can't swim as many events as they were able to in 1972. There are certain comparisons like the speed they both travel through water, but Matt is definitely not Mark. He is his own swimmer. Someday, people will be comparing another young swimmer to Matt. That's the way it works.

While some athletes don't mind the attention and, in some cases revel in it, Biondi didn't fit that mold. He preferred to reside in anonymity, but as his list of accomplishments grew, his ability to go unrecognized waned. Peaceful walks on the Cal campus changed to "that's him" pointing and requests for photographs made simple trips to the grocery store a chore. And of course, as the 1988 Olympics in Seoul crept closer, the glare of the spotlight intensified.

While Biondi flourished at Cal, where he also starred in water polo, what he did in international waters is what drove the headlines and interview requests. He wasn't a one- or two-event wonder but instead excelled in the freestyle and butterfly, his freestyle range stretching from the 50-meter sprint to the 200-meter distance. Making him even more enticing was his presence as a hammer in all three relays, someone the United States could rely on to shut the door on the opposition's chances.

To watch Biondi move through water was to witness near perfection, someone with a unique gift that is God-given and can't be taught. It was Thornton's job to mold that talent, similar to what Doc Counsilman did with Spitz and with what Bob Bowman did with Phelps.

"He was born with all the right tools," Thornton said. "He has an incredible feel for the water. It's hard to describe. It's the same feel a pianist has for the keys and an artist's brush has for the canvas. He is able to sense the water pressure on his hands. He sets his hands at the right pitch, like a propeller on a boat. He is able to pitch his blades at the right angle. A lot of people don't have that awareness."

As much as he yearned for a quiet and undetected lifestyle, Biondi wasn't ignorant of his changing status. He won seven medals at the 1986 World Championships in Madrid, including the title in the 100 freestyle, and he added six medals at the 1987 Pan Pacific Championships. Those efforts, coupled with the 1985 Pan Pacific Champs, marked three consecutive international competitions in which Biondi won at least six medals. And with the Olympic Games next up, there was no way he could fight off the hype that was about to come.

Every Olympiad, a few athletes are identified as showstopping talents, or as part of a riveting saga. For the Seoul Games, Biondi was selected as the guy who could take home a fistful of medals. Meanwhile, the 100-meter dash showdown between American Carl Lewis and Canadian Ben Johnson was recognized as the Games' can't-miss event. Biondi knew he was part of a complicated equation.

"I remember when I was training last year," he said.

> It compared a lot to the movie Rocky. You know, in the beginning he's such a basic person. He sleeps in this old bed. His alarm clock goes off really early in the morning. Well, that's what it was like for me last year. There was no pressure on me at all. The drive to do really well was within myself. But, remember Rocky III? By that movie, he's training and he's got about 150 people watching him, and girls come up and kiss him on the cheek and he's selling T-shirts and everything like that. That's what you can't let yourself get into. This year I still have the pressure within to do well, but unfortunately there's a lot of pressure everywhere else, and that's really changed the game.

Heading to Seoul, the most difficult challenge was the constant comparison to Spitz, and the one question he heard over and over: Can you match the seven gold medals of Spitz from 1972?

While Biondi was preparing to race against the likes of West Germany's Michael Gross and fellow American and rival Tom Jager, he was also racing the ghost of Spitz. There was no escaping that fact, especially with six of their events—three individual and three relays—matching. The only difference in their schedules was Biondi's entry in the 50 freestyle, a new event on the Olympic slate, as opposed to Spitz racing the 200 butterfly.

"When I said, 'Matt who,' little did I know he would become one of the greatest swimmers in history," Gaines said. "I always say I came along during a perfect time in history, post-Spitz and pre-Biondi. Matt had tremendous pressure put on him in 1988 because Spitz was still fresh in the minds of many Americans from what he accomplished 16 years earlier. He was a couple of tenths here or there from matching Mark. The guy was an amazing human specimen physically, but he was also a kind, gentle person outside of the water."

Biondi was a focal point of NBC's coverage of the Seoul Games, and he agreed to produce a regular diary for *Sports Illustrated*. Both media outlets were hoping for a replication of Spitz's achievements, which surely would have driven television ratings and magazine sales. But the possibility of that scenario unfolding quickly vanished.

The first event of Biondi's second Olympiad was, inarguably, the most difficult challenge on his schedule. Although he had a successful past in the 200 freestyle and was the American record holder, the race pushed Biondi to his maximum distance. So, when he earned the bronze medal behind Australian Duncan Armstrong and Sweden's Anders Holmertz, Biondi was satisfied with the performance, even if NBC Olympics host Bob Costas made it sound otherwise, noting the American "had to settle for the bronze," and would not have the chance to match Spitz's seven-gold haul from Munich.

Costas' assessment was equal parts ignorance about the intricacies of the sport and the unreasonable expectations placed on Biondi to equal what Spitz accomplished. For his part, Biondi gracefully accepted the outcome, paying plaudits to his foes and expressing his gratitude for standing on an Olympic podium for the first time in an individual event.

Two nights later, however, Biondi found himself in a far less accepting mood. In the final of the 100 butterfly, in which he was a co-favorite with Gross, Biondi led the field for 99 meters, only to be caught in the final stroke by Suriname's Anthony Nesty. In becoming the first Olympic champion from his country in any sport, Nesty posted a time of 53.00, clipping Biondi's mark of 53.01 by the slimmest of margins.

This time around, Biondi wore a look of disappointment and frustration, knowing he yielded a massive lead and lost out on gold due to a late error. As Biondi approached the wall, he found himself in between strokes and had to make a call: Glide to the wall or take a quick, short stroke. Biondi opted for the glide and when Nesty nailed his finish, Biondi was 0-for-2 in his quests for gold.

"I fouled up," he said. "I'd do anything to do it over again, but I can't. Maybe if I had grown my fingernails a little bit longer or kicked a little harder, I would have won. The wall came up at an odd time, at mid-stroke. I was caught halfway through a stroke and had to decide whether to take another stroke or kick in. I decided to kick to the wall."

As much as Biondi was angered over the outcome of the 100 butterfly, the setback may have served as fuel for his second race of the night. As the anchor of the 800 freestyle relay, Biondi delivered the fastest split in history (1:46.44) to rally Team USA past East Germany and to a world record of 7:12.51. Teaming with Troy Dalbey, Matt Cetlinski, and Doug Gjertsen, Biondi outsplit East German anchor Steffen Zesner by 1.99 seconds to register a come-from-behind victory. More, the leg generated momentum for Biondi, who turned out to be untouchable for the remainder of the meet.

The next two nights, Biondi added gold medals in the 100 freestyle and as a member of the 400 freestyle relay, with the final two evenings bringing gold medals in the 50 freestyle and as part of the 400 medley relay. After opening the week with a pair of minor medals, Biondi finished his Seoul sojourn on a five-gold streak, making him just the second swimmer—along with Spitz—to collect seven medals in a single Olympiad.

"To think of Seoul, I was able to distinguish myself not just in America, but as a great Olympian. That was my high-water mark," Biondi said. "That was a peak year. It's hard to think about it. Like other people, I'm a guy who will burn a bagel in the toaster, but I got to take that trail. It's kind of amazing."

The 50 freestyle was the standout performance of the week for Biondi, who set a world record of 22.14 on the way to gold and took down Jager, his longtime nemesis. For years, from collegiate to national to international competition, Biondi and Jager frequently dueled in the 50 free and 100 free, but it was the one-lap event, that pure test of speed, in which they engaged in numerous showdowns.

Between 1986 and 1992, Biondi and Jager appeared together on the podium at five international competitions. At the 1986 and 1991 World Championships, it was Jager who got the best of Biondi, which was also the case at the 1987 Pan Pacific Championships. For Biondi, his lone international gold ahead of Jager was in Seoul, although he won silver to Jager's bronze at the 1992 Olympics, where Russia's Alexander Popov won gold and took over the sprinting throne.

As is the case when any event is added to the schedule, it took a few years for the 50 free to become respected, and not just a circus discipline of flailing arms and legs. The fact that Biondi and Jager dedicated themselves to the event from the start enhanced its importance and made it more than a novelty.

"The 50 is psychological warfare. It leaves no room for error. It's an event of nerves, pressure and precision," Jager said. "If Matt hadn't swum the 50 these last few years, people wouldn't be giving me much respect now. Matt made the event respectable because he's such a great swimmer at other distances. Beating him means something."

After taking some time away after the Seoul Games, Biondi was back in form at the 1991 World Championships, supporting his runner-up finish to Jager in the 50 free with a world title in the 100 free. He also powered two American relays to the top of the medals podium. A year later, at the 1992 Olympics, Biondi added gold medals in two relays and raised his career total to 11 medals over three Olympiads.

A 1997 inductee into the International Swimming Hall of Fame, Biondi distanced himself from swimming shortly after his retirement and moved to Hawaii, where he embarked on a teaching career. In 2012, though, he returned to the United States mainland and joined the faculty of the Sierra Canyon School in Los Angeles while becoming the school's swim coach.

Biondi's stint at Sierra Canyon allowed him to continue a passion—giving back. During his career, and beyond elevating the presence of the 50 freestyle, Biondi sought ways to improve the sport for his fellow athletes. Together, he and Jager fought for more financial benefits for postgraduate swimmers, such as prize money, made-for-television match races, and increased stipends and support from national federations. In 2019, Biondi again took up the fight for improved financial opportunities for swimmers, as he was named the director of the International Swimmers' Alliance. With Biondi as the head of the organization, the goal is for swimmers to receive better pay and compete at a greater number of events that will reward them for their presence and performance.

Although Biondi is again active in the sport, albeit in a deckside position, he will always be remembered for what he achieved in the water.

"I always dream in the future," Biondi once said. "I think about the Olympics a lot, mostly when I'm walking between classes or home from swim practice. I run through a race in my mind, as if it's really happening. In that respect, I'm a dreamer. I'm like a little kid who thinks about being an astronaut and going to the moon."

He reached his goal—and more.

Chapter 2

THE LEGENDS (WOMEN)

Deciding the greatest female swimmer in history is a more difficult task than identifying the premier male. Still, the contenders are fairly obvious: Katie Ledecky, Tracy Caulkins, Krisztina Egerszegi, Janet Evans and Dawn Fraser.

KATIE LEDECKY

The scene was the 2012 Olympic Games, inside the London Aquatics Center. As Great Britain's Rebecca Adlington was introduced and made her way to the starting block in Lane Four for the 800-meter freestyle, the fans inside the venue—including the Duke and Duchess of Cambridge—erupted in applause and cheers. It was one of the loudest ovations of the week.

Four years earlier, Adlington won a pair of Olympic titles—the 400 freestyle and 800 freestyle—in Beijing, and now with the Games in her backyard, citizens of the United Kingdom yearned for a repeat in the longer distance on home soil. The pressure on Adlington was obviously immense, but she had become a sporting star and the way she was greeted during introductions was hardly a surprise and was an appreciation of her skills.

Just before Adlington walked onto the deck, much more mild applause welcomed 15-year-old Katie Ledecky to the deck. A slight grin on her face, Ledecky quickly sauntered to Lane Three, ready to compete in her first Olympic final. If she was a gold-medal contender, few of the spectators knew it. They were transfixed on Adlington, and Ledecky was an afterthought. A little more than eight minutes later, everything was different.

"I didn't know much about her, to be honest," Adlington said. "Going into the Olympics, the [Americans' top] story was Kate Ziegler making a comeback. [Ledecky] was so, so young. She had never faced this sort of competition. She'd never been to the World Championships. I knew next to nothing about her. She came into the heats and it was like, 'Wow, this girl is good.' My coach [Bill Furniss] pointed her out, but we knew nothing about how she raced."

They quickly learned.

Of the 16 laps in the 800 freestyle, Ledecky failed to lead for one. And by the time she took command permanently on the third lap, thanks to a surge that would become a trademark, it was clear the race was over. At an age when most teenagers are thinking about obtaining their driver's license or planning sleepovers with friends, Ledecky began to etch her legacy as the greatest distance freestyler in history and, in many books, the greatest female swimmer the sport has seen.

When Ledecky touched the wall, her time of 8:14.63 was just a half-second off the world record set by Adlington in Beijing and broke the 23-year-old American record of Janet Evans by more than a second. Meanwhile, silver medalist Mireia Belmonte of Spain was more than four seconds behind, with Adlington almost six seconds adrift in the bronze-medal position.

Katie Ledecky has redefined the distance-freestyle events, posting times never believed possible. Peter H. Bick.

"I gave it my all, but I knew I had nothing left in my tank," Adlington said.

> I knew the way the race was going, I couldn't crawl [Ledecky] back. I knew I couldn't hang on to her. Her feet kept getting further and further away from me. I thought, "She's gone." I thought she was getting my world record. It was so amazing. She was so switched on—not fazed by anything. And she was so lovely. After the race, she was so happy. I could tell how passionate she was for the sport. I definitely thought, "This is not the only time we're going to see this girl."

Adlington couldn't have been more accurate. What Ledecky showed in London was just the start, the opening scene in what has been a show-stopping career. Still, she was not yet the headliner for USA Swimming, as that role was occupied by Missy Franklin, who won five medals at the London Games and followed with six gold medals at the 2013 World Championships in Barcelona.

But even as Franklin reigned in 2013, Ledecky made a move to provide USA Swimming with No. 1 and No. 1A performers. Although Franklin was still the biggest name, Ledecky won the 400 freestyle, 800 freestyle, and 1,500 freestyle in Barcelona, the longer two events in world-record time, and cemented her status as a distance queen in development.

"I just tried to stay patient the whole week and focus on each of my races one at a time," Ledecky said. "I exceeded all expectations I had going into the meet."

The 1500 freestyle in Barcelona served as a clear indicator of Ledecky's unmatched talent. Entering the final, the world record for 30 laps stood at 15:42.54, posted by Ziegler in the summer of 2007. En route to the silver medal, Denmark's Lotte Friis beat Ziegler's standard by three-plus seconds. The problem? Ledecky was a further two seconds clear of Friis.

As Friis and the competition exited the pool in Barcelona, the writing was on the wall, and the Dane knew it. Her encounter with the brutal truth was only reinforced on the way to the Olympics in Rio de Janeiro.

"If Katie does what she has been doing the past four years, we are all swimming for second and third place," Friis said.

Outrageous expectations have been the norm for Ledecky, who is almost second-guessed when she does not challenge a world record. At the 2014 Pan Pacific Championships in Australia, she swept the 200 freestyle, 400 free, 800 free, and 1,500 free, completing The Quad for the first time in international waters. More, with Franklin hampered by back and shoulder injuries, she started to solely carry the banner for USA Swimming.

At the 2015 World Champs in Kazan, Russia, she pulled off The Quad for the first time against a whole-world field and set the stage for her second Olympiad. At the 2016 Games, Ledecky planned to chase gold medals in the 200 freestyle, 400 free, and 800 free, a feat pulled off by American teenager Debbie Meyer at the 1968 Olympics. No one else—man or woman—had been able to replicate the effort or win three freestyle crowns of any distance in a single Olympiad. Ledecky knew she could pull it off.

"I've seen Michael win eight medals in Beijing. That was hard-fought," said Frank Busch, USA Swimming's National team director, of Ledecky's quadruple. "I'm sure he'd be the first one to say Katie's a freak. She's a freak of nature in what she's done".

The emergence of Ledecky allowed Meyer to return to the spotlight nearly five decades after the end of her competitive career. Not only did she appreciate a distance swimmer who was willing to challenge herself and set herself apart from the pack in the way she did, but Meyer loved Ledecky's style, a take-no-prisoners approach that dared the rest of the field to go with her and, more difficult, keep up.

"She reminds me so much of me 48 years ago," Meyer said of Ledecky. "It brings back so many wonderful memories of when I was swimming, things that this old brain has forgotten. I love watching her

An attacking mentality has been a trademark of Katie Ledecky during her races. Peter H. Bick.

swim, absolutely love it. I love seeing that drive. I love seeing the way she attacks things. The way she swims is very much the way I tried to swim."

A 16-year-old at the 1968 Olympic Games, Meyer and her fellow competitors across all sports had to deal with the high altitude of Mexico City, which sits 7,300 feet above sea level. But because Meyer was an asthmatic, she was accustomed to working through breathing problems and may have had a built-in advantage. More, she was experienced on the international stage, having won a pair of gold medals at the 1967 Pan American Games.

Like the American teen who would follow her path nearly a half-century later, Meyer was considered untouchable in the 400 freestyle and 800 freestyle, and she proved those predictions accurate when she won the events in dominant fashion. While Meyer prevailed in the 400 freestyle by nearly four seconds, she won the 800 free by a staggering 11 seconds.

In keeping with the Ledecky parallel, Meyer's toughest chore was securing the gold medal in the 200 freestyle. Leading a podium sweep for the United States, Meyer got to the wall a half-second quicker than Jan Henne. The totality of what Meyer achieved was not lost on experts within the sport, including her coach, Sherm Chavoor.

"I still get goose bumps when I think about it," Chavoor once said. "She was a hell of an athlete. She was in a class by herself."

Ledecky can make the same claim.

In Rio, Ledecky had the luxury of sharing the spotlight with several teammates who were major storylines, none more obvious than Michael Phelps, who was in his fifth Olympics and on the way to raising his career total to 28 medals. But when she walked onto the deck, all eyes shot in her direction and anything less than a win would not suffice.

Ledecky was able to get her second Olympiad off to a sterling start, as she routed the field in the 400 freestyle on the second day of competition. Producing a world record of 3:56.46, the American registered a victory of almost five seconds over Great Britain's Jazz Carlin. That quickly, her pursuit of Meyer was going full force, although the chase encountered its biggest hurdle with the second of Ledecky's individual events.

In addition to the 200 freestyle being a sprint for Ledecky, the field was among the deepest of the Games. Also in the pool were Swedish star Sarah Sjostrom, Australian standout Emma McKeon, and Italian Federica Pellegrini, the 2008 Olympic champion. Ledecky was unfazed by her challengers and instead of relying on her closing speed, she had the lead for good by the end of the third lap. Ledecky touched in 1:53.73 for gold, Sjostrom (1:54.08) and McKeon (1:54.92) taking silver and bronze.

Ledecky's win in the 200 freestyle, coupled with her earlier triumph in the 400 free, made her equaling of Meyer a formality. Once the 800 free commenced, Ledecky was in total control. She set a world record of 8:04.79 to beat Carlin by more than 11 seconds and took her place in the annals of the sport.

"This is the end of a four-year journey," Ledecky said. "The Olympics are the pinnacle of our sport, and I have to wait another four years to have that moment, so I just wanted to enjoy it. The memories mean more than the medals to me. I hit all my goals right on the nose this week. I'm proud to be part of history."

For all Ledecky had shown in the lead-up to the 2016 Games, from multiple world records to superb range, there was still reason to doubt if she could match Meyer. After all, the sport had grown significantly deeper since Meyer raced, with some athletes targeting just one or two events to preserve energy and enhance their chances of emerging on top.

Even Phelps, the greatest athlete the sport has seen, has not been immune to increased depth. At the 2012 Games, Phelps suffered a surprise loss to South African Chad Le Clos in the 200 butterfly, along with posting a fourth-place finish in the 400 individual medley. Ledecky, though, found a way to navigate her schedule unscathed.

As a follow-up to Rio, Ledecky kept the heat on at the 2017 World Championships in Budapest, where she again won the 400 free, 800 free, and 1,500 free, but tied for silver in the 200 free. In 2019, however, the World Champs proved to be a struggle. Dealing with a severe stomach virus, Ledecky won the silver medal in the 400 freestyle, defeated by Australian rising star Ariarne Titmus, and was forced to withdraw from both the 200 free and the 1,500 free. Yet, she recovered enough by the end of the meet to earn a fourth straight gold medal in the 800 freestyle, her performance among the gutsiest of the week.

"It surprises me a little bit," Meyer said of Ledecky's ability to win a range of events in an era of greater depth.

> Swimmers today are so particular about what events they swim, and very rarely do you see a swimmer go from the 1500 down to the 200, and to see that surprises me. But when I look at who's doing it, it doesn't surprise me, either. I see her desire and her ability to be able to change speed when she swims, to change tempo. You can see it in her stroke. It's very minute, but somebody that knows swimming can see it. Your average person that watches the TV doesn't see a change.

Following her success in Mexico City, Meyer had every intention of pursing additional medals at the 1972 Olympics in Munich. After setting a world record during the 1969 season in the 1,500 freestyle, she followed with a global standard in the 400 freestyle in 1970. At the same time, Shane Gould was emerging as a force, and showdowns between Meyer and the rising Australian star were much anticipated.

Yet, at the beginning of 1972 and with the Munich Games just eight months away, Meyer decided to walk away from the sport. The 15-year-old Gould went on to shine in her lone Olympiad, winning five individual medals, including three gold. But like Meyer, she also exited the pool prematurely, choosing to retire in early 1973.

"At first I wanted to repeat in the 200, 400 and 800," she said.

> But I made up my mind to quit on Jan. 8, 1972. The practices weren't fun anymore and had become drudgery. I knew the time had come for me to hang up my suit. My times were still competitive, but I can't say how I might have done. There was a lot more competition in 1972. East Germany was just picking up and there was Shane Gould from Australia.

"I don't think there's any one thing (which stands out about my career). I think just the total package," Meyer said. "I loved every minute of it, even the days when I hated working out. I've had great memories. I just hope I can keep them fresh."

In Ledecky, Meyer found the perfect answer to keeping those memories alive, and her insight was frequently sought by journalists as Ledecky prepared for the 2016 Games. More, Meyer struck up a friendship with the Ledecky family and was in regular communication with Ledecky's mother, Mary Gen, during the Rio Games.

The difference between the cross-generational stars is Ledecky's decision to follow her Olympic triple with additional Olympic appearances. And with the International Olympic Committee adding the 1,500 freestyle to the schedule for women for the first time when the Tokyo Games are held in 2021, following a one-year postponement due to the coronavirus, Ledecky's racing slate will more resemble what she has encountered at the World Championships than what she has faced at the Olympic Games.

As aggressive as Ledecky is in the water, her deckside personality is altogether different. Ledecky is generally soft-spoken, gracious, and measured. Really, her eloquence runs in contrast to the woman who seemingly crushes her rivals' spirits within seconds of a race's start. Among her teammates, past and present, she is appreciated.

"Katie Ledecky is the student who takes 20 credits a semester at Harvard and gets a 4.0 every semester—and nobody likes that person," said two-time Olympic medalist Elizabeth Beisel. "But everybody loves Katie Ledecky. You just love to love Katie."

In her early twenties, Ledecky obviously has many more opportunities to bolster her impressive resume. Yet, she already ranks among the greatest female performers the sport has seen, alongside the likes of Tracy Caulkins, Janet Evans, Krisztina Egerszegi, and Dawn Fraser.

Regardless of her legacy, Ledecky has no plans to reflect on her status. Instead, she will rely on the traits that have helped her succeed.

"What I've done over the past couple years has been pretty great, but even that doesn't define my swimming," she said. "Working hard and doing everything I can to be successful should be my identity."

TRACY CAULKINS

The event didn't matter. Neither did the distance. If Tracy Caulkins was behind the blocks, preparing to race, she was a contender. It's not unusual for an athlete in the sport to stretch out into a range of events. Americans Michael Phelps and Ryan Lochte are the most recent examples of multi-event superstars. Count Hungarian Katinka Hosszu in that category, too.

But Caulkins was at another level when it came to her widespread skill set. From competition to competition, she could change her schedule—even alter it heavily—and still earn a bevy of medals against premier opposition, including those specializing in specific disciplines. The word "weakness" did not apply to the woman who surged onto the global scene in the late 1970s and left in the middle of the next decade as a legend.

For three decades, Caulkins was widely regarded as the premier female swimmer in history, her versatility putting her over the top in the debate, which also featured Hungarian Krisztina Egerszegi, American Janet Evans, and Australian Dawn Fraser. If an argument was made for one of the other contenders, versatility usually swayed the discussion in favor of Caulkins.

These days, active distance star Katie Ledecky is the consensus choice as the female GOAT [Greatest of All-Time], largely due to her epic world records, world-champion status at all freestyle distances from 200 through 1,500 meters, and her Olympic champion's identity in the 200 free, 400 free, and 800 free. But Caulkins isn't easily dismissed from the argument for the No. 1 spot. How could she be?

During her career, Caulkins set at least one American record in every stroke—freestyle, backstroke, breaststroke, butterfly, and the individual medley. That range was never previously approached and hasn't been sniffed in the years since her retirement. Simply, Caulkins was a

Swiss-Army knife in the pool, capable of excelling not only in multiple strokes but over a variety of distances.

"It became pretty clear to me at a young age that I would be a very good individual medley swimmer," Caulkins said. "I didn't really have a weakness, and if I had one, I was still quite competitive in it. It was also motivating because it let me choose (different strokes) and there was no monotony in my training. I was [proud] to be successful in a variety of strokes and that was something that kept me going for quite a while."

Born in Minnesota, Caulkins and her family relocated to Nashville, Tennessee, just before Caulkins began first grade. It was in Nashville, and under the direction of Paul Bergen, where Caulkins became a star. While she wasn't a significant factor at the 1976 Olympic Trials, her mere presence as a 13-year-old suggested she possessed a bright future. It wasn't long until her potential truly bloomed.

After setting American records in the short-course version of the 200 individual medley and 400 individual medley in 1977, Caulkins put on a dazzling display at the 1978 World Championships in Berlin. In what was a precursor to the 1980 Olympic Games in Moscow, Caulkins left her first global competition with five gold medals and a silver medal. Individually, she claimed victories in the 200 butterfly, 200 medley, and 400 medley, all in world-record time, and added a silver medal in the 100 breaststroke.

Caulkins' effort brought to fruition the belief by Bergen that she could be a special performer, perhaps one of the finest ever. As he worked with Caulkins, Bergen recognized her innate feel for the water and natural ability to make adjustments.

"I suggested that with her ability, she had a chance to be a great swimmer," Bergen said. "She was comfortable in the water. She was equally at ease at any stroke. Some kids don't like it when you turn them upside down, or right-side up. She was perceptive. She was able to focus on what she had to know to get better. Until we had video tape, some kids could never picture what a coach was trying to say, but Tracy always could."

Caulkins' performances in Berlin stymied what had been an unstoppable East German powerhouse over the previous five years. Fueled by a systematic doping program that fed its teenage girls with steroids, East Germany was accustomed to routing the opposition. At the 1976 Olympics, the communist nation won gold in 11 of 13 events and tallied 18 medals. Conversely, the United States captured one gold medal, to go with four silver medals and two bronze medals.

Tracey Caulkins is widely regarded as the most versatile swimmer in history. Peter H. Bick.

At the World Champs, each of the events won by Caulkins featured an East German on the podium, noticeably on a lower step. The biggest statement by Caulkins was in the 400 individual medley, where she destroyed East Germany's Ulrike Tauber by nearly seven seconds, and in the process wrested her world record away. In Caulkins, Team USA featured a teenage upstart who had not previously been exposed to, or was overwhelmed by, the East Germans' dominance. More, she didn't particularly care about what was unfolding behind the Iron Curtain, but instead was only concerned with her preparation and what she could do in her 50-meter lane of water. Years earlier, the goal of being an Olympian had seeped into her brain, and achieving that target was her focus.

"I remember watching the 1972 Olympics on television when I was nine," Caulkins said. "I had been swimming competitively for about a year and I remember thinking that was something I wanted to do. I wanted to go to the Olympics one day, and I want to win a gold medal. I think all kids need to have dreams. I think that dream was a real inspiration to me, and in the back of my mind throughout my developing years, that was a motivation."

A dominant showing at the World Champs in her pocket, Caulkins continued her Olympic tune-up work in successful fashion in 1979. Racing at the Pan American Games, her sweep of the medley events was complemented by silver medals in the 400 freestyle and 100 breaststroke. In a year, the results suggested, she would make her Olympic splash.

Politics, though, put that long-held dream on pause.

In January of 1980, a month after the Soviet Union invaded Afghanistan, U.S. president Jimmy Carter noted that he would not support American participation in that summer's Olympic Games in Moscow. While the words were concerning, the situation morphed to damning in March, when it became official that the United States would not send an Olympic delegation to the Soviet capital.

Along with hundreds of other American hopefuls across the sporting landscape, Caulkins was dealt the biggest blow of her career—and life. Hours of training were immediately nullified by political maneuvering, and a dream she had harbored since she was a nine-year-old was crushed. At the peak of her powers—as was the case with the likes of Rowdy Gaines, Craig Beardsley, and Mary T. Meagher—Caulkins would not have the chance to exhibit the prowess that vaulted her to the top of the swimming world.

"What really hits home to me about the boycott was the Soviets didn't pull out of Afghanistan for nine years," Caulkins said. "Did it put any pressure on them? No. It was just a missed opportunity for many athletes. It just doesn't seem fair."

With her Olympic aspiration squashed by the mix of sports and politics, Caulkins moved on with grace and determination, and set several American records during the 1981 campaign. By 1982, she was enrolled at the University of Florida and training under her third big-name coach, as Randy Reese joined Bergen and Australian Don Talbot as onetime mentors to Caulkins. As a freshman for the Gators, and with the NCAA rules more lenient than today about participation limits, Caulkins won five individual events at the NCAA Championships and helped Florida to the team title.

But as that 1982 season progressed, and despite the promise of the World Championships, Caulkins lacked her typical motivation. She was not in top form at the World Champs, where she was off her best times and claimed bronze medals in the 200 medley and 400 medley, both events won by East Germany's Petra Schneider.

In part, Caulkins was coming off a draining first year of college, where adaptations were necessary not only in her training but in her life. More, the 1982 season fell between what should have been her first Olympic foray and the next opportunity at realizing her dream, the 1984 Olympics in Los Angeles.

As much as 1982 was a down year by her standards, Caulkins regained her desire during the 1983 season. She once again flourished on the collegiate stage and won both medley events at the Pan American Games, where she also took silver in the 200 butterfly. With the Olympics on the horizon, and the chance to erase the pain of 1980, Caulkins was mentally and physically where she wanted to be.

"I was still doing OK nationally, but not internationally, and I had not improved much," she said of 1982. "I hadn't done a personal best at a major meet, and I just lost a little motivation. By the fall of 1983, I really started stepping up my training, though, knowing the '84 Games were coming around. Los Angeles was a major factor for me to turn things around."

The United States Olympic Trials are considered by many to be the most cutthroat competition in the world. Because only two athletes qualify individually in each event, and due to the U.S. power and depth, it isn't uncommon for a third-place finish to be an Olympic medal contender. For the athletes who were denied their chance to chase their Olympic dreams in 1980, the pressure to come through in 1984 was massive.

As expected, the United States Trials proved to be painful for a handful of athletes whose best Olympic hopes were tied to four years earlier. Beardsley, the former world-record holder in the 200 butterfly, was shut out in his prime event. Meanwhile, Gaines failed to qualify for the 200 freestyle or as part of the American 800 freestyle relay but benefited from a pep talk from Caulkins to qualify in the 100 freestyle.

As far as Caulkins was concerned, her races primarily worked out, and she handled the pressure she faced with aplomb. She had no trouble winning the 200 individual medley and 400 individual medley, and she also eked out a triumph in the 100 breaststroke. The fact that she finished fourth in the 200 backstroke and 200 breaststroke could not dampen her week, and the fact she had stamped her ticket to Los Angeles.

"What made her so amazing was she remained this calm, cool and collected person regardless of how she performed," said Gaines, who has remained close with Caulkins through the years. "She was even keel all the time. She really is the nicest person I've ever met, and she helped me tremendously as a friend at the Trials in 1984."

In retaliation for the U.S. boycott of the Moscow Games, the Soviet Union led a boycott of its own in 1984, as 14 Eastern Bloc nations chose to bypass the Los Angeles Games. Among those countries was East Germany, which meant Caulkins would face weakened fields and not get the chance, as she did in 1978, to take down the top East German women.

As Caulkins prepared for her first event of the 1984 Olympics, nervousness started to build. It wasn't a surprise, given that Caulkins had waited an additional four years for this opportunity, but she needed to reduce the jitters. That's when Reese stepped forward and calmed Caulkins' nerves.

"In the evening, I put a lot of pressure on myself," she said of the final of the 400 medley.

> I knew the East Germans weren't there, but I was just getting myself so worked up. I saw (Reese) before I went to the ready room, and even though he is not a man of many words, I was expecting some sort of a pep talk. Instead, I got a kiss on the cheek and he said, "Trace, have fun." I was like, "What? That's it?" But I was putting so much pressure on myself that I think that's exactly what I needed. I needed to enjoy the moment, and it did alleviate the pressure.

Her butterflies neutralized, Caulkins had no trouble capturing the first Olympic title of her career, as she won the 400 individual medley in an American record of 4:39.24. The time handed Caulkins a nine-second win and set in motion a highly successful week.

"It was a personal best and an American record, but all I could think about were the ups and downs of getting to that point and the exhaustion of finally getting there," Caulkins said of realizing Olympic glory. "When I touched the wall, I looked for my family and my coaches. It was like a dream come true."

Sparked by her success in her first event, Caulkins followed with an American record en route to victory in the 200 individual medley and picked up a third gold medal while handling the breaststroke leg on the U.S. triumphant 400 medley relay. In the 100 breaststroke, Caulkins finished just off the podium with a fourth-place finish.

After missing the Opening Ceremony to rest for the start of the swimming program, Caulkins had the chance to enjoy the rest of the Los Angeles Games and was present for the Closing Ceremony. At the same time, she knew a major decision awaited, and she was sure of the direction she was headed.

Having won four more individual NCAA titles in 1984, which raised her career mark to a record 12, Caulkins had one more year of eligibility remaining at the University of Florida. But instead of continuing her career, she opted for retirement and the life of a regular student. It was a difficult call to make, but Caulkins knew it was the right decision.

"When I got back from the Olympics, I had been training at a high level for a really long time. So after I thought about it, I realized I had accomplished everything I wanted to in the sport," Caulkins said. "There wasn't really an opportunity to turn professional back then, so it really came down to the fact that I didn't really have the motivation to train at the level I knew I needed to anymore. It was a very difficult decision because I really loved the team aspect of the sport in college, and I didn't want to let my teammates down. But I just wanted to concentrate on my studies."

The what-if game has always been part of sport, and Caulkins' career lends itself to wondering what might have been if President Carter hadn't pushed for the 1980 boycott. In dominant form, Caulkins was coming off a spectacular showing at the World Champs and could have won a fistful of medals and clashed again with the top East Germans. Then again, had she raced at the 1980 Games, would Caulkins have stayed active through the 1984 Olympics?

Inducted into the International Swimming Hall of Fame in 1990, Caulkins won 48 national titles and set 63 American records during her career. In 1978, she was the Sullivan Award winner as the top amateur athlete in the United States. To this day, her name is one of the first spoken when the discussion shifts to the best to dive into the pool.

"There is no doubt in my mind that she's the greatest swimmer this country has ever had, by far," Reese said at the conclusion of Caulkins' career. "Her sheer ability, her versatility in all four strokes, and her durability in being so great for so long. She's been amazing."

KRISZTINA EGERSZEGI

The population of Hungary sits a little below 10 million, which leaves the Central European nation just inside the 100-most populous countries in the world. Yet, when a gaze is given to the most successful nations in the history of Olympic swimming, Hungary rates toward the top of the list, evidence of its passion for the sport.

Through the years, some of the best athletes to grace the pool have been produced by Hungary, ranging from early stars such as Alfred Hajos and Zoltan Halmay to modern greats like Tamas Darnyi, Norbert Rozsa, and Katinka Hosszu. But there is no debate about the finest swimmer produced by Hungary, a woman nicknamed "The Little Mouse," who dazzled from the late 1980s into the middle of the next decade.

Outside of Europe, few in the sport knew anything of Krisztina Egerszegi as the 1988 Olympic Games in Seoul were about to begin. While she scared the podium as a 13-year-old in both the 100 backstroke and the 200 backstroke at the 1987 European Championships, the competition of a global field in Seoul was a more difficult gauntlet to navigate, and how a bright-eyed teenager would handle the pressure was of legitimate concern.

Except for one person.

When Laszlo Kiss started coaching Egerszegi, he knew he was working with a precocious talent, someone capable of achieving greatness. He immediately envisioned exponential success in the backstroke events, but, more important, Kiss recognized his obligation to be attentive and measured in his approach to Egerszegi's development.

"I quickly realized I had found a real pearl, whose sports career had to be nurtured with a lot of responsibility," said Kiss, who was inducted into the International Swimming Hall of Fame in 2012. "When I first diagnosed Krisztina's technique in the four strokes, I immediately realized that she was an ideal backstroker, with thin thighs, broad shoulders, large palms, loose and flexible shoulders, and an excellent buoyancy on the surface of the water. These characteristics enabled her to become a world-class backstroker. And she never felt pressure."

It all started in Seoul, where Egerszegi captured the gold medal in the 200 backstroke and added a silver medal in the 100 backstroke. The victory came at the expense of a pair of East Germans—Katrin Zimmermann and Cornelia Sirch—and made Egerszegi the youngest Olympic champion in swimming history at just 14 years and 41 days. The performance also launched her status as a Hungarian hero and sparked her nicknames of The Little Mouse and Queen Krisztina.

Like so many athletes through the years, Egerszegi found herself bitten by the East Germany doping bug at the 1989 European Championships. Her silver medals in both backstroke events and the 400 individual medley arrived behind women linked to the systematic doping program instituted by the communist nation between the early 1970s and the late 1980s.

By 1991, however, Egerszegi was an untouchable force in the backstroke events and surging in the 400 medley. Egerszegi began the pre-Olympic year by starring at January's World Championships in Perth, where she swept the backstroke events. But it was at the European Championships during the summer in which Egerszegi left her biggest mark.

Racing in Athens and providing what equated to a warning shot to the competition ahead of the next year's Olympic Games in Barcelona, Egerszegi claimed three gold medals. She broke world records in the 100

backstroke and 200 backstroke and added her third title in the 400 individual medley. The dominance with which Egerszegi prevailed was most
noteworthy. Not only did she win the 100 backstroke by one second, she
claimed the 200 backstroke and 400 medley by nearly five seconds each. In
the 200 backstroke, she sliced almost two seconds off the previous world
record and watched that effort, a 2:06.62 performance, endure as the global
standard for more than 16 years.

In Barcelona, the young queen's reign continued as she repeated her
trifecta in Athens on the biggest stage. Again, Egerszegi was overwhelming
in the backstroke disciplines, winning by more than a half-second in the
100 distance and by more than two seconds in the 200. Meanwhile, she
showed her grit in the 400 medley by fending off China's Lin Li by .19
and scaring Petra Schneider's steroids-boosted world record from a decade
earlier.

"I don't like to look back too much," Egerszegi said of her career. "It
always feels strange to see me competing in past competitions. But when I
do look back, the Barcelona Olympics was a fantastic experience. I remember the races. They meant so much."

The momentum of the Barcelona Games carried into 1993 for
Egerszegi, who pulled off her typical triple in the backstroke events and
400 medley at the European Championships and added a continental title
in the 200 butterfly. The fact that she won a European crown in another
event only spoke to her versatility.

But for as well as things went through 1993, the Hungarian star
experienced a bump during the 1994 campaign. At the 1994 World
Championships, Egerszegi was a stunning fifth place in the 100 backstroke
and was the runner-up to China's He Cihong in the 200 backstroke,
marking the first time she lost the event in an international meet since
1989. The loss to He came under controversial circumstances as Chinese
swimmers, who were previously minor players, suddenly took command
of the sport. Several months later, seven Chinese swimmers tested positive
for performance-enhancing drugs and while He was not among them, her
rapid ascent up the global ladder suggested she was benefiting from chemical assistance.

Initially planning to retire after the 1994 World Champs, Egerszegi
changed her mind and dedicated herself to two more years of competition,
her eye predominantly on the 1996 Olympic Games in Atlanta. The loss
to He was the trigger for extending her career, as she did not want to bow
out under unsatisfying circumstances.

At the 1995 European Champs, Egerszegi was back in familiar territory. She won the 200 backstroke and 400 individual medley and regained her confidence on the way to her farewell Olympiad. In Atlanta, Egerszegi picked up a bronze medal in the 400 individual medley, an event won by Ireland's Michelle Smith, and earned a third consecutive gold medal in the 200 backstroke. While she didn't contest the event individually, her leadoff time on Hungary's 400 medley relay was faster than the winning time in the 100 backstroke.

Egerszegi's final victory in the 200 backstroke handed her entry into an exclusive club of three-peat Olympic champions. Before Egerszegi pulled off the feat, only Australian Dawn Fraser had won the same event at three consecutive Games, doing so in the 100 freestyle in 1956, 1960, and 1964. Michael Phelps joined the club in 2012 by winning the 200 individual medley and 100 butterfly for a third straight time, and he made it four consecutive golds in the 200 medley at the 2016 Olympics in Rio de Janeiro.

"I love all my medals, but I think this one is the best," she said of her Atlanta triumph in the 200 backstroke.

During her three Olympics, Egerszegi won five individual gold medals, a record that stands today. Her gold total could be even more impressive had she not clashed with doping offenders throughout her career. In 1988, her silver medal in the 100 back was behind East German Kristin Otto, whose name, after the fall of the Berlin Wall and the release of Secret Police (Stasi) files, appeared on documents confirming performance-enhancing drug use. Meanwhile, Smith's stunning rise from also-ran to Olympic champion fueled doping allegations, assertions that were confirmed when Smith tampered with her urine sample during an out-of-competition test and was subsequently banned for four years.

Egerszegi was inducted into the International Swimming Hall of Fame in 2001 and has remained a highly respected athlete in her homeland. More, her former world-record time in the 200 backstroke, although nearly 20 years old, would have earned a medal at every Olympiad since her retirement, with the exception of the 2012 Games in London. That year, she would have finished fourth. When a discussion of the greatest female performers of all-time unfolds, Egerszegi is always in the conversation, alongside the likes of Katie Ledecky, Tracy Caulkins, Janet Evans, and Fraser.

A Hall of Fame member for his media work, journalist Craig Lord once wrote of Egerszegi: "Her ability to endure the pain of hard training was one of the key reasons why she was so far ahead of her rivals."

JANET EVANS

No one ever saw the time machine that dropped Janet Evans into the late 1980s, but it has always been assumed she came from an era far beyond the one in which she competed. That's the only explanation for what Evans achieved during her splendid career, which spanned three Olympiads and still holds up against the test of time.

If Evans raced the 800 freestyle at the 2016 Olympic Games in Rio de Janeiro, her best time would have earned the bronze medal, and finished just shy of the silver step on the podium. Yes, Evans was that much ahead of her generation—three decades to be precise—and ranks among the most spectacular performers the sport has seen.

There is no set lifespan for a world record. Some last a few months. Some endure a few years. In rare instances, a handful will push a decade. Evans, though, played in a different pool. In three events, she held the world record for at least 18 years. That longevity is difficult to comprehend for one event. To boast that kind of reign in three events is downright mystifying.

Evans was anything but the prototypical Olympic champion. At just 5-feet-5 and 105 pounds, she was a sprite in a sport filled with giants. She employed an unorthodox windmill stroke, a draining technique that would suck the life out of almost any other athlete. When needed, she would deviate from the traditional breathing pattern and go seven or eight strokes without a breath. She also possessed a cut-their-throat mentality that is more innate than teachable.

"The difference between good and great swimmers is good swimmers set a goal but let other things get in their way," Evans once said.

> If they want to miss a workout or go away for a weekend, they'll do it. You really shouldn't do that if you really want to have a goal. When I was little, swimming was something I did, and I didn't know better. Now, I know there are so many things a high school kid can do, and I don't get to do most of them. When I finally realized it, I was into swimming and enjoying it. And I think I've done a lot more than most high school kids have ever done.

A rising teenage phenom under the tutelage of Bud McAllister, Evans used the 1987 season to announce her name to a global audience. During that campaign, she set world records in the 800 freestyle and 1,500 freestyle as a 15-year-old and capped the year with a world record in the 400 freestyle as a 16-year-old. It was all a buildup to the 1988 Olympic Games in Seoul, where Evans delivered a performance that hadn't previously been achieved and hasn't been replicated.

The 1988 Games are remembered as a disaster for the American women, who managed only seven medals—three gold, a silver, and three bronze. It was Evans who accounted for each of the titles, and not without a daunting hurdle in her way. With the Berlin Wall yet to fall, the systematic doping program of East Germany was revving along, helping the communist nation to gold medals in 10 of 15 events, and to 12 minor medals.

But Evans was so dominant, even steroids-assisted opponents could not keep pace with the Californian. She opened her program by winning the 400 individual medley by nearly two seconds over Romania's Noemi Lung and followed by defeating East Germany's Astrid Strauss with an Olympic record in the 800 freestyle. The best was saved for last, as Evans set a world record of 4:03.85 in the 400 freestyle to easily beat East Germans Heike Friedrich (4:05.94) and Anke Mohring (4:06.62), who were suspected of using performance-enhancing drugs.

"It wasn't just David versus Goliath, but David versus Goliath and Goliath was taking steroids," Olympic gold medalist Rowdy Gaines said of Evans' duel with the East Germans. "(Evans) not only proved you could beat them [clean]. She proved you could do it at 17. Janet transformed the sport for women. She was able to take times to a place where nobody thought [was possible]."

The summer after Seoul, Evans set the last of her seven world records, taking the 800 freestyle mark down to 8:16.22 en route to gold at the Pan Pacific Championships. In Tokyo, she added Pan Pacs crowns in the 400 freestyle and 400 individual medley. Her time in the 800 freestyle, though, was the showstopper, considered on par with Bob Beamon's legendary world-record long jump at the 1968 Olympics in Mexico City.

Evans' standard in the 800 freestyle—her third in the event—remained in the record book from August 20, 1989, until August 16, 2008, when Great Britain's Rebecca Adlington clocked 8:14.10 at the Beijing Games. Although Adlington's effort was impressive, it is worth noting she had the benefit of a tech suit, which was banned effective January 1, 2010. Overall, Evans was the world-record holder in the 800 freestyle for more than 20 years. In the 400 freestyle, Evans owned the world record from December 20, 1987, through May 12, 2006 and she reigned in the 1,500 freestyle from July 31, 1987, until June 17, 2007.

During training, Evans was known for pushing herself to the extreme, and McAllister was never afraid to design workouts that seemed outrageous. Evans found motivation in those demands and was constantly in tune with how her training fit her competition needs.

"Janet likes to be challenged," McAllister once said. "I know she's always going to work hard. She'll tell me what she can do, and I'll stand

During her heyday, Janet Evans was untouchable in the distance-freestyle events.
Peter H. Bick.

there and time her, and she'll be right on it. An athlete like Janet knows her body better than anyone. She asks me to help her set her goals, but she tells me how she feels physically. And she keeps asking for more. She's the best I've ever seen at responding to pressure."

By the early 1990s, Evans was no longer shredding the record book, but she remained the preeminent distance performer on the planet. At the 1991 World Championships, Evans doubled in the 400 freestyle and 800 freestyle, and added a silver medal in the 200 freestyle. Her podium finish in the shorter event only emphasized the exquisite range of her skill set and set the stage for her Olympic sequel at the Barcelona Games of 1992.

During her second Olympic appearance, Evans repeated as champion of the 800 freestyle but was caught in the final strokes of the 400 freestyle by Germany's Dagmar Hase, who was connected to East Germany's systematic doping program before the fall of the Berlin Wall. Hase touched the wall in 4:07.18, with Evans right behind in 4:07.37, and more than three seconds slower than her gold-medal effort from four years earlier.

Evans entered the last lap nearly a second ahead of Hase, but her early pace proved to be too much, as she struggled over the final 50 meters. It was an unusual occurrence for a woman so accustomed to possessing an extra gear in the final stages of a race, just as her foes were grimacing through the pain.

"I took it out hard, and I was hurting at the finish," Evans said. "It's disappointing. But I showed that I could hang in there for four years."

Evans remained relevant for another quadrennial. In 1993, she won gold medals in the 400 freestyle and 800 freestyle at the World Short Course Championships and at the Pan Pacific Championships, and she followed in 1994 with a title in the 800 freestyle at the World Championships in Rome. But there were continued signs of decline, as Evans was fifth in the 400 freestyle at the World Champs and her times were well off what she formerly produced.

At the 1996 United States Trials, Evans earned her way onto a third Olympic team behind a victory in the 400 freestyle and a runner-up finish in the 800 freestyle, which was won by 16-year-old Brooke Bennett. At the Olympics in Atlanta, Evans failed to advance out of the preliminaries of the 400 freestyle and was sixth in the 800 freestyle, 22 seconds off her world record. The positive to the Atlanta Games was the way Evans finally appreciated the Olympic experience. However, she also discussed the difficulty of chasing the woman in the mirror, especially in the latter years of her career.

"It was hard to swim against myself for seven years," she said. "I never improved. For seven years, I didn't do a best time, and that was really hard. How do you get motivated when you're not improving? It was terrible."

Untouched for most of her career, Evans had a difficult time dealing with her decline and the emergence of challengers to her throne, particularly Bennett. Although Evans was a multi-time Olympic champion and 45-time national champion, Bennett claimed Evans was intimidated by her rising-star status. Bennett's confidence and bravado did not sit well with Evans, who took time to compare her peak performances with those of her new rival.

"Why is there so much attention on her," Evans asked. "You guys tell me. A lot of people say they see some of me in Brooke. But her times aren't anything that are going to be remembered in five years. Unless she goes faster, 10 seconds faster, then I'd say she reminds me of myself. I'm not really impressed."

Evans' pursuit of additional glory in Atlanta was complemented by her willingness to speak about the performances of Ireland's Michelle Smith, whose three gold medals and stunning rise prompted accusations of performance-enhancing drug use. A non-factor at the 1992 Olympics, where she finished toward the bottom of the results in her events, Smith rapidly vaulted up the world rankings on the road to Atlanta.

The unusual progression of Smith caught the attention of numerous athletes, and Evans was asked to comment on her development. Knowing that Smith failed to medal in any event at the 1994 World Championships and was now dominating the Olympic Games, Evans acknowledged there were concerns on deck.

"Are you asking me if she's on drugs?" Evans said. "Any time someone has a dramatic improvement there's that question. I have heard that question posed in the last few weeks about that swimmer. If you're asking if the accusations are out there, I would say yes."

Evans retired following her third Olympic appearance and did not feel the tug of the sport during the first decade of the 2000s. However, she embarked on a comeback in 2012, qualifying for the United States Olympic Trials in the 400 freestyle and 800 freestyle. Despite failing to advance out of the preliminary heats in either of her events, the 40-year-old served as an inspiration for maintaining fitness and a healthy lifestyle.

Despite missing out on a fourth Olympic berth, Evans was not deterred. She found a way to remain involved in the Olympic movement and was a key committee member in Los Angeles' selection as host of the 2028 Olympic Games. Still, Evans will be best remembered for her exploits in the water, which were eons ahead of their time, and were delivered via an unorthodox approach.

"No coach recommends her technique, but she makes up for it with guts," said Nancy Hogshead, an Olympic champion in 1984. "When some swimmers pull ahead, you wonder if they can hold the lead. With Janet, you never doubt that she will stay there."

DAWN FRASER

Find an expert on the sport and ask that individual to identify the greatest male and female swimmers in history. The answer for the guys is usually instantaneous: Michael Phelps. Truthfully, any other answer reveals foolishness. Obtaining a majority among the ladies is much more difficult. Tracy Caulkins and Janet Evans are in the conversation. Arguments are made for Krisztina Egerszegi. Despite her active status, Katie Ledecky has already achieved such greatness that votes are cast on her behalf.

The other contender for female GOAT status requires a trip back in time of more than a half-century. It also requires a trip Down Under. Back then, and there, is where Dawn Fraser is found. Hailing from a nation with a rich aquatic history, Fraser spent the middle part of the 1900s establishing herself as a freestyle legend.

There haven't been many stretches over the past century-plus in which Australia has been a non-player on the international scene. But when Fraser came along in the early 1950s, there was a lull in the Aussie ranks. It was Fraser who lifted her nation back to prominence, first capturing back-to-back gold medals at the 1956 and 1960 Olympics, and then using the Games of 1964 as a stage for history, for it was that Olympiad in which Fraser became the first swimmer to win three consecutive titles in the same event, doing so in the 100 freestyle.

Just how challenging is an Olympic trifecta? Consider this fact: The club of three-peaters still only features a trio of members: Fraser, Egerszegi, and Phelps.

Before celebrating Fraser's historic achievement from the 1964 Games in Tokyo, there must first be a look at how she came to pursue the triple. It can be easily argued that her rise to stardom hinged on her crossing paths in 1950 with Harry Gallagher, the man who would coach Fraser to excellence. While talent is obviously the key ingredient for any global success, it must be nurtured and molded, and Gallagher had the perfect approach for working with Fraser.

Fraser wasn't the easiest of pupils with whom to work. She could be hard-headed and rebellious. She was brash. She could be defiant. If she didn't want to go along with a suggestion, she didn't. She operated on her terms. Yet, Gallagher knew how to work with these traits and devised a blueprint that took Fraser's unquestioned skill set to the greatest heights

"Dawn was a horror," Gallagher once said.

> She told me I was a deadbeat, to drop dead, to piss off, to get lost. She wasn't going to do what I wanted her to do. No guy would ever get her to do what she didn't want to do. She had wild aggression. She reminded me of a wild mare in the hills that you had put the lightest lead on to keep her under control. She wanted to do her own thing. If you had to guide her, it had to be very subtly, so she didn't understand that she was being manipulated. I used to say that, you know, "Dawn,

no girl has ever done this before, and I don't think you can do it either, but you just might be able to do it." She'd say, "What do you bloody mean? Of course I can bloody well do it."

Before Fraser started down the path toward greatness, Lorraine Crapp was the premier Australian woman in the sport. A freestyler with range, Crapp won gold medals in the 110-yard freestyle and 440-yard freestyle at the 1954 British Empire and Commonwealth Games. Crapp and Fraser gave Australia a potent one-two combination, and Crapp, who was coached by Gallagher early in her career, provided Fraser with a target to chase.

Gallagher's psychological genius and Fraser's talent proved to be a perfect pairing. While Gallagher recognized how to work with his star athlete, Fraser understood the importance of Gallagher as a mentor, and a give-and-take relationship was established. At the 1956 Olympics in Melbourne, the partnership yielded the tandem's finest moment to date. Behind a world-record performance, Fraser defeated Crapp for gold in the 100 freestyle, simultaneously sparking her legendary status.

In what was a tantalizing rivalry, the order of finish was reversed in the 400 freestyle, where Crapp earned the gold medal and Fraser the silver. Together, they helped Australia to victory in the 400 freestyle relay. But what could have been their finest duel never came to fruition. Between Fraser's sprint skill and Crapp's distance excellence, a meeting in the 200 freestyle would have been a race to remember. While Fraser broke the 17-year-old world record of Denmark's Ragnhild Hveger in early 1956, Crapp took the mark down twice during the latter stages of the year. However, the 200 freestyle did not appear on the Olympic program until 1968, leaving a meeting between the women at their peaks to the imagination.

Following her Olympic breakthrough, Fraser etched herself as the globe's premier female swimmer. She set multiple world records in the 100 freestyle and 200 freestyle and entered the 1960 Olympics in Rome as the heavy favorite to repeat in the 100 free, considered the sport's blue-ribbon event. Indeed, Fraser prevailed in dominant fashion, as the Aussie bettered American Chris von Saltza by more than a second, an eternity in a two-lap event.

Had Fraser opted for retirement following the 1960 Games, she would have walked away as an icon. It was rare during that era for swimmers to hang around for multiple Olympiads, let alone three. But Fraser has always been known for bucking the system and prolonging her career and time on top only added to her legacy.

As the 1964 Olympics in Tokyo beckoned, Fraser continued to flourish. Additional world records fell, and, in 1962, she became the first woman to crack the one-minute barrier in the 100 freestyle. For all she had previously achieved, Fraser was getting better and was seemingly headed to her third Olympiad as an undeniable force. Of course, not all plans unfold smoothly.

Seven months before the Tokyo Games, Fraser endured a physically and emotionally crippling life event. Leaving a fundraiser, Fraser was the driver of a car that also carried her mother, sister, and a friend. During the ride home in the early morning hours of March 9, 1964, Fraser was forced to veer out of the way when her car suddenly came upon a truck. When Fraser swerved, her car flipped over, leading to tragic results. While Fraser, her sister and friend were injured, Fraser's mother was killed, pronounced dead upon arrival at the hospital. Fraser's brother initially informed her that their mother died of a heart attack prior to the crash, but as Fraser prepared to write her autobiography, she learned that her mother's death was actually the result of injuries suffered in the car accident.

"I was led to believe by my family for many, many years, that my mother had died prior to the accident," Fraser wrote in her autobiography. "I did not feel good inside, but I know I've wiped away that question mark in my mind. Over the years, I've realized you can beat yourself up at night, lose sleep . . . but you can't change the past. My parents taught me to accept things the way they were, the rights and the wrongs . . . and to learn from my mistakes."

With the car accident so close to the Olympics in Tokyo, questions rightfully arose concerning Fraser's ability to three-peat. Really, Fraser would have been excused had she bypassed a third Olympics. Not only was she carrying the enormous weight of her mother's death, but the crash left Fraser with a chipped vertebra that forced her to wear a neck brace for nine weeks. More, doctors advised her to not dive off starting blocks, due to the risk of aggravating her neck injury. It wasn't until the Olympics in which Fraser dove off the blocks with full force.

As Fraser prepared to chase a third straight gold medal in the 100 freestyle, she wasn't simply battling her own physical and mental demons. American Sharon Stouder had emerged as a prime challenger, and Fraser would have to produce one of the best efforts of her career to retain her crown. Ultimately, that is what the Aussie managed, as she came through in the final to clock an Olympic record of 59.5, ahead of the 59.9 produced by Stouder.

Although Fraser was expected to encounter difficulty during her third Olympiad, she found the path to the top of the podium smooth. Fraser was nearly a second clear of the opposition during the preliminary heats, then advanced to the final as the top seed by more than a second. While Stouder finished within a half-second of Fraser in the final, her latest victory was convincing. Fraser bolted into the lead off the start and never looked back, finishing almost a half-body length ahead of the American.

In less than a minute of race time, but with years of work and dedication providing fuel, Fraser had become the first swimmer to win the same event at three consecutive Olympiads. It was truly a remarkable feat, a triumph well ahead of its time. Years down the line, Egerszegi joined Fraser in the special club, winning the 200 backstroke at the 1988, 1992, and 1996 Games. Eventually, Phelps was given his key, too, and went a step further by winning the 200 individual medley at four consecutive Games (2004–2016). Phelps also won the 100 butterfly from 2004 to 2012. But Fraser will forever be President Emeritus of the Three-Peat Club.

It is worth noting that America's first sprint star, Duke Kahanamoku, could have beaten Fraser to the treble. Kahanamoku was the Olympic champion in the 100 free in 1912 and 1920 but had his 1916 Olympic opportunity stolen by the cancellation of the Games due to World War I.

"I put myself under a lot of pressure by deciding to go to Tokyo and I also put myself under a lot of pressure to compete in the same event in three Olympics," said Fraser, who was ultimately convinced to compete by her Aussie teammates. "I had, at the back of my mind, that this was for my mother because we were saving up for my mother to go to Tokyo with me. I just imagined that she was there and that I was doing it for her."

If Fraser's excellence in the pool cemented her identity as an all-time great, her third gold medal in the 100 free apparently wasn't enough of a souvenir from her visit to Tokyo. After completing her work in the pool, the rebellious Fraser set out on a night excursion with Howard Toyne, an Australian Olympic team doctor, and Des Piper, a member of Australia's field hockey team. The trio planned on obtaining some Olympic flags that lined the street leading to the Imperial Palace, the main residence of the Emperor of Japan.

After getting two flags in their possession, police were alerted, and Fraser and her countrymen were arrested, taken to the police station, and threatened with jail time. However, Fraser's prominence was soon revealed, and all three Aussies were released, the lieutenant of the police station allowing Fraser to keep one of the stolen flags.

"After showing them my gold medal and my dog tags, (the police) were still very disgusted that I'd . . . that it was me, that I would do that," Fraser said. "They explained to me that it was a stealing offense, it could mean a jail term. And they decided then because of who I was, Dawn Fraser, they let us off."

The Tokyo police may have been lenient with Fraser, but Australian Swimming was tired of its Glory Girl and her antics. The organization saw the flag incident as a third strike against Fraser. Prior to the flag shenanigans, Fraser—against team orders—walked in the Opening Ceremony in Tokyo, rather than rest. She also donned a suit for competition that she felt was more comfortable but was not the team-sponsored suit. The accumulated offenses led Australian Swimming to institute a ten-year ban against Fraser, a decision that led to her retirement.

Although the ban was lifted prior to the 1968 Olympic Games in Mexico City, Fraser didn't feel like she had the appropriate amount of time to come out of retirement and prepare for a pursuit of a fourth consecutive title in the 100 free. It was the end.

Even in this era of lengthened careers, three-peat success in an event at the Olympic Games remains a daunting challenge. Over the trio of Olympiads, fate must be on an athlete's side. In addition to peaking at the proper moments, which is far from easy, athletes must dodge the pitfalls of injury and illness. Maintaining a sharp mental edge is also mandatory.

Considering Fraser achieved her three-peat at a time when careers were primarily one Olympics and done only emphasizes that she was ahead of her time and set a spectacularly high bar to chase. Although it will never be known, one also must wonder if Fraser—a multi-time world-record holder in the event—could have also managed the accomplishment in the 200 freestyle, had it not taken so long to become an Olympic event.

As the International Swimming Hall of Fame opened in 1965, Fraser was an easy choice for induction. Despite being just a year removed from racing at the Tokyo Games, Fraser was honored alongside greats from earlier in the century, such as Johnny Weissmuller and Gertrude Ederle.

Memorable moments dot the Olympic landscape, and what Fraser achieved in Tokyo in 1964 will remain an iconic feat. History never disappears. Instead, it serves as a reminder of the past and the greatness that came before and should never be forgotten. For Fraser, she will always be the first swimmer to win Olympic gold in the same event at three consecutive Games, each victory defined in its own way, but the last defining history.

"I can remember precisely what I said," Fraser stated about the completion of her triple. "I said to myself, 'Thank God that's over.' "

Chapter 3

HISTORIC MOMENTS

*From barrier-breaking performances to breathtaking finishes, the sport
has offered its share of defining moments. Even as history continues to
be made, these special times will forever be remembered.*

A WOMAN'S WORLD

Not long after Hungarian Alfred Hajos became the first Olympic swimming champion, winning the gold medal in the 100 freestyle at the 1896
Games in Athens, Australia's Sarah "Fanny" Durack developed the urge to
learn to swim. It wasn't that Durack, a youngster at the time, was inspired
by Hajos' efforts or the performances by any other male swimmer.

Rather, Durack's desire to swim was triggered out of necessity and in
the pursuit of peace of mind. While on vacation as a nine-year-old, Durack
struggled with the surf in her native land, and it was that experience which
convinced her to become water safe. It was a decision that made Durack
swimming's first female superstar.

From 1896, when the first Modern Games were held in the birthplace
of the Ancient Olympics, through 1908, only men competed in swimming
at the Olympics. During that time, the likes of Hajos, American Charles
Daniels, Great Britain's Henry Taylor, and Hungary's Zoltan Halmay
emerged as the sport's standouts.

It wasn't like women were banned from the Olympics altogether during that stretch of time, as female athletes competed in events such as sail-
ing, tennis, and equestrian as early as the 1900 Games in Paris. Swimming,
though, didn't create a coed program until the 1912 Games, which were
held in Stockholm, Sweden.

When it was announced that women would be invited to compete in Stockholm, some countries jumped at the opportunity while others were disinterested. Only 27 women took part in the two swimming events—the 100 freestyle and 400 freestyle relay—with host Sweden and Great Britain sending six athletes each. Australia sent two swimmers—Durack and Mina Wylie—while the United States opted to send no women, despite fielding a team of seven men.

While Durack had put together an impressive career, Wylie actually held the upper hand over her countrywoman in the lead-up to the 1912 Games. Wylie beat Durack on several occasions at the Australian Championships. Getting to the Olympics, however, proved to be an issue for Durack and Wylie, with politics playing a role. Considering the role politics have played throughout the history of the Olympic Games, maybe it was fitting Durack and Wylie had to play a waiting game.

"The Aussie men in charge of selecting the team for the 1912 Games declared that it was a waste of time and money to send women to Sweden," wrote Craig Lord in an article for the former SwimVortex website.

> The rule book didn't help, either. The New South Wales Ladies' Amateur Swimming Association regulations held that no women could compete at events where men were present. A public outcry resulted in a vote and rule change at the association and Durack and Wylie were allowed to make the journey to Europe—provided they paid for themselves. The wife of Hugh McIntosh, a sporting and theatrical entrepreneur and newspaper proprietor, launched a successful appeal for funds and with money donated by the public, family and friends, Durack sailed for Sweden via London, where she was reported to have trained half a mile a day.

The competition pool was hardly high-tech in nature, constructed in Stockholm Harbor and consisting of saltwater. But Durack wasn't derailed by the conditions. Representing Australasia, a combined team from Australia and New Zealand, Durack opened her Olympic career in grand fashion, setting a world record of 1:19.8 during qualifying heats of the 100 freestyle. She followed by winning her semifinal easily and then captured the gold medal with a time of 1:22.2, more than three seconds quicker than Wylie.

Great Britain's Daisy Curwen was expected to be a medal contender in the final, but the former world-record holder was forced to withdraw from the competition after the semifinal round due to a bout of appendicitis. It was Curwen's world record that Durack broke during the qualifying heats.

With Durack and Wylie the only Aussies competing in swimming, Australasia could not field a squad for the 400 freestyle relay, although it tried. Durack and Wylie offered to swim two legs each if Australasia was given a chance to race, but officials denied the request and Great Britain's quartet of Belle Moore, Jennie Fletcher, Annie Speirs, and Irene Steer went on to win the gold medal by nearly 12 seconds over Germany. Fletcher was the bronze medalist behind Durack and Wylie in the 100 freestyle, and Fletcher spoke of the limited practice time she and her teammates had in preparation for the 1912 Games.

"We swam only after working hours, and they were 12 hours and six days a week," Fletcher said. "We were told bathing suits were shocking and indecent, and even when entering competition, we were covered with a floor-length cloak until we entered the water."

With only two women's events, as opposed to the seven on the men's program, there is no telling what Durack could have done if given a chance to contest additional events. But a lack of equality in the Olympic schedule has been more commonplace than not during the 100-plus years of the Games. From the first time women competed in swimming at the Olympics through the 1972 Games in Munich, men's events always outnumbered women's events.

And while men and women each competed in 13 events at the 1976 and 1980 Games, there were fewer women's events over the next three Olympiads. Since 1996, however, the number of events between the genders has matched, albeit with a caveat. Through the 2016 Olympics in Rio de Janeiro, there was inequality in the length of the longest events on each program. While men's distance swimmers contested the 1,500 freestyle as their gender's longest event, women covered just more than half that distance via the 800 freestyle.

A change will be made in the summer of 2021, thanks to the International Olympic Committee's decision to expand the men's and women's programs. At the Tokyo Games, which were postponed by a year due to the COVID-19 pandemic, women will race the 1,500 freestyle for the first time, with the 800 free added for men.

A parallel can be found in the history of track and field. It wasn't until the 1984 Games in Los Angeles in which women contested the marathon, and in some years prior, women's distances were capped at 1,500 meters while male athletes were given the opportunity to double in the 5,000 and 10,000.

"I was happy to see it," said world-record holder Katie Ledecky of the addition of the 1,500 freestyle. "I think adding the 1,500 was a long time coming. It's good that there's parity in the men's and women's distance events now."

From 1912 to 1918, Durack set 11 world records over various distances, including three in the 100-meter freestyle. Her fastest time of 1:16.2 from 1915 lasted as the world record for five years, until American Ethelda Bleibtrey won Olympic gold in 1:14.4. A Durack–Bleibtrey duel would have been a highlight event of the 1920 Games, but illness prevented Durack from racing.

After being denied the chance to defend her Olympic title in 1916 due to the cancellation of the Games by World War I, Durack was hoping to repeat in 1920, but appendicitis put an end to that dream. More, Durack came down with typhoid fever and pneumonia a week before Australia's athletes were scheduled to sail to Europe for the Antwerp Games.

In between competitions, Durack took part in numerous world tours, along with Wylie, in which they would race one another and demonstrate the Australian crawl, the stroke that Durack made famous and used to become a world-record holder. Durack's vast achievements earned her induction into the International Swimming Hall of Fame in 1967, the third year of the Hall's existence.

"Fanny Durack not only took on all comers the world over, but beat all comers the world over for eight years in the formative years of women's swimming," reads Durack's profile in the International Swimming Hall of Fame.

BETTER THAN THE MEN

Five: The number of men who had accomplished the feat.
Zero: The number of women who had succeeded.
One: The number of times she had already failed at the endeavor.
Sixteen: The number of hours the journey would take.

It was a little past 7 a.m. on August 6, 1926. Wearing a two-piece bathing suit and self-made goggles, Gertrude Ederle walked to the edge of the beach on Cape Gris-Nez, located in Northern France. She was covered in multiple layers of grease as she gazed at the choppy and chilly water that would be equal parts her friend and foe for the better part of the day.

It didn't matter that a year earlier, her quest to complete this 21-mile trek proved unsuccessful. It didn't matter that only men had managed the feat to this point. And it didn't matter that many observers felt her latest pursuit, simply because she was a woman, was going to fall short. On this day, Gertrude Ederle was convinced she would become just the sixth person—and first female—to swim across the English Channel.

Ederle was comfortable in the water from an early age. Growing up in New York City, she took swim lessons at a public pool and spent much of her summers at the New Jersey shore, swimming in the Atlantic Ocean. The ease with which she negotiated one of Mother Nature's most powerful forces led Ederle to be a superb competitor in races ranging from as short as 50 yards up to a half-mile.

In an era in which Ethelda Bleibtrey and Martha Norelius were stars for the United States, Ederle also held that distinction. She was a world-record holder over various distances and as the 1924 Olympic Games in Paris approached, Ederle was considered a gold-medal contender in three events—the 100 freestyle, 400 freestyle, and as a member of the American 400 freestyle relay.

While Ederle left Paris with three medals, she was surprisingly beaten in both the 100 freestyle and the 400 freestyle. In the shorter distance, Ederle finished behind American teammates Ethel Lackie and Mariechen Wehselau. Over the longer distance, Norelius and Helen Wainwright bettered Ederle, leaving her with the bronze medal. However, Ederle earned gold in the relay, as the United States set a world record.

The trip to the French capital may not have produced what Ederle envisioned in her individual events, but the journey itself sparked a dream that would come to define her life. As the ship carrying members of Team USA moved through the English Channel en route to Paris, Ederle was struck by the idea of swimming across the body of water, which spanned 21 miles at its narrowest point between Dover, England, and Calais, France.

After her Olympic appearance, Ederle sought to make her dream a reality. In 1925, she prepared for her initial English Channel challenge by successfully covering the 17.5-mile distance between Battery Park in New York City and Sandy Hook in New Jersey. Two months later, she entered the cold waters of the English Channel.

Between her pool and open-water careers, Ederle knew she had a special relationship with the water.

"To me, the sea is like a person—like a child that I've known a long time," she said. "It sounds crazy, I know, but when I swim in the sea, I talk to it. I never feel alone when I'm out there."

When Ederle made her first attempt to cross the English Channel, only five people before her had been successful, highlighted by Great Britain's Matthew Webb as the first in 1875. It wasn't until 1911 when the second successful crossing was recorded, this time by Britain's Bill Burgess.

Meanwhile, three men achieved the feat in 1923 and set the stage for Ederle to become the first woman.

Ederle was progressing adequately in her first Channel swim when a member of her team touched her during the swim, forcing an automatic disqualification. The team member thought Ederle was in trouble and in danger of drowning, while she was actually resting and preparing to again pick up the pace.

There is no guarantee Ederle would have completed the swim had she not been disqualified. However, some valuable data was collected, including knowledge of the ever-shifting currents and the most advantageous way to ride the waves.

"It was really just that they got the tide wrong and she hadn't prepared for it enough," said Gavin Mortimer, the author of *The Great Swim*, which chronicles Ederle's second English Channel assault. "You've got this ebb and flow tide, which changes every five to six hours. So, you don't swim in a straight line. You've got to zig zag to go with the tide."

The second time Ederle confronted the English Channel and chased history, experience played a key role. She was wise enough to apply multiple layers of grease to combat the cold water and she was more familiar with the battering waves and jellyfish encounters. She was also supported by a personal entourage aboard the tugboat, *The Alsace*. The crew included Ederle's father, sister, and Burgess, who followed his days as a Channel swimmer by becoming the American woman's trainer.

When Ederle needed to recharge, someone aboard the tugboat would extend her food to be fished out of a net. At times, the 20-year-old Ederle was seen eating fried chicken and drinking broth. Despite the greater familiarity with the Channel, Ederle took a beating during her 1926 sequel. She suffered bruises from the waves and, at one point, it was suggested by her support team that she abandon the attempt. To that suggestion, Ederle responded, "What for?"

As morning turned to afternoon and afternoon disappeared into night, Ederle consistently fought with the shifting tides and was taken significantly off course. But she demonstrated tremendous grit and determination and with the current eventually turning in her favor, Ederle was able to reach the English shore, stepping foot onto the beach near Kingsdown. There, she was greeted by applauding fans, some of whom had turned on car headlights to illuminate her achievement.

It was after 9 p.m. when Ederle reached land in England, and her time of 14 hours, 39 minutes not only made her the first woman to cross the English Channel but also made her the fastest person to make the trek—by nearly two hours. She proved she could rebound from failure and accomplish something that was previously believed capable by only men.

"It was just that everybody was saying it couldn't be done," she said. "Well, every time somebody said that, I wanted to prove it could be done. It took a Yankee to show them how. When I walked out of the water, I began thinking, 'Oh my God, have I really done it?' When my feet hit the sand, oh, that was a wonderful moment."

Dubbed the Queen of the Waves, Ederle was swarmed by the well-wishers on the beach, but she retreated to *The Alsace* for the night, and boarded a steamship, *The Berengaria*, for her return to the United States. As the ship got close to the United States, Ederle received a message to head to the top deck, so planes could drop bouquets of flowers from above.

Upon returning to the United States, Ederle was feted as a hero. New York City mayor Jimmy Walker orchestrated a ticker-tape parade and newspapers, which covered her epic crossing, continued their coverage of America's new hero. It was overwhelming for Ederle, who did not anticipate such fanfare and, upon embarking on a speaking tour following her achievement, had a breakdown over the attention.

Still, she knew the reaction was out of sheer appreciation.

"That was marvelous," she said of being welcomed home. "The whole thing was a surprise to me. I thought Mayor Walker would just give me a dinner. There were 2,000,000 people, and it looked like they all wanted to reach out and grab you and hug you, and I felt the same way about them."

As part of Ederle's celebration, Walker likened Ederle's crossing with Moses' parting of the Red Sea and George Washington crossing the Delaware River. Obviously, New York City's mayor was big into hyperbole, but this moment was spectacular. It, too, was taxing on Ederle's health.

As a child, Ederle contracted a bout of measles that left her with damaged hearing. Doctors suggested it would be intelligent to leave swimming behind, due to the possibility of further hearing loss, but Ederle was not about to part ways with her passion. Ultimately, her continued days in the sport, and her Channel swims, led to almost complete hearing loss. In turn, Ederle reached out to the deaf community and taught kids with hearing problems how to swim.

Meanwhile, Ederle's inspirational crossing of the English Channel fueled growth in swimming among women and encouraged water safety. Most important, she proved that women were not inferior to men.

"When Gertrude Ederle struck out from France, she left behind her a world which has believed for a great many centuries that woman is the weaker vessel," wrote *New York World* columnist Heywood Broun. "Much of government, most of law and practically all of morality is based upon this assumption. And when her toes touched the sands of England, she stepped out of the water into a brand-new world."

She proved doubters wrong. She broke down a barrier. She became a pioneer.

GOOD AS GOULD

Cameras couldn't get enough of Mark Spitz, the mustachioed American who adorned all sorts of newspaper front pages and magazine covers before, during, and after the 1972 Olympic Games in Munich. He was can't-miss television. Spitz's seven gold medals, and equal number of world records, equated to the greatest Olympic performance to date, and, on the Richter Scale of Olympic efforts, his showing shook the world.

Yet, Munich will also be remembered for sorrow, the deaths of 11 Israeli athletes and coaches via terrorism, which cast a pall over an Olympiad that tried diligently to emphasize global peace. It was heartbreaking television, defined by ABC anchor Jim McKay revealing the deaths with three poignant words: "They're all gone." On the Richter Scale of Olympic pain, the acts of Black September shook the world in a much different manner.

Largely forgotten in the Munich Games' conflicting storylines of brilliance and tragedy were the efforts of a teenage girl from Australia. In most other Olympiads, Shane Gould would have been the headliner, her five individual medals in the pool a female record then and still. But Gould was a victim of circumstance, the spotlight not shining as brightly as was appropriate for a young woman whose career was a sprint in duration.

The truth is, even the greatest coaches rely on good fortune when it comes to molding a special talent. As the cliché goes, they must be in the right place at the right time to have a uniquely gifted athlete walk through their doors. But coaches also must possess an eye and instinct for which youngsters have the potential to be developed into exceptional performers. Upon seeing Gould for the first time, Forbes Carlile knew this young lady was different.

Carlile is revered as one of the finest coaches the sport has seen, and probably the best from Australia. He and his coaching wife, Ursula, formed a potent tandem, and he was inducted into the International Swimming Hall of Fame in 1976, thanks to pioneering advances such as the two-beat kick, interval training, heart-rate monitoring, and tapering. In Gould, he and his wife had a special prospect.

"She was very good when she came to us," Carlile said of Gould. "She was a 12- or-13-year-old who had done well. We picked her as a future champion. As a matter of fact, when she first got into the pool with us, it was a question of when she'd break Dawn Fraser's world record (in the 100 freestyle), not if she'd break it. We trained her as an endurance athlete, and it carried her through, both in sprints and in distances. That was a new idea."

Gould appreciated Carlile's approach when she decided to join his program upon her family's move from Brisbane to Sydney. Carlile's penchant for pioneering the use of science stood out, as did his focus on providing feedback and keeping his swimmers abreast of what their foes were doing around the world. The variety and organic nature of Carlile's training regimen won out over Gould's other option, which was joining the more militaristic atmosphere and volume-focused approach of Don Talbot.

"I won the gold medals. I set the world records," Gould said.

> But Forbes as my coach certainly facilitated that with the type of training he put me through. I'm sure another coach and I wouldn't have been so successful. Forbes' style of coaching suited me and his approach of getting the best out of me worked. He made (coaching) a profession, a distinguished profession. He was systematic, had integrity in his research and study, and in his application. He never had his own ego attached to his methodology. He had a love for swimming instead because he was always open to exploring the nature of swimming. He had a terrific eye. He was really attentive when I was training. He would always cut to the business side of things. I was always trying to improve and I really wanted to receive instruction. I was hungry for feedback. He recognized that in me and gave me what I needed.

Carlile knew what was necessary to produce an Olympic-caliber athlete, having served as Australia's Olympic coach at the 1948 and 1956 Games and as the head coach of the Netherlands in 1964. Under Carlile's watch, it didn't take Gould long to reveal an immense skill set that has never been matched.

The first of Gould's 11 world records arrived when she was a 14-year-old, in April of 1971. As far as initial global marks go, this one was a doozy and can be argued as the preeminent world record of her career. For nearly 15 years, the world mark in the 100-meter freestyle had stood to the legendary Dawn Fraser, she of three consecutive Olympic titles in the event and iconic status in the sport. But at the Coca Cola International Swim Meet in London, Gould etched herself as the heir apparent to Fraser as the next Aussie female sensation.

Clocking a time of 58.9, Gould equaled Fraser's record, which was set seven years earlier and was the last of Fraser's 11 standards in the 100 freestyle. As much as Gould was compared to Fraser prior to equaling her world record, the performance only intensified the link between the two— one era handing the proverbial torch to another generation.

Gould's world record in the 100 freestyle was one of six she set in 1971, spanning five freestyle events. In what seemed to be a perfectly orchestrated run through the calendar of a pre-Olympic year, Gould set world records in the 100 free, 200 free (twice), 400 free, 800 free, and 1,500 free between April and December. Gould's run of success, given its frequency and range, remains one of the most impressive stretches in swimming history.

With every freestyle record simultaneously under Gould's name at the end of 1971, her wide-ranging skill set was on full display. She was as dominant a sprinter as she was a dominant distance performer and everything in between. Had the 50 freestyle been an event during that era, it's likely she would have owned that world record, too.

Not surprising, Gould was brimming with confidence, her results proof that her work with Carlile was paying dividends. As Gould prepared for her various meets, she believed world records were within reach. That feeling was evident ahead of the 400 freestyle at the Santa Clara International Swim Meet in July, where she posted a global mark of 4:21.2 to shave more than a second off the previous record.

"I'm pretty sure I'll get a record here," Gould said upon her arrival in Santa Clara. "I seem to improve every time I get in the water. I haven't finished a race yet where I felt I couldn't go a bit further."

In recent years, Gould's name returned to regular conversation within the sport when American Katie Ledecky emerged as a freestyle star over a span that mimicked the days of the Australian wonder kid. By winning gold medals at the 2016 Olympic Games in Rio de Janeiro in the 200 freestyle, 400 freestyle, and 800 freestyle, Ledecky matched the exploits of the United States' Debbie Meyer from the 1968 Games in Mexico City. But with Ledecky also the world-record holder in the 1,500 freestyle and a contributor to the American 400 freestyle relay, a comparison to Gould also surfaced.

"I think you would have to say the standard is Shane Gould," said Ledecky's former coach, Bruce Gemmell, ahead of the Rio Games. "Their range is similar. When you hold the world record at every (freestyle) distance from the 100 through the 1500, the standard is set pretty high."

As the Olympic year dawned, Gould delivered an immediate warning shot to her competitors when she broke her world-record tie with Fraser in the 100 freestyle. Racing at the New South Wales State Championships, she took the world mark down to 58.5, and generated anticipation for what she would accomplish at the Summer Olympics in Munich.

The hype surrounding Gould built gradually throughout the 1972 campaign, and media requests flowed in. The country knew she had the ability to be a headliner in Munich and her story became well known but also difficult to suppress.

"Six months out (from the Olympics), I was really conscious of making sure I did good training, kept good records of my moods and sleep and balance in my life," Gould said. "At the same time, there were a lot of media. I had to attend to the media. I didn't have Australian Swimming or a manager to filter that. It was my parents who did that. That can really suck the life out of you."

Gould's Olympic schedule was hardly a mystery leading to the Games. It was clear she would contest the 100 free, 200 free, 400 free, and 800 free, seeking to match or surpass Meyer's three freestyle titles from the previous Olympiad. But there was a surprise to her program when she added the 200 individual medley, a decision that allowed her to showcase her skill beyond the freestyle. Gould also considered adding the 100 butterfly but ultimately decided it did not adequately fit her schedule.

Her newest event jumpstarted her week in Munich, and it could not have provided greater momentum. Engaging in a battle with another rising teenage star, East Germany's 13-year-old Kornelia Ender, Gould set a world record of 2:23.07, edging Ender (2:23.59) by a half-second.

Boosted by her opening salvo, Gould was expected to go 2-for-2 when the 100 freestyle was held a day later. But Gould was missing her usual pop and settled for the bronze medal behind the American duo of Sandy Neilson and Shirley Babashoff.

"The 100 freestyle was one that I wanted to win," Gould said. "That's kind of like the blue-ribbon event. I knew as soon as I dived in and swam 10 meters, it was not my day for the 100 freestyle. I got to the end, and I thought, 'Third place. OK, let's do this again. Do better the next time. But that's it. You haven't got another chance.'"

Although the outcome of the 100 free was not what she wanted, Carlile ensured Gould was able to refocus and not dwell on what didn't go right. Her ability to move forward was exhibited in her next two events, as

Gould won the 400 freestyle and 200 freestyle, both in world-record times. After beating Italian Novella Calligaris by more than three seconds in the longer event, Gould got the best of the United States' Babashoff and Keena Rothhammer in the 200 free.

In the 800 freestyle, it was Rothhammer who prevailed, leaving Gould two-plus seconds behind for the silver medal. Gould went into the final of the 800 free at less than 100 percent, a chest cold developed during the demanding week. Still, her haul of five medals was an epic performance and bettered the four individual medals of Spitz. But since his solo hardware was all golden, and he also had three relay titles, it was Spitz who was the toast of the Games.

There is no doubt that Gould was hampered by Australia's lack of depth and inability to field contending relays. While she was a member of the Aussie 400 freestyle relay, her supporting cast was not strong enough and Australia finished eighth in the final. Meanwhile, the Australian 400 medley relay did not even advance out of the preliminaries, leaving Gould with no final to contest.

Philosophical in her approach to life, Gould has often reflected on her Olympic experience with pride and through a whole-world lens.

"A gold medal is like a stamp of achievement, but it's not the achievement in itself," she said. "What I feel most proud of is the process that got me to that point: Blocking out distractions; keeping on task; learning time management; and being adaptive. These are all life skills that people learn in many different ways as they work toward a high achievement, such as a university degree or raising a family. It's just that winning Olympic gold medals seems to get a whole lot more attention."

As Gould left Munich, few thought it was the last time she would be seen on the Olympic stage. In early 1973, Gould set the last of her world records, breaking the 1,500 freestyle standard at the Australian National Championships. It appeared she was headed to the inaugural World Championships later that year and, down the line, to the 1976 Olympic Games in Montreal, when she would be only 19 years old.

However, Gould had also traveled to the United States after her first Olympic experience and was intrigued by life beyond the pool. Eventually, she decided to walk away at the peak of her career, and at a ripe 16 years old. Not only would there have been increased pressure to match and exceed what she had already achieved, how could she maintain her internal drive? What was left to chase?

Gould's premature retirement raised several what-if questions beyond the obvious: How many more Olympic medals would have been secured?

There was also the question of how many more world records she would have set. More, East Germany was in the early stages of implementing its systematic doping program that made the country a global power deep into the 1980s. Even with the East Germans relying on performance-enhancing drugs, could Gould's talent have neutralized the benefits of anabolic steroids?

When Gould and Ender clashed in the 200 individual medley in Munich, it was supposed to be the first of many duels between the women. While Gould was the world-record holder in the 100 freestyle at the time, Ender went on to set ten consecutive world records in the event between 1973 and 1976. The East German added four world marks in the 200 freestyle and two in the 200 individual medley. Had Gould stayed active, could she have interrupted Ender's reign, and would Ender's chemically fueled talent have pushed Gould to event greater heights?

The answer will never be known.

"There was a whole series of things that happened," Gould said of her decision to retire.

> I went to America after the Olympics. I wasn't a happy chappy. I was wondering whether to swim or not to swim. I had a lot of hot chocolate fudge sundaes and doughnuts and didn't swim as much. So, I just blew up like a balloon, and that's not very good for competition swimming to be overweight. I was just confused. There was a lot of pressure for me to stay swimming, but I really had no goals to work toward and just in the confusion of it all, I had to run away.

The sport might have missed Gould's presence, but in retirement, the Australian found depth to her life, becoming much more than an athlete. She immersed herself in topics such as history and ethics, and she earned her doctorate in philosophy. Along the way, she also studied the culture of swimming and earned a degree in film study. Simply, she became a well-rounded person, not always an easy task in a sport that features many athletes struggling to find the next chapter beyond the water.

Gould has remained a hero in her homeland, and at the 2000 Olympics in Sydney, she was selected to be one of the torch bearers during the Opening Ceremony. It was an honor she ranks alongside the greatest accomplishments of her swimming career. She also maintains an appreciation for what her competitive career—as short as it was—provided to her life.

"You see there truly is something delightful about the experience of competing at an elite level, and it's not the extrinsic: The glory, the medals or the money," Gould said. "All of the motivation is intrinsic. You have to love to try, love to perform, love to compete, love to be disciplined and love the physical exertion. Most of all, it's the love of being good at what you do."

A TEAM OF EXCELLENCE

The 1927 New York Yankees. The 1995–1996 Chicago Bulls. The 1972 Miami Dolphins. The 1976–1977 Montreal Canadiens. Each of these teams, defined by championship seasons and star-studded rosters, can make a claim for being its sport's greatest squad in history. Yet, there will be a handful of arguments against the distinction, someone's preference not jiving with the consensus.

In the pool, there is no doubt.

At the 1976 Olympic Games in Montreal, Team USA put on a show that hadn't been seen prior, or since. Led by double individual champions John Naber and Brian Goodell, the United States captured gold medals in 12 of the 13 events contested, a statistic that just begins to characterize the dominance that was on display. Sixteen years before Michael Jordan led NBA players onto the basketball court for the first time in Olympic competition, this squad was the original Dream Team.

When the curtain rose for the 1976 Games, the athletes faced a daunting challenge. The previous Olympiad provided bountiful fireworks in the pool, American Mark Spitz surging to seven gold medals with as many world records, and Australian teenager Shane Gould winning five individual medals, highlighted by three titles. The efforts of Spitz and Gould were generational, and the risk of a letdown was real.

But the 1976 squad the United States sent to Montreal found a way to flourish in its own generational way. While there was no Spitzian performance on an individual basis, Naber and Goodell stood out as solo stars, and the sum of the team's parts equated to legendary status for this Red, White, and Blue roster.

"Nothing could be explained on a physical basis," said Gary Hall, a team captain alongside Steve Furniss. "It was an emotionally charged team. It led us to compete at a level beyond what we thought we were capable of."

One of the legendary figures in the sport, Doc Counsilman immediately recognized the special nature of the team he would oversee as the head coach of Team USA in Montreal. For one, several of his Indiana University swimmers, including Jim Montgomery and Hall, dotted the

roster. Meanwhile, Counsilman was aware of the talent he inherited from programs such as the University of Southern California (USC) and the Mission Viejo Nadadores, among others.

The key for Counsilman was connecting these rivals as teammates and convincing them to buy into a team approach. On the surface, that objective was not a simple task. At the time, Indiana and USC were fierce rivals on the collegiate scene, and with numerous athletes from the schools on the Team USA roster, how they would blend as teammates was a question.

Although he was not part of the coaching staff for the 1968 Olympics in Mexico City, Counsilman paid several visits to the Team USA training camp for those Games. During those stops, Counsilman saw a fractured team, one that featured obvious clicks and a lack of unity. The Indiana swimmers kept to themselves, as did the Southern California guys. Meanwhile, the Stanford and Yale athletes did not break ranks, either. The environment was not to Counsilman's liking, and, when he took the reins of the 1976 squad, a primary focus was breaking down barriers and bringing a united team to Montreal. Ultimately, Counsilman succeeded, and the Hall of Famer was able to paint a picture of vast success ahead of the Olympic Games.

"(Counsilman) began the training camp with a pep talk to the team," Naber said.

> He said, "Congratulations, gentlemen. I assume that each you have a goal for your performances in Montreal. Allow me to share my goals for this team with you. In the 13 men's events on the program, I think we can win every one. I believe we can win more medals than the rest of the world combined, and I think we can win more medals than all the other U.S. sports teams combined." With those words, he magically lifted our sights from what each of us might do, to what we could accomplish as a team. The backstrokers began to encourage the butterfliers. The sprinters helped the distance men. Medley swimmers pulled for the relays. No one was left behind. Doc also ordered that all club and school T-shirts and jackets be shipped home.

Counsilman had long been known as a master motivator, and this initial speech to the 1976 group worked wonders in breaking down walls between rivals and generating a belief that the team was unbeatable. The results from the Games proved—with one exception—that the team indeed was an unstoppable force. Even before Montreal, though, the level of racing was top-notch. As the athletes looked around the practice deck, they saw their biggest obstacles to Olympic glory. There was no mystery that the difference between a gold medal and a silver medal could be beating a teammate. Yet, Counsilman designed a training camp that kept both competitiveness and camaraderie high. Finding that balance perfectly positioned the team for the Games.

"Workouts were fun, but also intense," said Naber, who complemented his individual backstroke wins with a silver medal in the 200 freestyle and contributions to both winning relays. "Like events were trained together. George Haines had all the backstrokers, and we trained similar sets on similar sendoffs. Naturally, we were aware of what the others were doing. We often did broken swims and the sums of our times often were faster than the existing world records. There was a sense that this team was firing on all cylinders."

The belief by Counsilman that his team could win every event in Montreal—whether motivational or wholeheartedly truthful—nearly came to fruition over the week of racing. Only David Wilkie managed to prevent a sweep for the United States, as the British star won the gold medal in the 200-meter breaststroke in a world-record time, Americans John Hencken and Rick Colella taking silver and bronze.

"I wanted to win very badly, and I wasn't worried at all about the run of American successes," Wilkie said. "I just swam for myself and for Britain. A great deal of effort and hard work went into the achievement. I'll always cherish the moment."

If there was any doubt in the team members before the meet started, it was erased on the opening night of competition. The 200 butterfly was the first individual event on the schedule and East Germany's Roger Pyttel was the favorite for gold. When the swimmers touched the wall and looked to the scoreboard, an American sweep was revealed. Mike Bruner set a world record for the gold medal, with Steve Gregg and Bill Forrester picking up silver and bronze.

Counsilman met with the team each night before finals, armed with two objects. An American flag reminded the swimmers they were racing for their country. A broom was used to motivate the team toward event sweeps.

"After the 200 fly, we all looked at each other and thought, 'My God! He's right. We can do it,'" Hall said of Counsilman's belief. "It was one sweep after another."

The confidence ran so high from the start that the United States swimmers were willing to wager with the Australians when they came looking for bets on the outcome of the 1500 freestyle. The Aussies were

confident that Stephen Holland would win gold, but the U.S. saw no reason to doubt their momentum and backed Goodell and Bobby Hackett, who eventually stood on the top-two steps of the podium, Holland relegated to the bronze medal.

Simply, the Games proved to be a U.S. rout. Consider the team and individual achievements:

- In addition to winning 12 of the 13 events on the schedule, the United States accounted for 11 world records. Eight individuals won solo gold medals, Naber (100 backstroke/200 backstroke) and Goodell (400 freestyle/1,500 freestyle) emerging with a pair of solo crowns. Overall, 19 members of the team earned a place on the medals podium.
- With the Games allowing three athletes per country through 1980, the United States swept the podium in four events—200 freestyle, 200 backstroke, 100 butterfly, and 200 butterfly. Additionally, the United States captured gold and silver in the 100 freestyle, 400 freestyle, 1,500 freestyle, 100 backstroke, and 400 individual medley.
- Of the 35 medals the United States could have claimed, it tallied 27, or 77 percent.
- In the 11 individual events contested, the United States failed to earn two medals in just the 100 breaststroke, which was won by Hencken ahead of Wilkie and the Soviet Union's Arvydas Juozaitis.
- In relay action, the 800 freestyle relay prevailed by more than four seconds while the 400 medley relay was triumphant by more than three seconds.

If not for a change in the schedule from the previous Olympiad, the United States could have been more impressive. In a shift from 1972, the International Olympic Committee cut the 200 individual medley and 400 freestyle relay from the program. While the 200 medley could have produced another American sweep, the 400 free relay would have been a foregone conclusion based on the U.S. power and depth among its sprint freestylers.

The 1976 Games also served as a stage for one of the most significant barrier-breaking swims in history. When Jim Montgomery touched the wall to complete his victory in the 100 freestyle, the clock read 49.99, marking the first time a man had covered the event in under 50 seconds. Although South African Jonty Skinner, barred from the Games due to his country's Apartheid practices, broke that record less than a month later, the fact that Montgomery produced a barrier-breaking swim in Montreal fit perfectly with the virtuoso showing of Team USA.

Montgomery was largely unimpressed with his sub-50 effort, his gold medal the more meaningful achievement. Counsilman, though, told his pupil that the achievement would take on greater significance as time passed.

"He was exactly right," Montgomery said.

While the U.S. men shined and enjoyed celebration after celebration, the same could not be said for the American women. Although stacked with an impressive roster of their own, the U.S. ladies ran into the doping-charged women of East Germany. Fueled by the systematic doping program that was instituted at the government level and ran from the 1970s into the late 1980s, East German women were victorious in 11 of 13 events, posted gold-silver finishes in five events, and swept the medals in the 200 butterfly.

The East German dominance left the United States with just seven medals, a dreadful showing for a country accustomed to topping the medals standings. Shirley Babashoff, who won three silver medals behind East German titlists, didn't mince words in Montreal, and accused the East Germans of performance-enhancing drug use. Babashoff's willingness to speak out, ahead of the revelation years later that a state-sponsored doping program was at work, earned her condemnation in the press, including the nickname "Surly Shirley." The backdrop of the American men's success made the situation that much more difficult to accept, along with the International Olympic Committee's continued refusal to disqualify the East Germans known to dope and present medals to the rightful winners.

"From our side of it, the whole issue has been shoved under the carpet," Babashoff said.

> I think it is sad. So many women deserved their medals. They were cheated out of their medals at the Olympics. We would like to get what we earned. We were going for the medals, not the cash. We were amateurs. We worked so hard. We earned it, and it was stolen right in front of everyone's face, and no one did anything about it. It was like watching a robbery where they just let the crooks go and then say, "It's okay".

The efforts of the 1976 squad were the last for Team USA in Olympic action until 1984, due to the U.S. boycott of the 1980 Games in Moscow

A double gold medalist at the 1976 Olympics in Montreal, Brian Goodell was a member of the greatest team the sport has seen. Peter H. Bick.

over the Soviet Union's invasion of Afghanistan. That boycott denied a handful of members of the 1976 team from a second Olympic opportunity, most notably Goodell. As a 21-year-old in 1980, Goodell was in peak form and would have defended his gold medals in the 400 freestyle and 1,500 freestyle against the Soviet Union's Vladimir Salnikov. Instead, he watched bitterly as Salnikov won both crowns.

"I would have been in the prime of my career," Goodell said.

The power of the 1976 U.S. men's team also fueled a change in international competition. While nations were still allowed to enter three athletes per event at the 1980 Olympics, the entry limit was reduced to two beginning with the 1984 Games in Los Angeles. The decision hinged on preventing countries like the United States from dominating and sweeping podiums and giving other nations a chance for increased medal representation.

The possibility of a country matching or bettering the achievements of the 1976 U.S. men's Olympic Team is minimal. Aside from the two-per-nation participation rule, worldwide depth is more prominent than it was 40-plus years ago. Regardless of what unfolds in the sport's future, this 1976 squad will be remembered for its legendary status.

"At the time, our results were not astounding," Naber said. "They were what we were expecting. Each tipping point turned in our favor, and with each success, our momentum grew. Looking back on it now, I can see how significant it might seem, but at the time we just wanted to win."

They did. Again, and again.

THE AIR-GUITAR ASSAULT

More than 17,000 passionate Australian fans stood and yelled, anticipating a moment their country had long envisioned. The Sydney Aquatic Center was the focal point of the 2000 Olympic Games and, as the first night of competition neared its end, those who filled the stands in this swimming-crazed country sensed it was time for something special to unfold. In a little more than three minutes, the atmosphere would be either pure jubilation or complete sorrow.

In the months leading into the 27th Olympiad, Australia was deemed a major threat to the U.S. stranglehold on the 400-meter freestyle relay title. With two bona fide stars, veteran Michael Klim and teenage sensation Ian Thorpe, the Aussies featured stellar bookend options for the relay, the middle legs of Chris Fydler and Ashley Callus more than reliable. With the necessary ingredients present, Australia was confident it could capture—on home soil—the biggest Olympic victory in its history.

The 400 freestyle relay became part of the Olympic schedule at the 1964 Games in Tokyo, and in seven editions of the event, only the United States had mined the gold medal. (The relay was not contested in 1976 and 1980.) Actually, Team USA dominated the event, winning by an average margin of more than two seconds. Adding to the lore of the United States in the 400 freestyle relay was the fact that it was a perfect 8-for-8 at the World Championships.

Conversely, Australia didn't have much of a tradition in the event, having won just a silver medal (1984) and two bronze medals (1964/1968) in Olympic action. A positive for Australia, however, was its silver medal behind the United States at the 1998 World Championships. It was a loss by just 0.28 and came without the presence of Thorpe, who was certainly going to have an impact on the outcome in Sydney. More, the Aussies edged the United States at the 1999 Pan Pacific Championships, and while that competition didn't feature a worldwide field and the United States was without some big names, it was a confidence boost.

With Australia poised to flourish, the Sydney Organizing Committee for the Olympic Games (SOCOG) worked out a deal to have the Sydney Aquatic Center expanded. Originally designed to fit 15,000 spectators, an expansion of the East grandstand increased the venue's capacity to 17,500.

Playing a significant role in the expansion project was Glenn Tasker, who followed his duties as the executive director of New South Wales Swimming by becoming the Swimming Competition Manager for the Sydney Games. As Australia prepared to host the Olympic Games for the first time since 1956 in Melbourne, Tasker envisioned an atmosphere in which as many Australians as possible could enjoy the spectacle. He also appreciated the desire of fans to catch a glimpse of Thorpe, who Tasker had watched develop from a ten-year-old age-group sensation into an athlete pegged as a can't-miss superstar and the pride of a nation.

From 1998 to 2000, Australia was the hub of the swimming world. The nation hosted the 1998 World Championships in Perth, and Tasker served as the event manager of the 1999 Pan Pacific Championships in Sydney before serving in his role for the Olympic Games. Tasker was so successful as a sports administrator that he was the CEO of Swimming Australia from 2001 to 2008. When he died following a massive heart attack in 2019, countless sports figures in Australia spoke of the void that would be felt.

"It was his passion for the sport, the athletes, the coaches, the fans and the Sydney swimming community that made him stand head and shoulders above the rest," said Ian Hanson, the former media director for Australian Swimming.

Australia's optimism hardly dented the American belief that an eighth consecutive Olympic title was on the horizon. Despite the knowledge that this Olympiad would likely produce its biggest challenge, the United States boasted a daunting lineup of Anthony Ervin, an upcoming sprint star, Neil Walker, Jason Lezak, and Gary Hall Jr.

The son of a three-time Olympian by the same name, Hall was equally known for his ability in the water and an oversized personality. Hall was never afraid to express his opinions on a variety of topics, from doping to the opposition, and brought to the blocks a showmanship that was unusual for a generally conservative sport. One of Hall's calling cards was wearing

Despite a tremendous effort, Gary Hall Jr. and the United States fell to Australia in the 400 freestyle relay at the 2000 Olympic games. Peter H. Bick.

Apollo Creed-esque shorts, seen in the Rocky movies, and performing a shadow-boxing routine behind the starting blocks.

After emerging from the gauntlet that is the United States Olympic Trials as the champion of the 50 freestyle and runner-up in the 100 freestyle, Hall was slated to contest four events in Sydney—two individual and two relays. His first event would be the 400 free relay, and Hall felt the United States would establish early momentum.

"I like Australia, in truth. I like Australians," Hall said in an Olympic diary he kept for *Sports Illustrated*. "The country is beautiful, and the people are admirable. Good humor and genuine kindness seem a predominant characteristic. My biased opinion says that we will smash them like guitars. Historically the U.S. has always risen to the occasion. But the logic in that remote area of my brain says it won't be so easy for the United States to dominate the waters this time. Whatever the results, the world will witness great swimming."

As the teams made their way to the deck, the Aussie crowd was already in a frenzy. Earlier in the night, Thorpe fulfilled the massive potential that had been placed upon his shoulders when he won the gold medal in the 400-meter freestyle, setting a world record of 3:40.59. The 17-year-old was nothing short of spectacular, beating Italian silver medalist Massimiliano Rosolino by nearly three seconds and American bronze medalist Klete Keller by more than six seconds. Racing in his own realm, Thorpe provided his home nation with much to celebrate and delivered on his vast promise.

At the 1998 World Championships in Perth, a 15-year-old Thorpe became the youngest male world champion in history when he won the 400 freestyle. Simultaneously, he ignited conversation about becoming an Olympic champion and, potentially, establishing himself as one of his sport's all-time greats. This speculation did not just come from journalists seeking an angle ahead of the Sydney Olympics, but also from high-ranking individuals within the sport.

When asked about the potential of young athletes, most coaches will choose their words carefully, cognizant of not creating undue pressure. Don Talbot, Australia's head coach during the emergence of Thorpe, did not abide by that thought process. Rather, Talbot took a contrasting approach, speaking openly and audaciously about Thorpe's skill set and ability to handle the lofty expectations that were impossible to miss.

"I've never seen a better swimmer than him," Talbot said. "He's got a great feel for the water. He makes it look easy. His maturity, that's what you notice. He's 17, but he seems like he's someone in his 30s or 40s. It's almost spooky. It's genetics gone bloody crazy. He could be the swimmer of the century.

"I think he's coping, handling it well, but he's got to feel pressure. Nineteen million people want him to win. He's a young boy with an octogenarian's head. It's amazing. But he's got to feel the pressure. In Australia, it's always been that way. You're nothing until you win a gold medal. If you don't win gold at the Olympics, you're not one of the greats."

Indeed, Thorpe handled the pressure with aplomb, as was demonstrated in his triumph in the 400 freestyle. Through that victory, he proved he wasn't overwhelmed by having his image adorn the front of buildings and billboards, from having his name in countless headlines and from having an entire sporting venue chant, "Thorpey, Thorpey, Thorpey."

While Thorpe's win in the 400 freestyle elated the Aussies in attendance, and the millions watching on television, the 400 freestyle relay carried greater significance. It was a chance for Australia to supplant the United States, and it meant that Thorpe, although supported by three teammates, was carrying a nation's hopes on his shoulders and in his well-documented size-17 feet.

"As soon as I walked out there, it was like a gladiator walking into the Colosseum, hearing the sheer noise of the crowd," Thorpe said. "'I was ready to race.'"

Michael Klim's leadoff leg in the 400 freestyle relay produced a world record and carried Australia to gold at the 2000 Olympics in Sydney. Peter H. Bick.

Aside from the United States facing its biggest test in Olympic waters in the event, Hall's comments added to the race's intrigue. The Team USA veteran may have been complimentary of Australia as a country and recognized that a battle awaited, but he also predicted an American victory, taking a page out of the book of Joe Namath, the National Football League quarterback who famously predicted a New York Jets upset over the Baltimore Colts in Super Bowl III.

If Hall thought his comments were innocuous and were going to fly under the radar, he quickly learned otherwise. Newspapers throughout Australia picked up on the American's words and, in an instant, they were splashed across numerous front pages and websites. At the same time, Hall became a villain, the "smash them like guitars" portion of his statement seemingly the only part that received focus.

"We came down to the lobby and there it was on the front page of the paper," Klim said of Hall's infamous words from his diary. "To be totally honest, we really didn't take it too seriously and despite what people think, it wasn't really motivating for us. We knew we were walking into something that was going to be incredibly tough. The Americans had never been beaten at the Olympics and were world-record holders."

Minutes before the race was scheduled to start, additional drama unfolded off the deck. Following his win in the 400 freestyle, Thorpe ripped the suit he intended to wear in the relay. Australian team managers

Lynn Fowlie and David Wilson were given the chore of finding Thorpe's wet suit from his individual event and getting it on the teenage star in time for the relay.

As the teams walked onto the deck for the 400 freestyle relay, only three Australians were visible. However, by the time the Australian team was introduced, Thorpe was behind the starting blocks and prepared to carry his country into Olympic lore.

Following the prerace introductions, it took a few extra seconds for the crowd to settle down and allow the meet referee to start the race. As much as the Aussies in the crowd were excited for the possibility of home-turf success, there was an equal level of tension and nerves. What if Australia did not take advantage of this opportunity? How long would it take for another chance to arise? This one took nearly 40 years and the span of eight Olympiads and the prospect of not coming through was sickening.

"I had been to the previous four Olympic Games in Los Angeles, Seoul, Barcelona and Atlanta and although (Los Angeles) was an amazing Games, a great outdoor venue and a huge success for the home team, this was different," Hanson said. "The buildup was like nothing any of the athletes, coaches, administrators and the media had ever experienced before. Thorpe was a phenomenon. Along with (track star) Cathy Freeman, he was the face of the Games. His image was everywhere. And looking back on pressure in sport, then this was pressure personified.

"On the flip side, there was also a weird sense of calmness as well. He was at home. He was in familiar surroundings. As soon as we walked off the bus from the (Olympic) Village and into the venue, Ian was in his second home. This was his safe haven. It was a place where he had swum his earliest school carnivals. It was the place where he saw familiar faces, faces of ageless volunteers, officials who had followed this kid from his earliest races."

With the partisan crowd eventually quieted, the eight leadoff swimmers took to their blocks, but this race was about the United States in Lane Four and Australia in Lane Five. For the Aussies, the event could not have started any better.

Slicing through the water in powerful fashion, Klim propelled Australia into an early lead and continued to build an advantage over Ervin. While the American teenager produced an opening split of 48.89 to put the United States in second place, Klim covered his two laps in 48.18, which cut 0.03 off Alexander Popov's previous world record in the 100 freestyle of 48.21, which had stood for six years. Not surprising, the already amped-up venue was now roaring in overdrive.

"I wasn't going for a personal best or anything," Klim said. "I just wanted to get the guys a pretty good lead. I knew if I did that, the guys would do their jobs."

Staked to a lead of 0.71, Fydler entered the water second for the Aussies, with Walker handling the leg for Team USA. At the turn, the Australian lead had been all but erased by Walker, but Fydler was known as the better finisher and made up most of the ground he yielded in the final 15 meters. With Walker splitting 48.31 to the 48.48 of Fydler, the United States trailed at the race's midway point by 0.54.

Into the water third were Callus and Lezak, who engaged in a duel that resembled what was produced by Fydler and Walker. Lezak immediately pulled even with Callus and even gave the Americans their first lead at the 250-meter mark. But Callus was the stronger racer in the closing strokes and put the Aussies back in front as he touched the wall for the exchange to Thorpe. Off of Lezak's split of 48.42, compared to the 48.71 of Callus, the Australians were now in front by just 0.25.

For Lezak, Sydney launched a decade-plus-long stretch as a relay leader for the United States. On 13 occasions, Lezak won a medal for the United States in global action in either the 400 freestyle relay or the 400 medley relay, with eight of those medals gold. His crowning moment arrived in 2008 when Lezak etched himself in Olympic lore by pulling off an epic comeback in the 400 free relay. With the United States trailing France by a sizable margin on the final leg, Lezak continually reeled in Frenchman Alain Bernard and touched just ahead of him at the finish, the comeback win keeping alive Michael Phelps' march to eight gold medals. Those 2008 Games in Beijing also saw Lezak win individual bronze in the 100 freestyle.

The matchup of Thorpe and Hall on the anchor legs was a contrast of styles—in the water and on land. While Hall was a pure sprinter and went on to share the gold medal in the 50 freestyle with Ervin later in the week, Thorpe was best known as a middle-distance star. More, Hall's showman persona was countered by Thorpe's measured and quiet demeanor. What they shared was a desire to represent their countries and to perform in the spotlight, when the pressure was at its highest.

The next 100 meters produced an epic showdown between Thorpe and Hall and put the bow on one of the greatest races in Olympic history. As expected, Hall pulled even, then ahead of Thorpe, as the future Hall of Famers raced their first laps. At the turn, Hall held a half-body-length lead, but could he maintain that edge over his rival, who was unquestionably the better finisher? With 15 meters left and Hall tiring, Thorpe, who was clad in his trademark bodysuit, pulled alongside his foe and then ahead. As they hit the touchpads, the scoreboard flashed a world-record time of 3:13.67 for the Australians, the United States second in 3:13.86, also under the previous world record. Hall actually outsplit Thorpe, 48.23 to 48.30, but it was not enough and magnified the importance of Klim's spectacular leadoff leg.

Upon finishing the race, Thorpe thrust a fist in the air and wasted little time hopping out of the pool to celebrate with his teammates. Hugs, fist pumps, and waves to the crowd accounted for some of the celebratory actions from the Aussies, but the best was to come. Much to the satisfaction of the fans, the Aussies took part in an impromptu air-guitar performance, an obvious reaction to Hall's earlier comments. Although Klim initially tried to downplay Hall's comments when the Aussie claimed they did not serve as a motivating force, the deckside antics said otherwise.

"I think it was (Fydler) who suggested it," Klim said. "We whispered in each other's ears, 'let's do the air guitars.' That wasn't planned nor had we spoken about it. Hadn't been mentioned at all, but on the spur of the moment we did it. But I must say, Gary Hall was the first swimmer to come over and congratulate us. Even though he dished it out, he was a true sportsman."

"We had the presentation, then drug testing, then headed back to the village. I still remember walking into the dining hall, it was about midnight, maybe later, but there were still maybe 200 people there and we got a standing ovation. For the next two days wherever we went we were getting standing ovations."

Hall was nothing short of gracious as he analyzed the race, and his performance was superb. Not only did Hall generate a split that was slightly quicker than what Thorpe managed, but it was the third-fastest in the entire race, bettered only by Klim's leadoff and the 48.12 delivered by Lars Frolander on Sweden's sixth-place squad.

The rest of the week was sensational for Hall, who complemented his joint gold in the 50 freestyle with Ervin with a gold medal as a member of the American 400 medley relay and a bronze medal in the 100 freestyle. Four years later, Hall repeated as Olympic champion in the 50 free.

"I'd be a liar if I said it wasn't somewhat disappointing," Hall said of the relay loss. "In the same breath, I'd say we were close to a second under the world record. It's nothing to be ashamed of. Tonight was something the swimming world has never seen before. The last 50 meters were rather painful. I went after it. This is the Olympics, all or nothing. I doff my swimming cap to the great Ian Thorpe. He had a better finish than I had."

The setback to Australia in the 400 freestyle relay not only snapped the U.S. 15-race winning streak in the event in global competition but also started a drought for Team USA. In 2001, Australia won gold in the 400 free relay at the World Champs, with Russia winning the event at the 2003 World Champs, a year before South Africa won Olympic gold in Athens.

Meanwhile, Thorpe maintained—and elevated—his status as one of the sport's all-time legends. In Sydney, Thorpe guided Australia to a second relay gold, this time in the 800 freestyle relay, and was the silver medalist in the 200 freestyle, where he was upset by the Netherlands' Pieter van den Hoogenband. A year later, Thorpe set three world records (200/400/800 freestyle) at the 2001 World Champs and retained his titles in the 200 free and 400 free two years later in Barcelona. At the 2004 Olympics, Thorpe won the 200 free for the first time, exacting revenge on van den Hoogenband, and repeated as champion of the 400 freestyle.

For all Thorpe accomplished during his illustrious career, Sydney will always hold a special place in his memory.

"It would have to be the best day of my life, the best hour, the best minute," Thorpe said.

> To be able to dream and to fulfill it is the best thing an individual can do. It's amazing to be in this situation and to perform well. I'm one of the select few athletes who have performed at their best at the Olympic Games. The statistics on that are very slim. It's one of the things I wanted to do. It was pretty amazing in front of my own crowd and it was just fortunate I was able to perform well in front of them. It really was a dream come true. When you race in Australia, you can't let them down. I'm on such a high.

So was an entire nation.

RACE OF THE CENTURY

What would have happened?

It's a question that comes up frequently when discussing sports history, and fans try to gauge the outcome of a matchup between athletes from distinct eras. What would have happened if Wilt Chamberlain and Shaquille O'Neal regularly battled on the basketball court? Who would have dominated if Babe Ruth regularly faced Roger Clemens on the baseball diamond? How would Tiger Woods have fared against Jack Nicklaus on the golf course?

Although entertaining and thought-provoking, these cross-era queries can never be truly answered, and the responses offered will be conflicting.

But every now and again, a sport will find itself in a unique period in which a handful of all-time performers are simultaneously active and will duel on a big stage.

For more than a decade, the tennis world has been in the position of producing routine meetings between three greats of the sport—Roger Federer, Rafael Nadal, and Novak Djokovic. It is an era never previously seen, and, when it fades away, it will be deeply missed.

At the 2004 Olympic Games in Athens, swimming fans were treated to one of these rare moments when Ian Thorpe, Pieter van den Hoogenband, and Michael Phelps raced in the same pool, chasing the gold medal in the 200-meter freestyle. The event brought together—arguably—the three biggest names in the sport and was coined the Race of the Century, a nickname previously given to major showdowns in stopwatch sports.

In the first half of the 1900s, horse racing had its Race of the Century when War Admiral and Seabiscuit squared off at Pimlico Race Course. In 1954, Great Britain's Roger Bannister and Australia's John Landry ran track and field's version of the Race of the Century in the mile at the British Empire and Commonwealth Games.

In 2004, it was swimming's turn.

Because the new millennium was just four years old, anointing any clash as the Race of the Century seemed like hyperbole run amok. How could a race earn such a distinction with the century's future—96 years' worth to be exact—so uncertain? The answer is simple. So rare are the moments in which three legendary figures test themselves against one another, journalists immediately sought to define the moment with a moniker.

In the case of what unfolded under a blue, evening sky in the birthplace of the Olympic Games, perhaps it was acceptable to give this showdown a premature description. After all, in the water were two Olympic champions from the previous Games in Thorpe and van den Hoogenband and, in Phelps, a former phenom who had the potential to become the greatest athlete in his sport's history.

The perfect alignment of the stars may have brought Thorpe, van den Hoogenband, and Phelps together, but a look at the preceding years is necessary to appreciate how this Race of the Century took form.

The 2000 Olympics in Sydney marked the first international meeting between Thorpe and van den Hoogenband, both rising stars. Thorpe was the talk of the swimming community, his 1998 world title as a 15-year-old in the 400 freestyle fulfilling the vast potential he showed during his age-group years. And with the 27th Olympiad on Thorpe's home soil, there were off-the-charts expectations for what the teenager would do.

Before the Games, the Sydney Aquatic Centre seating capacity was expanded to 17,500 to meet the demands of a nation that adored the sport and had fallen in love with Thorpe, his beautiful stroke, and his size-17 feet. Fans and journalists alike anticipated a pair of individual gold medals for Thorpe, and his image was splashed all over newspapers, magazines, and billboards.

"I don't look at (the expectations) as pressure. I look at it as support," Thorpe said. "I guess that I will have a hometown advantage. I'm very excited at this stage. I want to savor these days leading up to the Games and savor the Games themselves."

Enjoying his first Olympic foray was easy on the opening night of the competition, as he delivered his first solo title by winning the 400 freestyle in world-record time. That same evening, Thorpe anchored Australia to gold in the 400 freestyle relay, the Aussies setting a world record and handing the United States its first Olympic loss in the event.

While Thorpe could not have designed a better start to the Games, van den Hoogenband found himself sitting around. A disqualification of the Netherlands in the preliminaries of the 400 freestyle relay left van den Hoogenband idle on Day One and yearning to get in the water in a competitive fashion. It was not an easy position for van den Hoogenband, who just missed the podium twice at the 1996 Olympics, following fourth-place finishes in the 100 freestyle and 200 freestyle.

He finally got the chance to get wet on the third day of the meet and immediately made noise. After advancing to the semifinals of the 200 free as the No. 2 seed, sitting behind Thorpe, van den Hoogenband eclipsed Thorpe's world record in the event in the first of two semifinals, going 1:45.35. While Thorpe answered in the second semifinal with a clocking of 1:45.37, van den Hoogenband's performance revealed the hometown hero had a serious challenge in front of him.

"I think the (semifinal) might have been a psychological blow," van den Hoogenband said of his world-record outing.

As the finalists in the 200 freestyle were announced, van den Hoogenband and Thorpe were calm awaiting their introductions, focused on the task ahead of them. After the Dutchman received ample applause, the spectators erupted in cheers for Thorpe. Once the athletes entered the water, they dazzled for nearly two minutes.

For most of the four laps, van den Hoogenband held a slight edge on Thorpe. But when the crowd expected Thorpe to pull even, and then ahead, with his customary strong finish, it was van den Hoogenband who slightly expanded his lead and got to the wall in the exact time he managed in the semifinals. Van den Hoogenband's world-record-equaling time of 1:45.35 was comfortably ahead of the 1:45.83 mark of Thorpe, who was nearly a half-second slower than the semifinals.

Realizing he had won the gold medal and slain the dragon in his home den, van den Hoogenband covered his eyes with his hands. Thorpe then swam over the lane line and greeted his rival with a congratulatory hug. For Hoogie, as he was known, it was merely the beginning of a sensational week, as he followed with another gold medal in the 100 freestyle and added a bronze medal in the 50 freestyle.

"It's unbelievable to be able to do this," van den Hoogenband said. "In (Thorpe's) home nation. In his home city. In his home pool. It's eerie. With 25 meters left, I didn't see him creeping up on me. I thought, 'Man, he's not going to touch me.' It's an amazing thing to beat the favorite."

A momentum shift in favor of Thorpe defined the rivalry between the friendly foes over the next few years. At the 2001 World Championships, where Thorpe set three world records in individual events, he covered the 200 freestyle in 1:44.06, leaving van den Hoogenband, who won three solo silver medals, well behind in 1:45.81. Two years later, with the World Champs in Barcelona, Thorpe again came out on top, this time beating van den Hoogenband by more than a second.

Van den Hoogenband might have been the reigning Olympic champion, but as the 2004 Games in Athens crept closer, there was no confusion concerning the favorite for gold. Thorpe had taken the world record to 1:44-low, and while Hoogie had gone 1:44.89 for the European title in 2002, his best was now nearly a second adrift.

The debut of Phelps to the hit show starring Thorpe and van den Hoogenband was akin to a highly rated television series adding a new character. While some changes disturb a successful dynamic, Phelps was a welcome addition by audiences, who saw the 200 freestyle elevate in status and become the can't-miss event of the 2004 Olympics, and one of the most anticipated events in Olympic history.

In his first Olympic appearance in 2000, where Thorpe and van den Hoogenband went head-to-head, a 15-year-old Phelps was just beginning to grab the attention of the world. The youngest American male swimming Olympian in 68 years, Phelps placed fifth in the 200 butterfly but, more importantly, signaled big things to come.

Phelps was more than an athlete who was ahead of his time from a performance standpoint. He exhibited an innate ability to focus and eliminate any outside interference. When he climbed onto the blocks, he looked as comfortable among the best swimmers on the planet as he was racing fellow teenagers in local meets around his Baltimore home.

"How do you stand this?" asked Mark Schubert, a multi-time Olympic coach, of Phelps' coach, Bob Bowman. "I have never seen anyone his age like him. You look at the Olympic Trials, the most pressure-packed meet in the world, and now the Olympics. He is truly phenomenal."

But Sydney was simply a launching pad.

By the next year, Phelps was the world-record holder in the 200 fly and secured a world title in the event, with the 2002 season boasting a world record in the 400 individual medley. At the 2003 World Championships in Barcelona, Phelps delivered his biggest statement, capturing gold medals and setting world records in the 200 fly and both individual medley events. Overall, the 2003 campaign featured eight world records from Phelps, who was challenging Thorpe—if not already passing him—as the sport's premier star.

Although the 200 freestyle had yet to appear on Phelps' international schedule, he won the event at the 2003 U.S. National Championships and he led off the U.S. silver-medal-winning 800 freestyle relay at the World Champs with an American-record time of 1:46.60. The national title and effort from the World Champs were enough to garner attention, and clues that Phelps, along with Bowman, was considering adding the 200 freestyle to his Olympic program for the following summer.

As 2004 rolled around, the 200 freestyle indeed became a focal point, and when Phelps won the event at the United States Olympic Trials, the Race of the Century was confirmed. That the race was slated for Athens, the home of the Olympic Games, added to the atmosphere.

"This is the best opportunity for me to swim in the fastest 200 (freestyle) in history," Phelps said. "I love a challenge."

The 200 freestyle, though, accounted for a single quiz in a multipart exam for Phelps, whose schedule included eight events—five individual and three relays. That arduous schedule was one focal point of the Athens Games, which had plenty of storylines in the pool. From the latest chapters in the breaststroke rivalry of Japan's Kosuke Kitajima and American Brendan Hansen to the United States' Amanda Beard medaling in a third straight Olympics, there was no shortage of interesting angles. But there was no event that could rival what the 200 freestyle featured—three living or developing legends fighting for glory.

"I don't see us as being animals and marking our territory," Thorpe said. "Not yet. I don't think there's anyone's territory. I enjoy challenging myself rather than it just being about who's in the race. I think Michael wanted to swim this race not just because I was in it, but you know, I think he wanted another challenge. For athletes, that's what we're here to do. I'm glad that I've had the opportunity to race against some of the world's best athletes in my event."

The final of the 200 freestyle was not scheduled until the third day of the meet, at which point each of the participants had raced at least one event in addition to the preliminaries and semifinals of the 200 free. On the opening day of action, Thorpe and Phelps secured their first gold medals of the Games, Thorpe winning the 400 freestyle and Phelps prevailing in the 400 individual medley. Regaining his crown from four years earlier, Thorpe had a tougher time in Athens, as he was pushed to the wall by countryman Grant Hackett. At the finish, Thorpe's time of 3:43.10 was just enough to get the job done, as Hackett touched in 3:43.36. As for Phelps, he won the 400 medley by more than three seconds over fellow American Erik Vendt, handing the 19-year-old what he longed to claim—an Olympic title.

A day later, Thorpe and Phelps were joined by van den Hoogenband in the 400 freestyle relay. While South Africa stunned the world with its gold-medal performance, van den Hoogenband's anchor split of 46.79 lifted the Netherlands to a surprise silver medal, the United States and Phelps taking bronze, and Thorpe and the Australians fifth and off the podium. Phelps' inclusion on the relay was the subject of controversy, particularly with veteran Gary Hal Jr., who loudly voiced his displeasure of being left off the relay for the final in favor of Phelps, despite the fact he did not contest the event at the United States Trials.

What wasn't controversial was the anticipation for the showdown between the sport's Big Three. Each man had no trouble advancing to the final, evident in how they were the top three seeds, and as their names were announced prior to the start of the 200 free, spectators in Athens' outdoor venue were fixated on the middle of the pool.

Looking to benefit from his natural speed, van den Hoogenband shot to the front of the field down the first lap, touching at the 50-meter mark in first, with Thorpe sitting in second and Phelps in fourth. At the midway point, van den Hoogenband still led Thorpe, 50.52 to 51.04, with Phelps now in third in 51.70. It was the third lap in which Thorpe began to make his move.

On the shoulder of van den Hoogenband in Sydney, Thorpe was unable to narrow the gap in front of his home crowd. This time around, the Aussie found the reserve power to reel him in. At the 150-meter mark, Thorpe had closed to within 0.20, 1:17.72 to 1:17.92, with Phelps back in 1:18.83. Over the last lap, Thorpe had van den Hoogenband's number. Thorpe's deficit at the turn was wiped out by the time the swimmers surfaced and the Aussie simply pulled away with each stroke, stopping the clock in 1:44.71, with van den Hoogenband earning the silver medal in 1:45.23. Thorpe split 26.79 for the closing 50 meters to the 27.51 of Hoogie. In grabbing the bronze medal, Phelps set an American record of 1:45.32 and posted the fastest last-lap split, going 26.49.

The typically reserved Thorpe looked to the scoreboard at the finish and raised an arm in the air at the realization of his victory, followed by a few short fist pumps. He and van den Hoogenband then shook hands, shared a hug, and exchanged a few words, in what was a clear display of appreciation for one another's talents and their rivalry.

"It was the final that excited a lot of people," Thorpe said. "This has been played out on three continents in the leadup to the Olympic Games, so it became a big deal. But I wasn't focused on that. I really wanted to concentrate on what I was trying to do, make sure I swam the race well. I was able to do that. For me, that's how I approached my races and I have been able to be successful in the past. I don't worry about that my competitors are doing."

> I said to (van den Hoogenband), "Well, I guess that makes it 1-1 and I'd like to see you again in Beijing. That brings up the question that was asked before, and you know I intend to be swimming it again. Pieter and I are good friends and it is a wonderful experience to be able to challenge yourself in this race, to prepare so hard in it. And you know, that's what I've done, and that's what Pieter's done. And Michael's done exactly the same thing. It's good to be able to go out there and experience that with people that you know well. People kind of have their fate and their destiny and that was what it was tonight. I've worked damn hard for this."

The 200 freestyle may have been the main attraction of the Athens Games, but it didn't mark the end of competition for the trio of combatants. Over his final five events, Phelps was perfect, claiming individual titles in the 100 butterfly, 200 butterfly, 200 individual medley, and adding relay golds in the 800 freestyle relay and the 400 medley relay to bring his week-long total to six gold medals and a pair of bronze medals. The U.S. victory in the 800 freestyle relay came at the expense of Thorpe, who couldn't rally Australia on the anchor leg and settled for silver.

Meanwhile, van den Hoogenband repeated as Olympic champion in the 100 freestyle, fending off South African Roland Schoeman by 0.06.

Earning the bronze medal was Thorpe, who demonstrated that his freestyle skill also included sprinting ability. For Phelps, the chance to race Thorpe and van den Hoogenband was something he couldn't pass up and was an experience he couldn't have envisioned as a youngster developing into a superstar.

"How can I be disappointed?" Phelps said of his finish in the 200 free-style. "I swam in a field with the two fastest freestylers of all time and I was right there with them. I'm extremely happy with that. It's a (personal) best time. It's a new American record. I wanted to race those guys and that's what I did. It was fun."

"It's a lot more emotionally draining than anything I have done before and it takes a lot out of you race to race, particularly tonight. When those guys are going so fast it makes it real exciting, but it's tough. I had an opportunity and I tried to do something that he [Mark Spitz] did, but I didn't. When I started to swim, I never thought I would have an oppor-tunity to go for seven."

The notion of a three-way rematch at the 2008 Olympics, as much as it was desired by the sport's fans, never neared fruition. Originally plan-ning a brief hiatus from the sport, Thorpe never pursued a place on the Australian squad bound for Beijing. Instead, he watched from afar as van den Hoogenband's competitive days wound down, and Phelps crafted a career that stands apart from any other in history.

Although out of the water, Thorpe still managed to drive Phelps, who was as superb finding motivation as he was powering off the wall. This time, it was Thorpe's words, not smooth strokes, that fueled Phelps' fire. Ahead of the 2008 Olympic Games in Beijing, Thorpe doubted Phelps' ability to capture eight gold medals, or even match the seven gold medals won by Spitz at the 1972 Games in Munich.

"I wish him all the best, and I'd love to see it, but I don't think he will do it," Thorpe said of Phelps' target. "There's a thing called competition. It won't just be one athlete that will be competing, and in a lot of events, he has a lot of strong competition."

Thorpe's assessment significantly missed the mark, and not only because Phelps completed his eight-gold pursuit. Competition endlessly drove Phelps, who deeply understood the obstacles he faced and was more than eager to embrace them. He also loved "he-can't-do-it" assertions, log-ging them into his mental vault for motivation.

After Phelps pulled off his Great Eight in Beijing, which included a world record of 1:42.96 in the 200 freestyle, Thorpe apologized for doubt-ing his former rival. Yet, he clearly didn't learn from the experience. As

Phelps announced his comeback from retirement for the 2016 Olympics in Rio de Janeiro, Thorpe noted Phelps might contribute to the American relays but would find it difficult to win an individual gold. Phelps again proved the Australian wrong as he left his final Olympiad with solo crowns in the 200 butterfly and 200 individual medley.

As for van den Hoogenband, the Dutchman was active in Beijing, but only in the 100 freestyle, where he was the two-time defending champion and placed fifth, 0.08 shy of the podium. But the 200 freestyle was not part of his Olympic schedule, and the reason was directly tied to what transpired at the previous year's World Championships in Melbourne.

As Phelps stormed to seven gold medals and five world records during his work Down Under, many of his results were expected, including the world records he produced in both medley events and the 200 butterfly. In the 200 freestyle, Phelps was certainly a contender for the gold medal, but when he broke Thorpe's six-year-old world record of 1:44.06 with a performance of 1:43.86, eyes opened wide. Suddenly, he was faster than the best man the event had ever seen.

Meanwhile, van den Hoogenband received an up-close view of Phelps' sharpened talents since their previous meeting, as he earned the silver medal in 1:46.28, more than two seconds off the pace. While van den Hoogenband was within 0.17 of Phelps at the midway point and within 0.43 at the 150-meter mark, Phelps unleashed a statement down the final length, outsplitting the Dutch star by 1.99 seconds. That finish convinced van den Hoogenband that his days in the 200 freestyle were over, the event now in another domain and not worth his focus.

"I was swimming OK," van den Hoogenband said of the 200 free in Melbourne. "But after every turn, he was pushing off and kicking through the water extremely fast. I was like, 'Let's see what he's got left for the last 50.' Well, he had a lot left. I thought the 200 freestyle record by (Thorpe) would last for 10, maybe 20 years."

Following the Beijing Games, van den Hoogenband joined Thorpe in hanging up his suit and goggles, but Thorpe got the urge to try a comeback in 2011. Thorpe's goal was to qualify for the 2012 Olympic Games, but his inability to advance out of the semifinals of the 200 freestyle and the prelims of the 100 freestyle at the Australian Trials ended the bid.

Phelps, of course, continued onward from Beijing. He won six medals in 2012 in London and followed, after a brief retirement, with six more medals in 2016 in Rio. Overall, Phelps won 28 Olympic medals during his career and combined with Thorpe (nine) and van den Hoogenband (seven), the centerpieces of the Race of the Century combined for 44 Olympic medals, along with 56 medals from the World Championships.

For one night in Athens, they gathered in one pool, and for one race and provided the sport with an iconic moment.

"It was special to be part of," Phelps said.

It was special to watch.

AN ANCHOR FOR THE AGES

The race was over, or so the 17,000 spectators inside the Water Cube believed. With France out in front and its superstar handling the anchor leg, the Tricolor was poised to hang in the rafters as "La Marseillaise," the French national anthem, echoed from the speakers.

Also over, or so it seemed, was the much-ballyhooed chase of eight gold medals by American superstar Michael Phelps. Looking to surpass the seven gold medals won by Mark Spitz at the 1972 Olympic Games in Munich, Phelps was only on Step Two of his grand plan and it had already short-circuited.

Every Olympiad is stamped with a few defining moments. In 1936, Jesse Owens ran away from the field in the 100-meter dash as Adolf Hitler looked on. In 1968, 200-meter dash medalists Tommie Smith and John Carlos stood on the podium with raised, gloved fists to protest racism and injustices against African Americans. In 1996, despite torn ligaments in her ankle, gymnast Kerri Strug scored high enough on her final vault to propel the United States to its first gold medal in the team competition.

At the 2008 Olympics in Beijing, two moments shined as iconic.

On the track, Jamaican sprinter Usain Bolt wowed the world when he captured gold medals and set world records in the 100- and 200-meter dashes. Unleashing never-before-seen speed, Bolt covered the 100 meters in 9.69 and blistered the track in the 200 meters in 19.30. The effort ushered in a new era in sprinting and launched Bolt to global fame.

The other iconic moment from Beijing unfolded across the street from where Bolt did his work. Inside the Water Cube, the venue which appeared like it was covered in bubble wrap, an improbable comeback became the headline story of Day Two's finals. As important, it ultimately proved to be a history-saving performance.

The hype leading into the men's 400 freestyle relay was considerable, the United States, France, and Australia touted as the gold-medal contenders. Each team featured not only depth but a top gun capable of carrying his country to victory. For the United States, Phelps was tabbed to handle the leadoff leg and given the opportunity to prove his worth in what was only his sixth- or seventh-best event. For France and Australia, they were respectively bolstered by Alain Bernard and Eamon Sullivan, two men who over the previous six months had combined for six world records in the sprint-freestyle events.

Still, what unfolded in just over three minutes of racing surpassed all expectations, and the man responsible was Jason Lezak. If the veteran entered the Beijing Games as an appreciated member of Team USA, thanks to his consistent efforts in international competition, Lezak left his third Olympiad as a relay legend and his place in Olympic lore firmly etched. All it took was the greatest relay split in history, a 46.06 mark that remains untouched more than a decade later and carried the United States to a world record and an improbable comeback over France.

"Whenever I watch it, I still get pumped up," Lezak said. "It's pretty amazing to see. I look at it as a spectator, and it's awesome."

The record book shows that the United States won the 400 freestyle relay in Beijing in 3:08.24, a scant 0.08 faster than what France managed. Both nations went under the previous world record by nearly four seconds, but the result tells only part of the story. The full tale requires a look at the race's ebb and flow, at history and at the pursuit of an achievement that is unlikely to be matched.

Prior to the 2008 Games, the 400 freestyle relay had not gone the way of the United States in back-to-back Olympiads, an unfamiliar development, given the way Team USA had dominated that relay since its inception at the 1964 Olympics in Tokyo. In the first seven editions of the event, the United States was unbeaten and hardly challenged, only two of its victories arriving by less than a second.

At the 2000 Games in Sydney, the United States was edged at the finish by Australia, which relied on a world record from Michael Klim on the leadoff leg and the anchor effort of Ian Thorpe to make history. Racing on home soil, the Australians ended the U.S. invincibility and celebrated the victory with an air-guitar performance on deck that was a direct response to Gary Hall Jr.'s prediction that the United States would "smash them like guitars."

Four years later, South Africa delivered a stunning triumph at the Athens Games, with the United States relegated to a disappointing bronze medal. Following a terrible performance on the opening leg from Ian Crocker, the United States was never in contention and had to battle back to earn a place on the podium.

The common denominator between the 2000 and 2004 American squads was Lezak, though it would be inaccurate to suggest he was the reason for either setback. At the Sydney Games, Lezak managed a split of

Jason Lezak is credited with producing the finest anchor leg in Olympic relay history, as he rallied the United States to gold in the 400 freestyle relay at the 2008 Games in Beijing. Peter H. Bick.

48.42, and easily bettered the 48.71 mark posted by Aussie Ashley Callus, who raced alongside the American. Four years later, as the United States scrambled for bronze, Lezak handled the anchor leg, going 47.86. That effort was bettered by only the Netherlands' Pieter van den Hoogenband and assured Team USA wouldn't be shut out of the medals.

Despite doing an admirable job on his legs, Lezak was burdened by the results of his first two Olympiads, and the fact that he was the only man to appear on both non-winning relays. He saw Beijing as an opportunity for atonement, and to return the United States to where it so long stood and, in his mind, belonged: on the top step of the medals stand.

"There was a lot leading up to that race that a lot of people don't know," Lezak said.

> My first Olympics in 2000, we lost that race for the first time in Olympic history. I grew up w-atching that race and the USA dominated and I wanted to be part of that domination. They played the air guitar in our faces and it was a defining moment. And then we lost it again at the next Olympics. Another disappointment there. It wasn't just about, "Let's go win a race." There was a lot of history behind it. And for me it was important. We never had four guys come together as a team and swim to our abilities. As captain, I tried to get these guys focused on doing it together.

The mistake Hall made in 2000 clearly did not serve as a lesson for France, which looked sharp on paper and felt the gold medal was its to lose. If that sense was supposed to be kept private, Bernard was unaware of the plan. Five months before the Beijing Games, Bernard was sensational at the European Championships, breaking the world record in the 50 freestyle and twice setting a global standard in the 100 freestyle.

In quick fashion, the Frenchman established himself as a leading medal contender for the summer and gave France the luxury of a stalwart anchor leg on the 400 freestyle relay. An imposing figure with an Incredible Hulk–like physique, Bernard's confidence was on display when he was asked to handicap the relay and the impending clash with the United States.

"The Americans? We're going to smash them," Bernard said. "That's what we came here for. I'll start my Games in the final (of the relay), confident that my pals will have qualified easily. If the relay goes according to plan, then we'll be on a roll."

Bernard's bravado did not sit well with at least one of his teammates. Fred Bousquet, who raced collegiately in the United States for Auburn University, knew the Americans would use Bernard's comments as motivation. But Bernard could not retract his words and his faith in his teammates and France's attempt to extend the U.S. winless streak in the event to three Olympiads was immediately tested when Phelps stepped onto the blocks for the leadoff leg. Although not known as a pure sprinter, Phelps was a slam-dunk choice to jumpstart the American hopes, as he clocked just under 48 seconds at the Olympic Trials and possessed unmatched rise-to-the-occasion talent.

As expected, Phelps delivered for his team, his opening split of 47.51 good for an American record and 0.40 quicker than the time posted by France's leadoff man, Amaury Leveaux. In the hierarchy of Phelps' events, the 100 freestyle sat down the road, and yet he set a national record. It can be argued that history hasn't appreciated the performance adequately, for without Phelps' lid-lifting excellence, the United States wouldn't have gotten the job done.

"I went into that relay wanting to do all I could for Team USA," said Phelps, who earlier in the night contested the semifinals of the 200 freestyle. "I tried to save as much energy as I could for that relay. I knew I needed it."

As sharp as Phelps looked, he was only the second-fastest man on the opening leg. Giving Australia a boost on the way to a bronze medal, Sullivan was untouchable. Covering his two laps in 47.24, the Aussie set a world record, bettering Bernard's previous standard of 47.50. The chase for gold was on, and it was a heated battle.

With the crowd roaring for Sullivan's world record and the three-country battle that was unfolding, the second leg featured another unheralded split for the United States. The winner of both sprint freestyles at the Olympic Trials, Garrett Weber-Gale kept the United States in the lead behind a time of 47.02, the fastest performance of any man racing in the No. 2 slot. While France's Fabien Gilot yielded just 0.03 to Weber-Gale, Australia fell back from the lead to third place after Andrew Lauterstein clocked a split of 47.87.

In hindsight, the performance of Weber-Gale was his finest of an otherwise disappointing Olympiad. Individually, Weber-Gale struggled in Beijing as he failed to advance out of the semifinals in the 100 freestyle and followed with another semifinal elimination in the 50 freestyle. But in a team role, Weber-Gale was more than reliable, with his split ranking as the fourth-fastest among the 24 swimmers contesting the second through fourth legs.

The momentum rapidly shifted over the third leg as Bousquet rallied France into the lead and battered American Cullen Jones in their head-to-head duel. While Jones was timed in a solid split of 47.65, Bousquet was more than a second quicker, going 46.63 to hand the French an advantage of 0.59 heading into the anchor leg.

Bousquet was the best known of the French quartet to the Americans, due to his Auburn training ground and NCAA championship portfolio. And when he exited the water, it looked like Bousquet had given France an insurmountable lead, particularly considering Bernard's status as the world-record holder when the Olympic Games started.

"When I made the turn at the 50-meter mark, I realized I was in the lead," Bousquet said. "I realized I had passed the Australian and the American. I said to myself, 'Fred, you have to go. You can't crack. You have to get even more ahead to ensure victory when you give the relay to (Bernard).' I gave him the relay with a 1.5 meters lead. I thought nothing could happen to us. We were going to be Olympic champions."

Bousquet wasn't the only person in the venue who believed Bernard's leg was a French coronation. As he entered the water, ahead of Lezak for the United States, Bernard put his power on display. By the time he turned at the 350-meter mark, France's lead had widened, and the country was one length of the pool away from its first triumph in an Olympic relay.

Members of the media mentally prepared their story angles, which would combine France's breakthrough title with the end of Phelps' chase for eight gold medals. Even Lezak didn't think the gap he faced could be overcome. Another loss in the 400 freestyle relay was about to be added to his resume, and it didn't feel good.

"The guy I was swimming against wasn't some chump," Lezak said of Bernard. "The thought entered my mind for a split second. I thought there was no way I could catch him. But then I changed. I thought, 'That's ridiculous. I'm at the Olympic Games. I'm here for the United States of America. I don't care how bad it hurts. I'm going after it.' I just got a super charge."

Over the next 50 meters, Lezak made history. With Bernard making the mistake of racing next to the lane line, he allowed Lezak to draft and expend less energy than if Bernard remained in the center of his lane. With each stroke, Lezak pulled closer to the Frenchman, the dynamic of the race changing in stunning fashion.

On the NBC television coverage, which was handled by longtime broadcast partners Dan Hicks and Rowdy Gaines, a sense of shock emitted from their voices. As the swimmers came off the final turn, Hicks' play-by-play sounded like this: "The United States (is) trying to hang on to second. They should get the silver medal." Within seconds, the narrative shifted, with Hicks noting that Lezak had narrowed Bernard's lead and was closing the gap even more.

As Bernard continued to tighten up over the final 15 meters, Lezak remained strong. At the touch, there was no doubt that Lezak had the most momentum leading into the wall, but it wasn't until the scoreboard flashed the results that the U.S. victory was confirmed.

"That was just unbelievable," Phelps said of Lezak. "His last 50 meters were absolutely incredible. He had a perfect finish".

Upon realizing the American win, Phelps and Weber-Gale flexed their muscles while Lezak tossed his cap onto the deck. After he got out of the water, the foursome embraced and took in the adulation of the crowd. The French, meanwhile, were stunned. While Leveaux stared blankly ahead, unable to comprehend what occurred, Bernard rested his arms on the side of the pool and lowered his head. In position to secure the biggest win for France in the sport's history, Bernard knew he let a rare opportunity slip away. Although he was timed in an impressive split of 46.73, Lezak's effort of 46.06 was other-worldly.

"Alain is wounded," said Claude Fauquet, France's National Team director. "When you are the last swimmer in a relay and you have the opportunity to bring a title of this importance to your country, you don't get out of this unhurt. But I don't think that Alain lost the race. It's Lezak who won it."

Jason Lezak solidified himself as a longtime relay stalwart for the United States. Peter H. Bick.

Stunned by their loss to the United States, the Frenchmen were also angered by events that transpired just 90 minutes before the start of the relay final. In the months leading into Beijing, the members of France's relay provided input that solidified a relay order of Leveaux, Bernard, Gilot, and Bousquet. While Leveaux was a superb starter, Bernard's second-leg placement was designed to take advantage of open water and enable France to build a sizable lead.

But the French coaching staff opted to rearrange the order ahead of the biggest race in the country's history. According to Bousquet, French officials were so confident they would win, they moved Bernard to the anchor leg to receive the adulation that is placed on the man capping off an Olympic victory. The decision irked Bousquet, who had to be calmed down by Bernard. To this day, he has not forgiven the coaching staff for its decision, citing the disruption as the main reason for France's loss.

"They messed up the race," Bousquet said of the coaches. "How could they destabilize us in such a way? We didn't understand and we were lost. It's been years since it happened and when I talk about it, the same emotions stand out. They spoiled our moment. It's still difficult to talk about."

The loss was certainly a blow to Bernard, whose season had been a dream to that point. But the French star also showed heart in the days following the relay. Bouncing back in impressive fashion, Bernard first set a world record in the semifinals of the 100 freestyle, going 47.20. Although that mark was bettered a few minutes later by Sullivan, who won his semi-final in 47.05, Bernard got the best of the Aussie in the final.

Producing a time of 47.21, Bernard earned the gold medal ahead of Sullivan (47.32), with Lezak and Brazil's Cesar Cielo sharing the bronze medal in 47.67. A few days later, Bernard added a bronze medal in the 50 freestyle to give him a rainbow of medals for the Olympiad.

"I can't believe it," Bernard said. "I know I was feeling down after the relay, but I didn't want to get beaten. I have been working for years and years. I didn't panic during the race. When I looked at the board, I thought, 'Wow, I did it.' It's a great joy to be here. I want to enjoy the moment."

For Phelps, Lezak's heroics kept alive his hunt for eight gold medals and helped secure his place atop Mount Olympus.

With a schedule featuring 17 races between his five individual events and role on three relays, it was almost assured Phelps would need a little luck at some point during the eight-day meet. Although Phelps was the undisputed king of the sport, his energy level was undoubtedly going to lessen with each passing race—both physically and mentally. Meanwhile, he had several double-event sessions in which his freshness would be tested.

As for his foes, it's not like Phelps was racing against middle-of-the-road competition. Rather, he was facing the best of the best, including duels with American rival Ryan Lochte and Serbian Milorad Cavic, who placed his emphasis on the 100 butterfly and was sure to benefit from a full gas tank. A little luck? To the mainstream media, it didn't make sense. Many reporters simply saw Phelps as a once-in-a-lifetime talent and considered his eight-gold chase a mere formality. What those journalists missed was the nuanced nature of Phelps' pursuit and the fact that Phelps, particularly in the relays, was not entirely in control.

"You have to have all your stars aligned," Phelps said. "Everything had to fall into place perfectly."

It did.

Following the 400 freestyle relay, Phelps still had six events to tackle. While the 200 freestyle, 200 individual medley, 800 freestyle relay, and 400 medley relay went smoothly, Phelps had to navigate a speedbump in the 200 butterfly and needed the greatest finish of his career to prevail in the 100 butterfly.

In the 200 fly, Phelps' goggles filled with water at the start, forcing him to race his four laps with minimal visibility. Phelps, racing by feel, still managed to set a world record of 1:52.03, but his reaction at the finish, in which he tossed his goggles onto the deck, revealed a level of disgust.

The 100 fly was more dramatic. For 99 meters, Phelps trailed Cavic by a considerable margin, the hopes of a perfect Olympiad seemingly gone in his seventh event. But at the finish, Cavic glided to the wall while Phelps took an extra half-stroke to emerge on top by the slimmest of margins, 0.01. Phelps' decision to squeeze in an extra stroke was innate, and the latest example of Phelps doing what was necessary to beat the competition.

By pulling out the 100 fly in epic fashion, Phelps equaled Spitz's record of seven gold medals and all but confirmed he would go 8-for-8. Indeed, his eighth gold medal arrived on the final day of competition, when Phelps handled the butterfly leg on the U.S. world-record-setting 400 medley relay. The week was nothing short of spectacular, Phelps mixing dominance with drama to produce the greatest Olympic exhibition in history. What Lezak meant to the week has not been lost on the Phelps camp.

"Lezak's swim was critical to keeping the pursuit of eight golds alive," said Phelps' coach, Bob Bowman. "His transcendent swim produced an energy that (Phelps) and Team USA fed off for the remainder of the meet. I remember thinking that our quest might be over before it really got going in the early stages of the relay. It wasn't until the last 15 meters that I thought we might have a chance. And, of course, the rest is history."

Four years after Lezak's mind-boggling performance, France got revenge on the United States by winning gold in the 400 freestyle relay by 0.45. Leveaux and Gilot retained their roles in the final for the French, while Phelps and Jones returned for the United States. In an ironic twist, the two men who dueled down the stretch for the title in Beijing were missing from the final, although Bernard and Lezak each earned medals due to their contributions in the preliminary heats.

For Lezak, the silver medal in London was his fourth medal in as many Olympiads in the 400 freestyle relay. Obviously, his gold from Beijing is the most memorable.

"On the second lap, I looked at (Bernard) on every stroke," Lezak said. "I saw myself getting closer and closer. The last 15 meters, I felt this extra surge and I was able to maintain my speed to the wall while his stroke fell apart. I looked at the scoreboard and saw pretty quickly that we won. It just meant so much, especially with my history (in the event). It was a special moment."

One of the greatest in history.

Chapter 4

˙GREATEST RIVALRIES

Rivalries add to the excitement of sports in their ability to enhance drama and draw on stories from the past. Through the years, there has been no shortage of rivalries in competitive waters.

BREASTSTROKE BRAWL

During an interview in the mid-1970s, British breaststroke ace David Wilkie referred to himself as a quiet personality. He wasn't one to exuberantly celebrate his victories and accomplishments, and he was relatively reserved when discussing the characteristics that made him a world-record holder and set him down the path to Olympic glory.

If Wilkie was considered on the quiet side, then American John Hencken had to be viewed as silent, so few were the words he offered to explain his exploits in the sport. Never mind his standing as—perhaps—the greatest breaststroker in history, Hencken offered little during interviews. Simply, he was the shy type who didn't need attention.

As much as Wilkie and Hencken preferred to steer away from the spotlight, their skills wouldn't allow for such avoidance. For the first half of the 1970s, they engaged in one of the best rivalries in the sport, and possibly the best rivalry the breaststroke has ever seen, although Kosuke Kitajima and Brendan Hansen can make an argument, too.

Although their names were known, it was the 1972 Olympic Games in Munich that launched this rivalry toward global acclaim. In the shadow of Mark Spitz winning seven gold medals and setting as many world records, Hencken and Wilkie won gold and silver, respectively, in the 200-meter breaststroke, with Hencken adding a bronze medal in the 100 breaststroke, an event in which Wilkie finished eighth.

"That was a good race," Hencken said of his Olympic triumph, which arrived in world-record time. "I was pretty happy with it."

For a guy who reached the pinnacle of athletic success, one would think a greater dissection of the accomplishment would be provided. But Hencken was a man of few words, and the minimal would do as far as he was concerned. Really, he was someone who let his achievements do the talking, and they certainly spoke volumes.

Over the next four years, the rivalry between Hencken and Wilkie further bloomed, their duels unfolding on both the collegiate stage and in international waters. While Hencken, a California native, remained in-state and chose Stanford University for his college career, Wilkie stayed true to his globetrotting ways. Born to Scottish parents in Sri Lanka, Wilkie spent the first 11 years of his life in South Asia, before attending school in Great Britain. When it was time to enroll in college, Wilkie opted for the United States and the University of Miami, which was coached by Bill Diaz.

Collegiately, Hencken and Wilkie were showstoppers at the NCAA Championships, clashing annually from 1973 to 1976. Ultimately, Hencken came away with five NCAA titles, with Wilkie accounting for three crowns. But anything more than head-to-head showdowns there wasn't, as Hencken and Wilkie kept their distance on the deck.

"It's not exactly a clash of personalities," Wilkie said of the distance with his foe. "In fact, maybe it's because our personalities are too much alike that we don't speak with one another. He's quiet and so am I. We're friendly rivals, but there's not much communication between us. We say one or two words after the race, but I don't think we've ever had a conversation that exceeded 10 words. It's not because we hate each other. It's because we respect each other and we're rivals."

Hencken, not surprisingly, didn't think much of the distant relationship, and it wasn't worth his time to examine the reasons.

"I don't know exactly why, but we've always avoided each other," said Hencken. "I guess we're trying to psych each other out or something."

The split of championships evident at the college level was replicated when Hencken and Wilkie dueled internationally. More, it became more obvious that while each man was a versatile breaststroker and capable of excelling in both events, Hencken and his powerful stroke were better suited for the 100 distance, and Wilkie and his long, smooth stroke were better geared for the 200 distance.

At the 1973 World Championships, Hencken and Wilkie indeed prevailed where they were strongest. The American set a world record in the 100 breaststroke, where Wilkie was fourth, while the British star earned gold in the 200 breaststroke, his world record of 2:19.28 necessary to fend off Hencken, who also went under the previous world record.

The next year, Hencken set three world records between the 100 breaststroke and the 200 breaststroke, while Wilkie flourished at the European Championships and Commonwealth Games. Wilkie collected gold in both the 200 breaststroke and 200 individual medley at Europeans, a surprise world record coming in the medley. The effort proved the Brit beyond the event for which he was primarily known.

Although they met during the NCAA season, the 1975 campaign—like the previous summer—did not offer a meeting between Hencken and Wilkie. At the World Championships, Wilkie won the 100 breaststroke and 200 breaststroke, but without his American rival in the mix. A year ahead of the 1976 Olympics, Hencken opted to skip the World Champs and focus on his studies. The absence only enhanced the intrigue on the way to the Montreal Games.

Adding to the interest were minor subplots that spoke to the men's personalities. Wilkie became the first swimmer to don goggles and a cap during competition. The goggles were designed to fight Wilkie's allergy to chlorine, with the cap corralling his long hair. Meanwhile, Hencken earned the nickname "Rocket Man" for his penchant to entertain teammates by sending model rockets into the air during downtime.

Coming off the 1972 Olympics in Munich and Spitz's spectacular show, the 1976 Games in Montreal faced a tough act to follow. Yet, the strength of the U.S. men quickly grabbed headlines, and Hencken played a front-and-center role. After equaling his world record in the preliminaries of the 100 breaststroke, Hencken lowered the standard in the semifinals to 1:03.62. The best, though, was delivered in the final, as Hencken clocked 1:03.11 to beat the 1:03.43 of Wilkie, who also went faster than Hencken's world mark from the semifinals.

The fact that Wilkie went that fast in the 100 breaststroke was a positive sign for the 200 breaststroke, and the Scotsman knew it. Still, he paid close attention to what the opposition was doing. Slated to race in the fourth and final prelim heat, nerves had Wilkie repeatedly ask his coach, David Haller, for the times of the other swimmers. The questions didn't stop until Wilkie climbed the blocks and clocked an Olympic record of 2:18.29 for the top seed in the final. It was then that the mental games started.

After the heats, David Haller and I walked past the American coach, Don Gambril, and David shouted in a voice that couldn't fail to be heard: "Well, David, a 2:15 tonight, then." It was a laugh, but we weren't joking. We were serious. I was very confident. (Hencken) was three seconds behind me in qualifying and I knew for him to beat me that night, he would have to drop six seconds on his time because I fully intended to swim another three seconds quicker. Logically I knew, after the heats, that there was no way he or anybody else could win.

Wilkie couldn't have been more correct. Although Hencken was even with Wilkie through the first half of the final, Wilkie pulled away over the last two laps. With every stroke, he lengthened his lead and dazzled the fans in attendance. When Wilkie touched the wall, the scoreboard revealed a time of 2:15.11, a mark more than three seconds quicker than the previous world record.

Hencken wasn't anything less than spectacular, thanks to a silver-medal performance of 2:17.26, nearly a second quicker than the existing world record. The American simply ran into a buzzsaw that wasn't going to be beaten. Wilkie finally had the Olympic gold he yearned to earn, and he was able to celebrate with Haller and his Miami coach, Charlie Hodgson.

"I stopped even being aware of (Hencken), for our contest was over, and it just became a race against the clock and getting as good a time as possible," Wilkie said.

I knew I had won easily, so I took my time before I turned around to see what time I had done. It felt like 10 seconds. I wanted to capture the whole glory of the moment and finding out my time was going to be the icing on the cake. And when I did look around and saw 2:15.11 on the scoreboard, I couldn't believe it. When you have broken the world record and your own best by more than three seconds, it's a great feeling.

Wilkie's effort in the 200 breaststroke is known today for keeping the United States from a perfect showing at the 1976 Olympics. Of the 13 events contested in Montreal, the American men won 12, with Wilkie's triumph the only blemish. The performance was so impressive that it remained the world record for six years.

Additionally, Wilkie provided Great Britain with its first Olympic gold medal in the pool since Anita Lonsbrough won the title in the 200 breaststroke at the 1960 Games in Rome. Among the men, it was Great Britain's first Olympic crown since Henry Taylor won gold in the 400 freestyle and 1,500 freestyle at the 1908 Games.

"He was absolutely phenomenal," Haller said of Wilkie. "His swim in 1976 is still probably the greatest individual performance I have witnessed. The most beautiful, fluid technique, powered by the strongest legs in swimming. It was like watching a periscope cut through the water when he charged up the third or fourth lap of a 200."

While Wilkie faded away, Hencken forged ahead, unwilling to accept that a swimmer's career had to end after college. Although extended careers are the norm in the modern era, Hencken was a trailblazer during his era. He pushed toward the 1980 Olympic Games in Moscow, but his dream of competing in a third Olympiad was squashed by President Jimmy Carter's decision to have the United States boycott the Games.

Despite Carter's decision, Hencken attended the Olympic Trials in the summer and qualified for the Team USA roster in both breaststroke events. Although not at his peak, it would have been interesting to see if Hencken could have dialed up some of his past magic and advanced to a final. Even after the 1980 boycott, he remained active and, at one point, considered pursuing a berth to the 1984 Olympics in Los Angeles.

"I believe it's a myth that swimmers are over the hill after college," said Hencken, one of the many stars churned out by the Santa Clara Swim Club. "They should be able to continue improving until at least 30, but that's up to the individual. Obviously, certain priorities change. Some people stop enjoying the sport when it competes with family and job obligations. At that point, it's no longer worth the time and energy."

Wilkie was inducted into the International Swimming Hall of Fame in 1983, with Hencken enshrined in 1988. Otherwise, their careers have always been connected and will continue to be intertwined long into the future.

NO LOVE LOST

One was known for an icy stare, everything around him shut out when it was time to work. The other operated via a looser approach, comfortable, entertaining, and connecting with the crowd up until go time.

One was tenacious in his training approach, regularly logging thousands of meters during a workout. The other took a freer approach to training, shorter workouts the norm and, occasionally, held in the ocean and not the pool.

One was eager to test himself at most international competitions, seeking world and continental crowns alike. The other was much more selective with his schedule and made it clear the Olympic Games were his main—and often only—priority.

They couldn't have been more different.

Over the course of a decade, from the mid-1990s into the mid-2000s, Russia's Alexander Popov and the United States' Gary Hall Jr. engaged in one of the best rivalries the sport has seen. The fact that they were opposites in several ways supplied a layer of intrigue to their duels, as did the back-and-forth insults that were exchanged.

But it was their sheer speed that was most enticing, spectators enthralled by their epic battles for the title of Fastest Man in Water. From Atlanta to Sydney to Athens, and with stops in between, Popov and Hall were showmen, and jointly wrote a chapter in the sport's history that will be long remembered.

The best rivalries are those that endure. When given a chance to grow, they often develop depth that goes beyond the black-and-white results shown on the scoreboard. They reveal differences in personality. They pit athletes from different countries. They can be friendly or hostile. The days of Popov vs. Hall featured some of these traits.

But before the Russian and American tangled in a sequel to the Cold War, they were preceded by a gentler conflict. It was a rivalry that captivated the sport, built hype around the sprints, and served as a red carpet to the Popov–Hall era.

Between 1985 and 1991, the sprint-freestyle events belonged to the tandem of Matt Biondi and Tom Jager. When they stepped on the blocks during their heydays, it wasn't a matter of whether the Americans would finish on the podium, but on which step. While Jager won back-to-back world titles in the 50 freestyle in 1986 and 1991, Biondi claimed bronze and silver, respectively. In the 100 freestyle, it was Biondi who repeated as world champion, Jager snaring bronze in 1986.

In between the World Championships, Biondi swept the sprints at the 1988 Olympic Games in Seoul. Jager was the runner-up in the 50 freestyle and teamed with Biondi to lead the United States to gold in the 400 freestyle relay by nearly two seconds over the Soviet Union.

During this stretch, Popov was busy honing his skills as a teenager with limitless potential.

Entering the 1992 Olympics in Barcelona, either Biondi or Jager had been ranked first in the world for seven straight years and, at one point, combined for 24 of the 25-fastest times in the history of the 50 freestyle. Meanwhile, Popov didn't make his first international dent until he won the 100 freestyle at the 1991 European Championships. That victory certainly provided a career boost, along with Popov's mental approach, which was an outlook that provided no mercy for the opposition.

"When I go to competitions in Europe or America, or even here in Australia, I am always looking for potential challengers," Popov said. "If I see any, I have to swim faster and make them feel sick. If they have a little potential, you must get on top of them and kill that enthusiasm right away so they will lose their interest in swimming."

As veterans, Biondi and Jager were not going to succumb to the intimidating nature of Popov, but the Russian's belief that he could compete at the same level as two legends was evidence of his toughness. His confidence ultimately led to the greatest achievement of his career—at least to that point.

Racing the 100 freestyle at the 1992 Olympics in Barcelona, Popov easily took care of the field, as he recorded a time of 49.02 to finish 0.41 ahead of Brazil's Gustavo Borges, with Biondi back in fifth in 49.53. Two days later, Popov put on another speed display, winning the 50 free in 21.91, Biondi and Jager completing the podium. It was clear that Popov had ascended to the top of the sprint mountain. Hall, for the record, was a teen with aspirations to be in the mix one day.

"Popov obviously had the courage to stand up to Matt Biondi and Tom Jager and take them down," Jager said. "The first person in the world to do that. I take my hat off to Popov. He has a great career ahead of him."

Olympic titles now on his resume, Popov—who was nicknamed "The Tsar"—moved forward from Barcelona with a wrecking-ball approach. He was the 1993 European champion in both sprints and replicated that feat at the 1994 World Championships in Rome. Another sprint sweep followed at the 1995 European Champs, leaving Popov to surge into the 1996 Olympics as a seemingly unstoppable force.

Popov's success followed a major life change. In late 1992, Popov's coach, Gennadi Touretski, accepted the head-coaching position at the Australian Institute of Sport in Canberra. Popov didn't think twice about leaving Russia and joining his mentor in the Australian capital. Obviously, the shift in locales wasn't a disruption in the slightest.

For his part, Hall used the 1994 World Championships to put his name in the spotlight. He might not have beaten Popov, but he gave a glimpse of the next great American sprinter, the guy who would take the baton from Biondi. On the way to a pair of silver medals behind the Russian, Hall also showed he was a different breed than Biondi, who was a measured and stoic

Gary Hall Jr. was known for his prerace showmanship. Peter H. Bick.

figure. Hall had an opposite personality. He liked to play to the crowd and was brash with his words, confident he could back them up.

The combination of Hall's threatening status and loud demeanor did not sit well with Popov, whose oversized ego made his disdain for Hall a paradox. So, when the 1996 Olympics in Atlanta opened, Popov not only sought defense of his gold medals but had a deep desire to muzzle his American rival on his home soil.

As was the case at the World Champs two years earlier, Popov emerged triumphant in both sprints at the Atlanta Games. He prevailed in the shorter distance by 0.13 over Hall, with a margin of 0.07 separating the combatants in the 100 freestyle. By capturing back-to-back Olympic victories in the 100 freestyle, Popov became the first man to repeat in the event since the legendary Johnny Weissmuller doubled in 1924 and 1928.

"He talks too much," Popov said. "He always says he's going to beat me. He likes talking about himself. If you're going to say something, you have to go out and do it. If you're not the best at something, you may as well go and look for something else to do. I like to let my results speak for themselves."

Popov undoubtedly had the upper hand in the rivalry through Atlanta, but Hall wasn't about to accept a permanent bridesmaid identity. He knew his peak years were in front of him, and he simply needed to follow the blueprint he had mapped out.

Hall hailed from a family with a rich tradition in the pool and he took pride in carrying his family legacy forward. His grandfather, Charles Keating Jr., was the 1946 NCAA champion in the 200 breaststroke for the University of Cincinnati, while his uncle, Charles Keating III, finished fifth in the 200 breaststroke at the 1976 Olympics in Montreal.

The lineage runs strongest, though, with Hall's father, Gary Sr., a three-time Olympian who excelled for Indiana University. Under the guidance of legendary coach Doc Counsilman, the elder Hall molded himself into an all-around standout for the Hoosiers and for Team USA. In an era in which Olympic careers were short-lived, Hall was an anomaly, racing at the 1968, 1972, and 1976 Games, and earning a medal in each Olympiad.

Known for enduring grueling workouts and pushing himself beyond what Counsilman designed, Hall set world records in four different individual events, a testament to his versatility. But for all his success, which earned him induction into the International Swimming Hall of Fame in 1981, Olympic luck was never on Hall's side.

After Hall claimed the silver medal in the 400 individual medley and just missed the medals in the 200 backstroke following a fourth-place finish at the 1968 Olympics in Mexico City, he seemed poised for major success at the 1972 Games in Munich. While Hall won the silver medal in the 200 butterfly, he placed fourth in the 200 individual medley and fifth in the 400 individual medley, events in which he entered the Olympics as the world-record holder.

Four years later, Hall closed out his Olympic career with a bronze medal in the 100 butterfly, an effort that was somewhat surprising given his talent was better suited to the 200-meter distances and up. At those 1976 Games in Montreal, Hall was part of an American squad that won 12 of the 13 events on the schedule and is regarded—almost without argument—as the greatest team in swimming history.

Always on the hunt for a mental edge, Popov didn't miss an opportunity to take a shot at the Hall family as his rivalry with Gary Jr. heated up. Aware of the younger Hall's penchant for shorter workouts and his father's history, Popov went on the attack in 1997.

"He doesn't work hard," Popov said of his rival. "He's doing 1500 meters? That's what I swim in warmups." "(Hall) says he will be at the Sydney Olympics and that he will win both sprint titles. I don't know how he can say that. His father was never an Olympic champion, and he never will be either. It's a family of losers."

When Popov's words got back to Hall, the American responded, feeling the need to defend not only his reputation but the honor of his father.

"(Popov) is the epitome of unsportsmanlike conduct," Hall said.

In the world of swimming, Alexander brings a new definition to the word shallow. What really upsets me is that in order to make himself feel better, Alexander must put down the Olympic accomplishments of his opponent's father. I am embarrassed for this coward of a man. He ought to quit now because that road is going to be a long and hard one. Or, he can learn the words of the Star Spangled Banner because that's what Olympic audiences will be hearing for years to come.

What didn't unfold was a meeting between the athletes at the 1998 World Championships. While Hall anchored a pair of U.S. relays in Perth, he was absent from the 50 freestyle and 100 freestyle, leaving his next showdown with Popov until Sydney. And before they would meet again, much transpired out of the water.

A little more than a year shy of the 2000 United States Olympic Trials, Hall was dealt news that not only complicated his pursuit of a gold medal but brought adversity to his daily life. In March 1999, Hall was informed he had type 1 diabetes, a disease in which the body does not produce enough insulin or does not effectively use the insulin created by the body.

Upon his diagnosis, doctors informed Hall that his career—almost certainly—would be short-circuited, leaving him to retire at his peak. Initially, Hall was devastated by the news and the knowledge that all his work and goals were crushed by a medical issue beyond his control. In short time, however, Hall flipped the script and didn't buy into the doctors' career-ending diagnosis.

After researching the disease and discussing his situation with medical experts and his coaches, Hall focused on creating the proper balance between treating his condition and the preparation necessary to earn a ticket to the Sydney Olympics. While Hall had to give himself as many as eight insulin injections each day, he managed to adhere to a training program that allowed him to remain one of the world's premier sprinters.

Sure, there were speed bumps along the way, including blurred vision and rapid fatigue. Ultimately, though, Hall responsibly monitored his blood-sugar levels and drafted a tutorial for how to battle the disease and maintain an active, demanding, and healthy lifestyle. More, he used his platform as an Olympic champion to raise awareness of the disease.

"The diabetes was really a major factor in my life, not just my swimming career," Hall said. "The travel took something out of me. It affected my blood-sugar levels. But I paid attention to what I ate and made sure I got the right amount of insulin. It was so scary when I was diagnosed. I heard these horror stories and the statistics. My reaction was it's just a matter of time. I've only got so much time before these things happen."

"But the quality of life a person with diabetes can have really comes down to the individual and the management that individual can provide. Other people have been able to successfully manage this disease and avoid very serious complications that stem from this disease, so it can be done. If there are complications, it's difficult to blame anybody but yourself."

With a plan in hand to manage his diabetes, Hall still had to get through the United States Trials and qualify for Sydney. It turned out that Hall accomplished that feat in emphatic fashion, an American record of 21.76 providing Hall with a narrow victory over Anthony Ervin, a rising star on the sprint scene.

The month following Trials was a critical time for Hall and Ervin. Under the guidance of coach Mike Bottom at the Phoenix Swim Club, the Americans trained side by side every day and helped one another hone their skills for Sydney. Also under the mentorship of Bottom, and adding to the competitive atmosphere, was Poland's Bart Kizierowski, a European champion. Simply, practices emulated an international showdown.

The setup, in which three medal contenders trained together, needed to be handled delicately by Bottom, and the veteran coach delivered. Each day, Bottom provided his swimmers with what they individually needed.

"Mike Bottom graduated near the top of his class in psychology," Hall said.

> It was applied every day, at every practice. Unlike any other coach I've ever met, Mike was able to alter his approach with each individual. Unlike any therapist, he was able to measure results to one hundredth of a second. What motivates and demotivates varies from individual to individual. Three personalities required three different approaches. Though our end goal was the same, our needs were all very different. We knew that we would be competing against each other at the end of the season. We competed against each other every day in practice, jockeying for minute advantages. This is the nature of the sport. Teammates and friends compete against each other. There was a lot of psychology

involved, in how we all interacted with one another, through the training and competitions. Not just between coach and swimmer, but also between swimmers. Mike was so skilled at shepherding this lively, and sometimes volatile, dynamic.

As much as Hall recognized Ervin as a top contender for gold in Sydney, he knew Popov would be an equally daunting figure. Like Hall, Popov encountered a medical emergency on the road to the 2000 Games, but the Russian's situation was a case of bad timing.

In August of 1996, just weeks after he swept the sprint-freestyle events at the Atlanta Olympics, Popov was walking with friends on a Moscow street when members of his party got into an argument with watermelon vendors. The exchange of words quickly escalated into a physical altercation and one of the vendors stabbed Popov in the stomach. Popov was rushed to a hospital where he underwent a three-hour surgery to treat damage to his lungs and kidney.

Popov spent 45 days in the hospital and resumed training three months after the incident, with his return to major competition arriving at the 1997 edition of the Santa Clara International Swim Meet, 10 months after the stabbing. After winning the 50 freestyle in Northern California, the only hint of his near-death experience was the six-inch scar on his chest.

"You know, we probably could have gotten out of the situation if it had been handled differently," Popov said. "But they approached us, and somebody started talking with them, and they misunderstood us and started to fight. The men didn't know who I was. We were in the wrong place at the wrong time."

With Hall's diabetes managed and Popov's incident in the rearview mirror, the sprint stars were able to direct their attention to the 2000 Games. Although Hall and Ervin headed to Sydney in fine form, Popov looked to be the sharpest of the bunch. At the Russian Olympic Trials, Popov took advantage of a time trial and unleashed a world record of 21.64 in the 50 freestyle. The effort cut 0.17 off Jager's global standard, a sizable chunk of time for any event, but especially for a one-lap sprint. From Moscow, a message was sent.

As the two-time defending Olympic champion, Popov was in position to make history as the first man to win the same event at three consecutive Olympiads, and he had two opportunities to pull off the feat. This fact was not lost on the Russian.

"If you win the Olympics once, you're good," Popov said. "Win the Olympics two times, you're great. Win the Olympics three times, you're history."

The 100 freestyle was the first individual showdown between Popov and Hall, although both had raced in the 400 freestyle relay on the opening day of competition. While Popov's Russian squad was disqualified, the bigger news was the U.S. silver-medal finish with Hall on the anchor leg. Fueled by Michael Klim's world record on the leadoff leg, Australia snapped Team USA's Olympic unbeaten streak in the event at seven. The defeat was a tough loss for Hall to accept since he predicted a U.S. victory prior to the Games, going so far as to claim the United States would "smash (Australia) like guitars." When he was out-touched at the wall by Ian Thorpe, Australia's teenage superstar, the Aussies celebrated with an impromptu air-guitar routine. Still, Hall carried himself with grace, acknowledging Thorpe and his teammates for their stellar performance.

By the time the final of the 100 freestyle was held, Popov and Hall had settled into their routines and were ready for the latest chapter of their feud. The problem was a Dutchman inserted himself into the middle of the fray and decided it was his turn to reign. The rising talent of Pieter van den Hoogenband was not unknown to Popov or Hall, who raced against him at the 1996 Olympics in the 100 free, where van den Hoogenband placed fourth to just miss the podium. Meanwhile, "Hoogie" was fourth at the 1998 World Championships before capturing the 1999 European crown over Popov.

Van den Hoogenband was also coming off a stunning victory over Thorpe in the 200 freestyle, the Dutchman setting a world record of 1:45.35 in the semifinals before matching that time in the final. His defeat of Thorpe hushed the Aussie crowd and confirmed what had been suspected for a few years: van den Hoogenband would emerge as one of the sport's greats.

At half the distance of his initial Olympic triumph, van den Hoogenband was equally impressive. Turning in third place at the midway mark, he blasted the field over the second lap to touch in 48.30, with Popov earning the silver medal in 48.69 and Hall taking the bronze in 48.73. The result left Popov short of history in his initial pursuit of a treble, but Hall was thrilled with his podium finish. As for van den Hoogenband, he recognized the enormity of the moment.

"I like to race against him," van den Hoogenband said of Popov. "He's such a legend. If you beat him, it means a little more than beating anyone else."

There wasn't much turnaround time between the end of the 100 freestyle and the start of the 50 free, the one-lap dash where a single mistake proves deadly. None of the big guns had any difficulty advancing out of the preliminaries and Hall, van den Hoogenband, Ervin, and Popov went into the final as the top four seeds, separated by a tenth of a second.

As the final approached, the familiar verbal jabs between Hall and Popov had ceased, each athlete merely focusing on his job. Perhaps it was evidence of maturity in both men, or maybe their quiet nature was affected by the fact that Ervin and van den Hoogenband were significant threats to the sprint throne.

Off the blocks faster than their fellow finalists, Hall and Ervin—as they had so many times in preparation for Sydney—engaged in a stroke-for-stroke duel at the Sydney Aquatic Center. The difference from practice was that this clash was viewed by more than 17,000 spectators and the prize was what all world-class swimmers strive to claim: Olympic gold.

As Hall and Ervin approached the wall, it was impossible to determine which man was in front, and for good reason. When the scoreboard flashed the results, a pair of 21.98 performances were listed. One was produced by Hall. The other was courtesy of Ervin. For the first time since 1984, there was a tie in an Olympic swimming final, and the guys who shared the top step of the podium just happened to see each other every day.

"The first thing you do is check your name and see the number next to it," Hall said of the finish. "It took me awhile to realize there was another '1' up on the board, and then I thought it was [van den Hoogenband] who had tied with me. When I realized it was Anthony, I was very happy. I couldn't have shared this medal with a nicer guy."

The sprint events are considered the macho disciplines of the sport. There is a lot of testosterone on the deck, and the miniscule margin for error tends to create stress and tension among the combatants. Somehow, though, Hall and Ervin successfully navigated those chest-thumping land mines and proved to be supportive on the road to Sydney. Throughout training, Hall could only recall one spat with Ervin, a flareup that quickly subsided and was forgotten.

For Hall, gold was the realization of a family dream, one that started with his father as a Team USA stalwart in the 1960s and 1970s. For Ervin, his emergence as an Olympic champion sparked discussion of whether he could etch himself as one of the greatest sprinters of all time.

"We pushed each other every day in training," Ervin said. "We got up and raced and I think that prepared us. It's an honor to share the gold with him. (Hall) is someone I look up to. He is very misunderstood. Until I roomed with him at the Olympics, I had never really gotten a true glimpse of what Gary is like. He's very deep, and well-spoken. We're similar in a lot of ways."

A two-time Olympic champion in the fifty freestyle, Gary Hall Jr. is one of the greatest sprinters in history. Peter H. Bick.

Touching behind Hall and Ervin for the bronze medal was van den Hoogenband, who pulled off the rare—and impressive—feat of medaling in three freestyle distances. Back in a surprising sixth was Popov, who never found his usually unmatched speed and watched another opportunity at a three-peat get washed away. In a way, Sydney witnessed a changing of the guard in the sprint realm, the formerly untouchable Popov surrendering his kingdom to new blood.

As he was wont to do, Hall went off the radar between Sydney and the Athens Olympics of 2004. Appearing at the World Championships was never a high priority, so he skipped the global competitions of 2001 and 2003. Really, Hall's approach was simple: He cared only about the Olympic Games, and he was confident he could excel without racing frequently, or against the best in the world.

Popov, too, vanished into the shadows the year after the Sydney Games, but the Russian was back in action at the 2002 European Championships. In Berlin, Popov finished fifth in the 50 freestyle but confirmed he wasn't slipping when he won the silver medal behind van den Hoogenband in the 100 freestyle.

There was more to come.

With the 2003 World Championships scheduled for Barcelona, Popov was eager to return to the city where he celebrated his initial Olympic success. The visit could not have unfolded in more perfect fashion as Popov decisively won both sprint-freestyle events. At 31 years old, he set a championship record of 21.92 in the 50 free and captured the 100 freestyle in 48.42, van den Hoogenband back in second place.

"Barcelona has always been a special city in my life," Popov said after winning the 100 freestyle. "This is the place where I started and, well, Barcelona is where we continue."

Coming off his age-defying and surprise double at the World Championships, Popov headed into the 2004 Olympic year with momentum. Hall? His lack of competition prompted a question mark. It also didn't take Hall long to make waves as part of a controversy within the Team USA camp.

With the help of Hall, the United States had no trouble qualifying for the final of the 400 freestyle relay on the second day of the meet. But when the lineup for the final was revealed, and Hall was not one of the listed names, Captain America voiced his displeasure. As one of the two-fastest Americans from prelims, Hall felt he earned his spot on the evening relay. The coaching staff, headed by University of Texas coach Eddie Reese, opted to bring back only Neil Walker from the prelim squad and use Jason Lezak, Ian Crocker, and Michael Phelps for the other three legs. Lezak and Crocker were locks, based on their one-two finish from the United States Trials. But Phelps' selection generated controversy since he didn't contest the 100 free final at Trials.

When the United States managed only bronze in the final in Athens, marking its worst Olympic showing, there was considerable disappointment. Crocker's leadoff leg, in which he was eighth, proved to be too much to overcome, and even the inclusion of Hall would not have affected the outcome. Still, a precedent had been bypassed in the selection of Phelps, and the decorated Hall was the man who got the boot.

"I was disappointed in the decision," Hall said. "I don't think it was the right decision. (Reese) said he wasn't going to second-guess himself and that's fine, but it's something I have to live with and something that I take personally. That relay, I wanted very much to be a part of it."

After his relay snub, Hall had several days to focus on the defense of his title in the 50 freestyle. Popov, meanwhile, had the 100 freestyle two days after his Russian team tied for fourth in the 400 freestyle relay. The event did not go according to plan as Popov's ninth-place effort in the semifinals left him shy of the final.

If Popov saw the 100 freestyle as a disappointment, then the 50 freestyle was a disaster. The two-time champion of the event experienced a premature ouster from the prelims of the dash after posting a time that was nearly a second slower than his world record. Since the effort arrived just a year after Popov was crowned world champion, shock filled the air.

Hall didn't encounter similar difficulties. After easily advancing through the preliminaries and semifinals, Hall joined Popov as a repeat champion of the 50 free. Winning by the slimmest of margins, 0.01, Hall touched the wall in 21.93 to edge Croatian Duje Draganja. Hall engaged in a muted celebration, raising his hands to acknowledge the crowd.

"Gary's a racer," Bottom said. "Nothing surprises me from Gary. He steps up. He's got heart, he's got soul, he's got desire. He's also creative in what he does. He doesn't swim miles and miles in the pool every day. He goes out and swims in the ocean. He goes to Costa Rica. He enjoys his life."

Their trophy cases each filled with two Olympic gold medals from the 50 freestyle, Popov and Hall went different directions after Athens. Popov announced his retirement in early 2005, while Hall made a final run at the Olympics at the 2008 United States Trials, coming up short of a trip to Beijing following a fourth-place finish.

As long as the history of sprinting and great duels is discussed, the decade-long rivalry between Popov and Hall will be mentioned. They spent years trading insults and playing mind games with one another. But most important, they spent years producing epic races and raising the bar in the sprint game.

"I hated Alex. And he hated me," Hall said. "He was such an asshole the first time we met, in the ready room before finals at the (1994) World Championships. I was a threat and he was going to do anything he could to gain an advantage, trying to get inside my head. It was a legitimate rivalry. Like any rivalry, it fueled us both."

A RIFT BETWEEN TEAMMATES

Like many rivalry stories, the tale of Jenny Thompson and Dara Torres is about opposites. Thompson was raised by a single mom where financial struggles were common. Torres was raised in Beverly Hills, money never an issue. Thompson is quiet and reserved, preferring to go unnoticed. Torres seeks out the spotlight, never one to pass up the chance to promote her brand. Thompson went into the medical profession after her swimming days. Torres' post-pool endeavors included broadcasting and modeling.

But in the pool, there were few differences. They both moved through the water with world-class speed. They raced the same events. They possessed high intensity levels and aimed for lofty goals. And in the Olympic campaign of 2000, Thompson and Torres dueled in spectacular fashion—in and out of the water—and provided the sport with an all-time rivalry.

Torres fits the mold of one of those teenage sensations who frequently emerge in the swimming world. As a 14-year-old, Torres announced her presence in a major way by winning the national title in the 50 freestyle, a crown that required her to defeat Olympian Jill Sterkel. In a little more than 20 seconds, Torres made it known she would be a factor in the sprints. What couldn't be predicted was the longevity she would eventually display.

Behind an equally efficient and powerful stroke, Torres punched her first Olympic ticket to a home Olympiad in Los Angeles in 1984. At those Games, where she was surrounded by veterans such as Mary T. Meagher, Rowdy Gaines, and Tracy Caulkins, Torres garnered the first Olympic medal of her career, as the United States prevailed in the 400 freestyle relay.

Over the next four years, the success continued for Torres, who became an NCAA and Southeastern Conference champion for the University of Florida and earned her second Olympic nod for the 1988 Games in Seoul. At those Games, Torres won silver and bronze medals in relay action and finished seventh in the 100 freestyle.

Just after Seoul, Thompson started to emerge as a U.S. future hope, an identity claimed through three medals at the 1989 edition of the Pan Pacific Championships. In Tokyo, Thompson won gold in the 50 freestyle and took silver in the 100 freestyle to strengthen the American sprinting contingent.

It wasn't until 1992, however, that Thompson and Torres competed at the same Olympics, albeit without crossing paths as competitors. While Thompson won the silver medal in the 100 freestyle and was fifth in the 50 freestyle, she joined Torres on the victorious 400 freestyle relay. But with Thompson recognized as one of the world's rising stars, Torres was ready to retire, and any potential rivalry was impossible to foresee.

With Torres gone and Thompson recovered from nagging injuries that hampered her 1994 season, she again put her name on the global radar

Jenny Thompson established herself as a hall of famer in the butterfly and freestyle events. Peter H. Bick.

in 1995 by medaling in three Pan Pacs events, including a gold in the 100 freestyle. On the road to her second Olympic Games, Thompson appeared poised to strike in Atlanta.

"I'm pleased with how everything went," Thompson said. "I think this was a good stepping stone toward the Olympics."

The 1996 Olympic Trials were supposed to be a formality for Thompson. Entered in four events, she was expected to hop into the pool, take care of business, and look ahead to the Games in Atlanta, where she could claim a fistful of medals. Instead, there was no way to describe Thompson's performance in Indianapolis other than with one of the most-hated words in sports: choke. The pressure got to Thompson, and when she struggled early on, a snowball of negativity became an avalanche of doubt.

Thompson entered her first event, the 100 freestyle, as the American-record holder and heavy favorite to win. But a third-place finish left Thompson with only relay duty in Atlanta and, more damning, damaged her psyche. She followed with a seventh-place finish in the 200 freestyle and a fourth-place finish in the 100 butterfly, and by the time the 50 free-style arrived as her last event, Thompson was done. Her third-place finish in that event was, simply, a last kick to the gut.

"People automatically assumed I would make the Olympic team," Thompson said. "I was a basket case. At those Trials, my mind was all over the place. Maybe I wanted something so bad, I lost my focus."

Although Thompson qualified for the Atlanta Games in the 400 freestyle relay, the coaching staff also used her on the 400 medley relay and 800 freestyle relay, allowing Thompson to win three gold medals. More, she served as a mentor to the younger athletes on the Team USA roster, imparting her wisdom from previous international meets.

By rallying from a disastrous Olympic Trials to perform admirably at the Olympic Games revealed a toughness in Thompson that hadn't been seen before. Her story was one of perseverance and making the best of a situation and doing so in a fishbowl. Not surprising, Thompson's tale was a major storyline of that summer.

"I've been proud of her in a lot of things, but how she handled the disappointment of how she finished at the Olympic Trials and the way she prepared for the Games, I think has taken an enormous amount of character," said her coach, Richard Quick.

> I really admire her because she hasn't looked at the short side of things. She's looked at the long side. It's a tremendous honor to be on the Olympic team. It's a tremendous honor to be on two Olympic teams. This is her second one. It carries a responsibility with it that Jenny recognizes. And she's accepted that responsibility. She knows the best way to prepare is to race all these races as if she were swimming all her events. Instead of feeling sorry for herself, she has been ready to do anything she can for the U.S. as a relay member.

The disappointment of 1996 did not linger with Thompson, whose next three years were nothing short of remarkable. Between the 1997 and 1999 Pan Pacific Championships, Thompson totaled 12 medals, 11 of which were gold. At the 1999 version of the event in Sydney, where she won three solo golds and six overall titles, Thompson took down Meagher's 18-year-old world record in the 100 butterfly.

In between Pan Pacs, at the 1998 World Championships, Thompson was the dominant athlete. In addition to claiming world titles in the 100 freestyle and 100 butterfly, Thompson powered a pair of American relays to gold medals and helped another relay to silver. The three years that followed her 1996 struggles clearly proved she had moved forward.

"It was probably the worst meet of my life," Thompson said of the 1996 Olympic Trials. "I definitely would not be here today if I'd had the dream Olympics I wanted to have in Atlanta."

As Thompson roared into the Olympic campaign with momentum from Pan Pacs, Torres embarked on her first comeback, putting an end to a seven-year absence from the sport. During her hiatus, Torres was not out of the spotlight, having done broadcasting work for several networks and appearing in commercials for the Tae Bo fitness program.

When Torres announced her comeback and reached out to Quick to seek his guidance on the road to Sydney, Thompson welcomed the opportunity to train with another world-class sprinter. The initial belief was that Thompson and Torres would push each other during practice and reap the benefits at the 2000 Olympic Games. It was a setup that worked at the Phoenix Swim Club, where Gary Hall Jr. and Anthony Ervin trained together under the watch of Mike Bottom.

But not long after they began sharing the same water, it was clear Thompson and Torres needed to be separated. The practices became too intense and instead of each athlete focusing on fine-tuning their strokes and meeting Quick's expectations, Thompson and Torres were more concerned with beating one another. Consequently, Quick split them up, opting to train Torres at another time.

"If you are training for the same event, every day, twice a day, both going after the same thing and only one is going to get there, it can be very intense," Torres said. "We're friends. We're not like enemies. I just think, in a way, it's better to keep us apart so there wouldn't be as much intensity in the workouts."

The separation of Thompson and Torres added to the hype of the Olympic Trials, as they were scheduled to clash in three events—the 50 freestyle, 100 freestyle, and 100 butterfly. Journalists were eager to tell the tale of two women, opposites in personality, who couldn't coexist in the same pool. The rivalry made for good copy.

For his part, Quick didn't try to sugarcoat the tension that built when they trained together. He was open and honest about the situation, and, to his credit, Quick did a fine job of preparing both women to excel at the Olympic Trials.

"Every day in practice was like an Olympic final. I had to train them separately," Quick said. "I just made the decision as a coach, because of the chemistry of the situation, to have them train at different times. There was a kind of chemistry situation that needed to be addressed. They deserved individual attention and I wanted to give it to them. They deserved it and they somewhat demanded it. When dealing with athletes who compete in the same events, that's not so unusual."

Once the Olympic Trials rolled around, Thompson and Torres engaged in their expected showdown, with Thompson coming out on top in the 100 freestyle and 100 butterfly. Torres, meanwhile, finished first in the 50 freestyle. Although they were foes chasing the same hardware in

Sydney, Thompson and Torres were teammates again, as was the case at the 1992 Olympics in Barcelona.

In Sydney, Thompson and Torres partnered toward a pair of gold medals, as they made up half of the U.S. 400 freestyle relay and 400 medley relay. Torres got the best of Thompson in the 100 butterfly, winning bronze while her rival was fifth, and she also took bronze in the 50 freestyle. But it is what transpired in the 100 freestyle that is only believable because it is logged in the history books.

Placing behind the Netherlands' Inge de Bruijn and Sweden's Therese Alshammar in the 100 freestyle, Torres and Thompson tied for the bronze medal, thanks to matching times of 54.63. It was a fitting outcome and one that Torres called ironic based on the lead-up to Sydney.

"There are three [things] to describe why I am where I am right now: Hard work, dedication and sacrifice," Torres said. "I feel I've done everything I possibly can the right way to get where I am. I know it seems a little amazing because I'm 33 and I was out seven years. But for some reason, this was supposed to happen, and I'm just enjoying the ride."

Following the 2000 Games, Torres opted for her second retirement while Thompson began her medical-school studies at Columbia University. After a year, Thompson returned to the pool and put together superb performances at the 2002 Pan Pacific Championships and 2003 World Championships. Thompson won the 50 free at Pan Pacs, to go with bronze medals in the 100 freestyle and 100 butterfly, and followed a year later by winning five medals at the World Champs, including gold in the 100 butterfly. It was a perfect setup for Thompson's final Olympics, the 2004 Games in Athens.

At 31 years old, Thompson was seventh in the 50 freestyle and fifth in the 100 butterfly. Yet, she added the final two Olympic medals of her career as the United States won silver in the 400 freestyle relay and 400 medley relay. Afterward, it was back to medical school, with the knowledge she had finished her career on her terms.

"What keeps me going is finding out how far I can push myself," she said. "How fast can I be? How long can I stay on top? That striving for excellence, that feeling of knowing you have trained till you don't have one drop of energy left, that's what keeps me happy."

The retirement of Thompson figured to put an end to the days of America's T&T tandem, until Torres made a second—and improbable comeback—in 2007. Upon returning for a second time, Torres didn't waste time emphasizing the seriousness of her comeback. She won national titles in the 50 freestyle and 100 freestyle in 2007 and followed a

Dara Torres competed in five Olympics and twice made epic comebacks from retirement. Peter H. Bick.

year later, as a 41-year-old, with berths to the 2008 Olympics in Beijing in both sprint-freestyle events, an American record defining her win in the 50 free.

At the 2008 Games, Torres captured three silver medals, two of them earned in a 35-minute span on the final night of action. A silver already claimed in the 400 freestyle relay from earlier in the meet, Torres was the runner-up in the 50 free and as a member of the 400 medley relay. Her second-place finish in the 50 freestyle was by the slimmest of margins, as Germany's Britta Steffen beat Torres, 24.06–24.07, a poor finish by Torres denying her the first solo gold of her Olympic career.

Torres became the oldest swimmer in history to medal at the Olympics and by raising her career total to 12 medals, she tied Thompson as the second-most decorated swimmer in Olympic history, behind Michael Phelps.

She also became an inspiration to women around the world, proving that age does not have to be a hindrance.

"If it helps anyone else out there who is in their middle-aged years and they put off something they thought they couldn't do because they were too old or maybe thought that because they have children they can't balance what they want to do and be a parent, then I'm absolutely thrilled," she said.

The first five-time Olympian for USA Swimming, Torres made another run at an Olympic bid in 2012 but finished fourth in the 50 freestyle at 45 years old. The sheer improbability of what Torres has achieved has been appreciated in many circles but has been questioned in others. Despite offering to be additionally tested, Torres has been accused of benefiting from performance-enhancing drugs.

"It's too bad," Torres said of the doping speculation. "Why do people have to emphasize drugs because someone does something really fast? I don't have words to describe it. It infuriates me. People think that because drugs are used so much in sport. Everyone has a conscience. For me, I know I've done everything I can do to get where I am the right way."

The shortcoming shared by the Hall of Fame inductees is the lack of an individual gold medal on either woman's ledger. But what Thompson and Torres achieved over a combined nine Olympiads outweighs the missing achievement. More, they gave the sport—and each other—something to follow in the Olympic campaign of 2000.

"We're both very competitive," Thompson said, at the height of the rivalry. "We're friendly when it comes down to it, but it hasn't always been easy. We make the best of it. The rivalry definitely has pushed me to be better. It put me out of my comfort zone and made me have to step it up."

BREASTSTROKE BRAWL: PART II

The year was 1999 and the World Short Course Championships were held in Hong Kong. Representing the United States in the breaststroke events was teenager Brendan Hansen, a rising star in the American arsenal whose primary objective was to garner international experience. Japan's Kosuke Kitajima did not compete.

The year was 2000 and the 27th edition of the Summer Olympics was held in Sydney. Representing Japan in the breaststroke events was Kitajima, a rising star in the Pacific Rim who just missed the medals podium with a fourth-place finish in the 100-meter breaststroke. Hansen did not compete.

American Brendan Hansen and Japan's Kosuke Kitajima enjoyed one of the greatest rivalries in swimming history. Peter H. Bick.

On opposite sides of the new millennium, Hansen and Kitajima found themselves debuting in the caps of their respective nations. But for the better part of the ensuing decade, they were basically inseparable in breaststroke competition, and comfortably distanced themselves from the opposition. In addition to developing a rivalry that was not just top tier from a performance standpoint, Hansen and Kitajima crafted a rivalry that brought intrigue and drama to the sport.

The rich breaststroke tradition in Japan dates to the first half of the twentieth century, when Yoshiyuki Tsuruta doubled as Olympic champion in the 200 breaststroke in 1928 and 1932 and Japan regularly placed athletes on the medals podium in Olympic competition. Yet as Kitajima came along, the country was in a major drought, having gone since 1976 without an Olympic medalist in a breaststroke event.

Kitajima wasn't the typical Japanese athlete. There was a swagger about this son of a butcher, as he was the antithesis of the demure and quiet temperament widely adopted in Japanese culture. In the pool, Kitajima was known to aggressively pump his fist or slap the water to celebrate a victory. Holding back was not in his nature.

Hansen, meanwhile, was a workmanlike athlete from a country that didn't know the meaning of a drought—in any event. Growing up outside of Philadelphia, Pennsylvania, Hansen—just months after graduating from high school—nearly qualified for the Team USA roster for the 2000 Olympic Games in Sydney, a pair of third-place finishes in the 100 breaststroke and 200 breaststroke at the United States Trials leaving him one spot and hundredths of a second from realizing a career goal.

When Hansen came up short of earning a trip to Sydney, there wasn't a sense of dread or a woe-is-me sentiment. Rather, he looked ahead, using the pain of his near misses as motivation for the future. His ability to focus and grind through workouts was immediately apparent as Hansen arrived at the University of Texas to begin his collegiate career.

"There were a few days when I didn't see the light at the end of the tunnel. It was hard," Hansen admitted. "But I'm going to use what happened as a positive. You can't regret what happened in the past, but you can use it as motivation, for myself and my teammates. I'm a man on a mission."

After missing each other during the first two years of their international careers, the opening chapter of the Hansen–Kitajima rivalry was written at the 2001 World Championships in Japan. In his homeland, Kitajima raced all three breaststroke events. Hansen, meanwhile, competed in only the 200 breaststroke, a scenario that allowed him to place his focus on a solitary event.

The initial round ultimately went to Hansen, who broke through with a gold medal in the 200 breast, his winning time of 2:10.69 placing the American 0.52 ahead of Kitajima, who took the bronze medal for his first piece of international hardware. It may not have been known at the time, but Hansen and Kitajima were just starting to engage in a battle that would endure for rounds and feature plenty of figurative uppercuts.

"His swimming at the (Olympic) Trials was a great indicator of his ability," said Eddie Reese, Hansen's coach at the University of Texas. "To get third in both events (at Trials) would floor most people. Not Brendan. He took no time to get back on his horse and get back to work."

Shifts of the upper hand were the norm in the Hansen–Kitajima rivalry. After they each won a race at the 2002 Pan Pacific Championships, Kitajima took command. The Japanese star first broke Mike Barrowman's iconic ten-year-old record in the 200 breaststroke in late 2002, then followed the next year by winning gold in the 100 breaststroke and 200 breaststroke at the World Championships, the shorter distance in world-record time. At the World Champs, Hansen settled for silver in the 100 distance and bronze in the 200 distance.

But at the 2004 United States Olympic Trials, control returned to Hansen, as he dominated his events and took both breaststroke world

A six-time Olympic medalist, Brendan Hansen is one of the top breaststrokers in history. Peter H. Bick.

records from Kitajima. The American's reign, however, was short-lived, as the Olympic Games belonged to Kitajima—but not without controversy.

With USA Swimming typically holding its Trials in close proximity to the Olympic Games, it hasn't been unusual to see some American athletes' performances fall off from the Olympic Trials to the Games. Hansen was one of the affected athletes in Athens, evident in the fact that he was nearly a second slower at the Olympics in the 100 breaststroke, where he won the silver medal, and more than a second slower in the 200 breaststroke, which produced a bronze medal.

Despite Hansen's struggles, his inability to replicate his form in the 100 breaststroke was not the reason for finishing second to Kitajima. Off the start and turn, underwater cameras showed Kitajima using a dolphin kick to propel him through the water. The maneuver was illegal at the time, but officials monitoring the race did not call the violation. With dolphin kicks deemed to boost efforts by about 0.20 per length, Kitajima's tactics almost surely provided the difference in his victory, which Kitajima took, 1:00.08 to 1:00.25.

Upon looking to the scoreboard and realizing his triumph, Kitajima launched into celebration, his trademark fist pumps and splashing complemented by several loud screams. In the adjacent lane, Hansen only knew he had been beaten and was unaware of Kitajima's dolphin kicks and the controversy that was about to hit the deck.

When the underwater footage was seen by members of Team USA, Hansen's teammates—most notably Jason Lezak and Aaron Peirsol—came to his defense. Peirsol was the most vocal, calling for Kitajima to be disqualified and for the gold medal to go to Hansen. But with officials not calling the violation during the race and replay not allowed for postrace review, the result was not going to change.

"He knew what he was doing," Peirsol said of Kitajima. "It was cheating. Something needs to be done about that. It's just ridiculous. You take a huge dolphin kick and that gives you extra momentum, but he knows that you can't see that from underwater. He's got a history of that. Pay attention to it."

Hansen took the high road as the controversy unfolded, choosing not to call out Kitajima. He also defended the officials by noting their difficult jobs and placing his faith in their willingness to make the proper decisions when necessary.

Kitajima initially refused to discuss the allegations levied against him by Peirsol, but eventually defended himself as playing by the rules. A few days after the controversial finish in the 100 breaststroke, Kitajima stormed away from the field for the title in the 200 breaststroke, Hungarian Daniel Gyurta earning silver to put an extra place between Kitajima and Hansen.

"There's nothing about the race I actually remember," Kitajima said when asked to discuss the final of the 100 breaststroke. "I got in and did the best I could. I just remember when I finished and I won, I was as happy as I've ever been. A lot of people will now start to pay attention more than before. When I heard the comments by Peirsol, I was really surprised because I always try to have fair competition. I'm always trying my best within the regulations. I have never, ever been cautioned by the official judges."

Hansen and Kitajima met one final time at the 2004 Games, with Hansen claiming a gold medal as a member of the United States' victorious 400 medley relay. Kitajima, meanwhile, added a bronze medal to his collection as Japan placed third in the relay.

The next three years of the rivalry belonged to Hansen, who bounced back from his Olympic disappointment in dominant fashion. Not only did Hansen win the 100 and 200 breaststroke events at the 2005 World Championships, his 2006 campaign featured world records over both distances and wins over Kitajima in both breaststroke events at the Pan Pacific Championships. At the 2007 World Champs, Hansen again beat Kitajima, this time in the 100 breaststroke. While Kitajima won the 200 breaststroke at Worlds, the final was missing Hansen, who was stricken with a stomach bug and forced to withdraw from the event.

Once again, though, the Olympic campaign was all Kitajima.

While some rivalries are friendly in nature, that description obviously didn't fit the temperament between Kitajima and Hansen, whose frigid relationship couldn't be overlooked. There was no love lost in the water, and their lack of camaraderie extended to the deck. Although Kitajima and Hansen could put on a diplomatic show, the true sense of their rapport could be found in the barbs they occasionally exchanged through the years. The disdain was evident during the 2008 United States Olympic Trials.

Although Trials started smoothly for Hansen, in the form of a win in the 100 breaststroke, he was surprisingly fourth in the 200 breaststroke, a setback that left him with a lighter schedule for the upcoming Games in Beijing. With Hansen down, Kitajima took the opportunity to inflict some more damage.

"For a swimmer of his level, it shouldn't be that difficult to qualify," Kitajima said. "He didn't seem to set his goals and rise to the challenge just one month before the Olympics."

Hansen fired back, noting the difference in competition levels between the United States and Japanese Trials.

"I don't really care what he has to say," Hansen said. "I can't control that. I know I didn't hold up my end of the bargain, and I'm disappointed with what happened. What can you do? It is what it is. At his Trials, he didn't have anything to deal with. The competition isn't close to what it is at our Trials".

The Olympics didn't go any better for Hansen. In their sole individual clash in Beijing, Kitajima thumped Hansen, setting a world record of 58.91. Hansen finished fourth in 59.57, kept off the podium by France's Hugues Duboscq, who was timed in 59.37. Although Hansen added another gold medal in the 400 medley relay, in the process helping Michael Phelps complete his record eight-gold showing, he left Beijing disappointed and under the impression that he was done with the sport.

On his way out, Hansen took a moment to congratulate his rival.

Japan's Kosuke Kitajim is the only man to win both breaststroke events at back-to-back Olympics. Peter H. Bick.

"I just said, 'Congratulations, man, that's an awesome swim.' " Hansen said. "And I know that if I had done that in front of him, he would have done the exact same thing. You've got to take your hat off when somebody goes 58.9 in the Olympic final."

With Hansen leaning toward retirement, Kitajima also took time away from the pool, opting to skip the 2009 World Championships in Rome. But he was back in action by the 2010 Pan Pacific Championships, where he won each of his primary events. At the 2011 World Championships, though, Kitajima managed just a silver in the 200 breaststroke and fourth place in the 100 breaststroke. It was the first sign of a drop-off from the overwhelming dominance he had long displayed.

As Kitajima fought to maintain his status, Hansen returned to training in 2011 to focus on qualifying for a third Olympiad, a feat he accomplished in the summer of 2012. As was the case in 2008, Hansen got the job done in the 100 breaststroke, but came up short in the 200 breaststroke, finishing fourth. Headed to the London Games, Hansen was far from a top threat, and the way racing began for the American, hopes of a medal seemed minimal.

After advancing through the preliminaries of the 100 breaststroke in tenth place, Hansen appeared like he would miss the final when he finished sixth in the first of the two semifinals. But when the second semifinal only saw two swimmers beat his time, Hansen moved into the medal round as the eighth and final seed. For his part, Kitajima was sixth entering the chase for the medals.

With nothing to lose and racing on his own out in Lane Eight, Hansen turned up the pace on his second lap, rallying from sixth place at the turn to shockingly finish in the bronze-medal position, gold going to South Africa's Cameron van der Burgh in a world-record time of 58.46, with silver claimed by Australian Christian Sprenger. Kitajima was fifth, marking the first time Hansen had beaten his rival in an individual Olympic event.

"This is the shiniest bronze medal ever," Hansen said. "It's definitely the hardest one I ever won. When I came back, I wasn't thinking about winning a medal. I outperformed myself."

Several days later, Hansen concluded his Olympic career with a third gold medal in the 400 medley relay, as the United States fended off Japan, which took silver with Kitajima fittingly handling the breaststroke leg. The race also signaled the end of Kitajima's Olympic days.

After the 100 breaststroke, Hansen and Kitajima each used social media to congratulate the other on a stellar career. More, following a press conference, the two found a moment to pose for a picture and exchange a quick hug, a fitting way for the men to wave goodbye as competitors. For all the years they battled, both in and out of the water, respect permeated the rivalry.

There is no question that Kitajima performed his best in Olympic waters, and he remains the only man to twice double as Olympic champion in the 100 breaststroke and 200 breaststroke. However, a look through a wider lens reveals that each man set five individual world records during his career and Hansen led with four solo world titles to three for Kitajima.

"We definitely went at each other for a long time and we had some terrific races," Hansen said. "It was a great rivalry."

AN ERA OF EXCELLENCE

All sports, especially those of an individual nature, have defining rivalries that attract fans' attention. Boxing had Ali–Frazier. Tennis had

Borg–McEnroe and Navratilova–Evert, and now features the triangular rivalry of Federer–Nadal–Djokovic. Look to golf for Palmer–Nicklaus and Woods–Mickelson.

The beauty of a rivalry is how it can take a variety of forms. A battle of conflicting styles. A clash of personalities. A fight for supremacy. A duel between the aging veteran and the talented upstart. All these versions are intriguing, and sometimes they will overlap with one another to make for an even tastier tale.

Such was the construction of the rivalry between Michael Phelps and Ryan Lochte.

When Phelps broke onto the international scene as a 15-year-old finishing fifth in the 200-meter butterfly at the 2000 Olympic Games in Sydney, it was a matter of time before his talent projected to additional events. And, indeed, by the 2003 World Championships, there was Phelps, capturing three gold medals and a silver medal in solo events to etch himself as his sport's undisputed king.

By all methods, Phelps was the measuring stick in the sport, this still-developing force who could do a little bit of everything—and at a peak level. At the 2004 Olympics in Athens, his six golds and two bronze medals made him the first athlete to win eight medals in an Olympiad, his multidiscipline pursuits generating nonstop comparisons to the legendary Mark Spitz.

In Athens, a much quieter ascension was also unfolding. As Phelps won gold in the 200 individual medley, the silver medalist was Lochte, nearly two seconds back. More, Lochte handled the second leg on the U.S. gold-medal-winning 800 freestyle relay that put an end to Australia's six-year international reign in the event. The week was Lochte's assurance that he belonged at the elite level.

"I just came here to have fun and right now I'm having a blast," Lochte said of his Olympic debut. "It's amazing to swim for the USA at the Olympics."

Over the next four years, through the 2008 Olympics in Beijing, the Phelps–Lochte rivalry echoed what was witnessed in Athens: Phelps was Batman, and Lochte was Robin. To think the rivalry was anything but super-hero and sidekick would have been foolish, as evidenced by Phelps' over-whelming dominance. In races with Lochte in major competition, defined as the Olympics, World Championships, Pan Pacific Championships, and Olympic Trials, Phelps owned a 12–0 advantage over Lochte.

At that time, Phelps actually had a more-balanced rivalry with Ian Crocker. The two had battled in the 100 butterfly since 2003, with

Crocker holding the world record and winning world titles in 2003 and 2005. Phelps, meanwhile, won Olympic crowns in 2004 and 2008 and captured the world title in 2007. But the combination of Crocker retiring and Phelps facing Lochte in multiple events made the rivalry with Lochte more visible.

Although Lochte had been unable to beat Phelps through Beijing, it would have been unfair to state Lochte was not making progress. His times in the medley events continued to drop and he was a regular presence on international podiums. Meanwhile, at the 2007 World Championships in Melbourne, Lochte snapped Aaron Peirsol's six-year unbeaten streak in the 200 backstroke by setting a world record. At the Olympics in Beijing, he again defeated Peirsol and further lowered his global standard. Although he wasn't beating Phelps, Lochte proved himself capable of taking down a giant in the sport, and the success provided confidence that Phelps, too, could be toppled.

"I believe in myself," Lochte said. "A lot of people look at Michael and think he can't be beaten. That's not me. I know I can beat him. That's that competitive edge that I have. I never feel like I'm going to lose, not matter who I'm racing. I always feel like I can win".

With Beijing in the past, Lochte used the summer of 2009 to ascend to the top of the world in the medley events—albeit with Phelps absent and focusing on other events. At the World Championships, Lochte doubled

Ryan Lochte, left, has spent much of his career chasing the bar set by Michael Phelps.
Peter H. Bick.

in the 200 I.M. and 400 I.M., but it was what he managed the next summer that truly changed the dynamic of the rivalry. Competing at the 2010 United States National Championships, Lochte finally got the best of Phelps in a high-profile race, winning the 200 individual medley by more than a second.

The momentum generated by Lochte carried into the 2011 World Championships, where Lochte won four individual gold medals and beat Phelps in the 200 freestyle and 200 individual medley. While Phelps was skipping practices and not as dedicated as he was earlier in his career, Lochte changed his diet and elevated himself to World Swimmer of the Year.

The losses to Lochte certainly didn't sit well with Phelps, who was unaccustomed to being upstaged. And even though he knew he hadn't adhered to his typical training program, that knowledge did little to alleviate his frustration.

"(Lochte) is super focused right now, and I think you can see that," Phelps said.

> He keeps putting the races together that are helping him win. To be honest, he's just more prepared. That's really what it comes down to. Races are always won by people who are most prepared. Give Ryan credit. We've been racing for years and he did the work to improve and put himself in the best position possible. I'm kind of playing catchup now. I think it's more motivating. I remember back in 2000 and 2001 when I was trying to climb and climb and, finally, I got there. Being back in this position, I think, will be kind of fun.

The 2012 Olympic campaign brought split decisions to the rivalry. While Lochte beat Phelps at the Olympic Trials in the 400 individual medley, the outcome at the Olympic Games was surprising. It wasn't stunning that Lochte won gold in the event, but that Phelps finished fourth and off the podium. It was the first time since his Olympic debut in Sydney in which Phelps contested an event at the Olympics and walked away without a medal.

Phelps rebounded, however, when the men clashed in the 200 individual medley. Defeating Lochte by 0.63, Phelps earned his third straight Olympic crown in the shorter medley. It was then off to retirement for Phelps. In his foe's absence, Lochte continued to add to his world-title count and, with Phelps making a comeback, they engaged in a final showdown at the 2016 Olympics in Rio de Janeiro.

After prevailing at the Olympic Trials, Phelps punctuated the rivalry with his fourth straight Olympic gold in the 200 medley. While Phelps won by almost two seconds over Japan's Kosuke Hagino, Lochte finished out of the medals in fifth. As far as the rivalry was concerned, it had come full circle, with the original king on his throne.

"The competitive environment between those two guys has always been good," said Gregg Troy, Lochte's longtime coach. "Even at their own testament, they both say they bring out the best in each other. And I think there's a mutual respect, but also they're very competitive and neither one has wanted to give in or go home."

In the water, Phelps and Lochte might have shared the unique ability to shine over all strokes. Out of the pool, though, they were very much different.

"Ryan is the personality," Austrian Olympic medalist Markus Rogan once said. "Michael is the machine. It's such a dramatic difference. Ryan is more like a Dennis Rodman. Michael is more like a Tim Duncan."

Phelps' demeanor never changed from competition to competition or event to event. When it was time to race, Phelps viewed the pool as his office or boardroom. Business was at hand, and moments for joking and smiling would wait. Via headphones or earbuds, the music pumping into Phelps' ears was the only external noise he heard. Otherwise, he stared straight ahead, laser-focused on the task that awaited.

Lochte was the antithesis of Phelps. It's not to say that he wasn't dedicated to his craft and rising to the top of his events. One doesn't attain the level of success Lochte realized without genuine focus. He just handled his business in a more lighthearted manner, bringing a surfer-guy and goofy persona to the deck. On various podiums throughout his career, including at the 2012 Olympic Games, Lochte wore decorative dental grills on his teeth. He was also known for his footwear style, as he always donned multicolored sneakers for his walks to the starting block.

"My shoes with the teddy bears. My grill. That stuff was meant to lighten the mood," Lochte said. "I mean, this world is so negative. If I can put a little bit of fun in people's lives, then I'm cool with that."

The problem for Lochte was that his frat-boy identity—at times— overshadowed the talent he possessed. If some fans of the sport were enamored by his silliness, others viewed Lochte as a clown, and his decisions didn't help assuage those notions. In 2013, he appeared on the E! Network's "What Would Ryan Lochte Do?" It was an eight-episode reality show that chronicled Lochte's life, and frequently focused on his drunken escapades with friends.

More, on the final night of swimming competition at the 2016 Olympic Games, Lochte became embroiled in controversy when he and three U.S. teammates, all intoxicated, urinated on private property at a Rio de Janeiro gas station and Lochte pulled a sign off a wall. The athletes were then confronted by armed security guards and forced to pay for the damages they caused. A day later, Lochte embellished what took place, claiming one of the guards pressed a gun to his forehead, and the story took off, making headlines around the world. For his actions and exaggeration of the night's events, Lochte was handed a ten-month suspension by the United States Olympic Committee and USA Swimming.

"You learn from your mistakes," Lochte said. "Am I going to be perfect? No."

Phelps hasn't been perfect either.

For all his achievements and accolades, Phelps stumbled several times during his career. Twice, he was charged with DUI, the second infraction leading to a stint in rehab in which Phelps looked deep within himself and confronted personal demons. Meanwhile, he was also photographed smoking marijuana at a party in 2009. Like Lochte, Phelps served multiple suspensions for his poor decisions but acknowledged learning from the mistakes.

Regardless of what transpired away from the pool, Phelps and Lochte will always be remembered for their vast accomplishments on the competitive stage. For Lochte, Phelps served as a motivating figure, a benchmark to chase. For Phelps, Lochte served to remind him that he could not rest on past laurels, and he was not unbeatable.

Overall, Phelps left the rivalry with a 16–4 edge in major competitions.

"Racing against him has been an honor," Lochte said. "He's one of the world's greatest swimmers ever. For me to be a part of that era—to be able to push him, or even to beat him—has been an honor. And it's been fun. Michael raised the bar and gave me something to chase. I had to get better and up my game to compete with him and that's what I did."

It is what rivalries are all about.

Chapter 5

CONTROVERSY REIGNS

*Controversy has played a regular role in the sport, ranging from judges'
decisions to political influence. The truth is, controversy is always going
to be part of the sporting fabric, only it is impossible to determine when
it will arise.*

A JUDGE'S VERDICT

His career included NCAA championships for the University of Southern
California. He was a world-record holder in multiple events. He was the
first man in history to break the minute barrier in the 100-meter butterfly.
He was enshrined in the International Swimming Hall of Fame as a member of the Class of 1980.

What Lance Larson did not claim during his career was an individual
Olympic gold medal, the defining achievement of any athlete in the sport.
But that missing tally on Larson's ledger was no fault of his own. Rather,
Larson was the victim of robbery, his name forever linked to one of the
biggest controversies in Olympic lore.

At the 1960 Olympics, automatic-timing technology was still in its
infancy and, therefore, not trusted as the ultimate judge of the races contested in Rome. Instead, the chore of identifying the finishing order was
handed to 24 judges—3 officials for each of the eight lanes in the pool.
Meanwhile, the timing system was viewed as a backup device to be used
only under extenuating circumstances. Through Olympic history, the use
of judges had never been a problem, and there was no reason to believe
anything would change.

An assessment of the 100-meter freestyle suggested the battle for the gold medal was a two-man affair, matching Larson and Australian world-record holder John Devitt. While Larson was riding a wave of momentum after winning the event at the United States Olympic Trials in 55.0, Devitt held the fastest time in history at 54.6. Barring an upset, those men were going to take gold and silver. But in what order?

After the final concluded, there still wasn't a clear answer.

Devitt entered the 1960 Games as an Olympic veteran, having won the silver medal in the 100 freestyle in 1956. With a pair of world-record performances in a ten-day span in 1957, Devitt stamped himself as the man to beat on the way to Rome. But Larson was no pushover, his credentials as the world-record holder in the 100 butterfly and 200 individual medley reflecting his versatility. However, neither of those events appeared on the 1960 Olympic schedule, which meant Larson had to place his focus elsewhere. The 100 freestyle was his choice.

Larson and Devitt had no trouble winning their respective heats in the preliminary and semifinal rounds, their showdown in the final a much-anticipated affair. Could Devitt improve from silver to gold and follow countryman Jon Henricks onto the top step of the podium? Or, would Larson restore the title in the sport's blue-ribbon event to the country that produced former champions and legends Duke Kahanamoku and Johnny Weissmuller?

As expected, Larson and Devitt battled side by side for their two laps, the Australian slightly ahead at the 80-meter mark. But a flourish in the final strokes by Larson enabled the American to pull even with Devitt, the men seemingly touching at the same time, Brazil's Manuel dos Santos back in the bronze-medal position.

As frenetic as the race was, it couldn't match the confusion and controversy that erupted at the finish. Of the three judges who were charged with determining the first-place finisher, two cited Devitt as the winner. However, the three judges selecting the second-place finisher were also split in their decisions, two choosing Devitt for second place and one selecting Larson as the runner-up. When the results of the six judges were combined, there was a deadlock over the winner. Three picked Devitt. Three named Larson.

When the automatic-timing system was consulted, another story was told. All three stopwatches assigned to Devitt revealed a time of 55.2. For Larson, the stopwatches returned times of 55.0, 55.1, and 55.1. At that point, technology deemed Larson the winner of the race, and because the stopwatches were considered the backup timers, Larson was viewed as the presumptive gold medalist.

That thought was quickly reversed.

Despite no written language in the bylaws allowing for the chief judge to rule on the outcome of a race, Germany's Hans Runstromer declared Devitt the champion and Larson the silver medalist, much to the chagrin of Larson and the U.S. contingent.

"I don't understand," Larson said. "I don't understand."

Larson wasn't the only individual perplexed by the decision. Max Ritter, the U.S. delegate to FINA and a founder of the international governing body, knew the chief judge was not to have a say in the case of a tie. Rather, he knew the referee was expected to consult the backup timing system and abide by its readouts. In this case, Larson would have been declared the gold medalist, with Devitt taking the silver medal. But Runstromer remained firm in his decision and added insult when Larson's final time was changed to 55.2, simply to match Devitt's mark and to make the outcome look reasonable. After all, the Olympic champion couldn't possibly have a slower time than the silver medalist.

Irate with the decision, Ritter called the situation "unbelievable." Meanwhile, the United States appealed the decision, citing the rule that the electronic-timing system should have been consulted, and Runstromer should not have involved himself in the selection of the winner. As for Devitt, he was not pleased with the U.S. decision to challenge the result.

"All I did was swim," Devitt said. "(Larson) took it badly. But he can't be crooked on me. I don't know who won, and Larson can't know either. If the judges change their placings, I am perfectly willing to give the medal back. I have always been taught to accept the judge's decision."

With the gold medal in his pocket, it was easy for Devitt to announce he would respect a judge's verdict against him. However, placed in Larson's shoes, would he truly have accepted the outcome? He never got the chance to fulfill his words, as FINA rejected the U.S. appeal.

In Rome, Devitt added a bronze medal in the 800 freestyle relay while Larson won a gold medal for handling the butterfly leg on the United States' victorious 400 medley relay.

Although Larson's Olympic days ended without a solo crown, he remained a prominent figure in the sport. As a Masters swimmer, he registered times that were on par—and sometimes faster—than when he was setting records during the prime of his career.

"I think it's the competition that motivates me more than anything else," Larson said of his Masters involvement. "I enjoy winning, and the recognition that goes along with it. It's sort of like being on stage again. Sort of an ego trip."

If there was a positive development out of Larson's loss, it was the decision by FINA to prominently utilize electronic-timing systems and eliminate the guessing game that arose in Rome. Of course, the move in that direction came at a price and left a black eye on the sport.

STOLEN GOLD

Other than being members of the Olympic fraternity, there was no reason why their names would be intertwined. They were born nearly 60 years apart. One was of Native American lineage. The other was a Northern Californian. One was a multi-sport star, his days as a decathlete followed by professional baseball and football careers. The other was a one-sport phenom, his attention focused on the pool.

But at the 1972 Olympic Games, a permanent link was established between Jim Thorpe and Rick DeMont. Albeit for different reasons, Thorpe and DeMont are Olympians who were stripped of their gold medals.

Thorpe is recognized as one of the greatest athletes in history, the gold medalist in the decathlon and pentathlon at the 1912 Olympic Games in Stockholm. He followed by playing Major League Baseball and then flourished in the National Football League. However, Thorpe had his Olympic titles rescinded in 1913 when it was learned he played professional baseball before his Olympic appearance, a violation of the era's strict rules governing amateurism.

In the case of DeMont, he headed to Munich as a precocious 16-year-old defined by beyond-his-years talent and innocence. Although he was a rising star for Team USA, DeMont was overshadowed by some of the sport's biggest names, including Mark Spitz and John Hencken. But he was also a threat to reach the podium, due to his world-record prowess.

At the United States Olympic Trials in Chicago, held a month before the Olympics, DeMont made his presence known by qualifying for Munich in the 400-meter freestyle and by breaking the world record in the 1,500 freestyle. In the longer event, DeMont didn't just clip the previous standard; he cut more than four seconds off the previous record.

As DeMont prepared for the Munich Games, he met with United States Olympic Committee officials as part of the athlete processing protocol. During the meeting, which included medical personnel, DeMont completed paperwork and noted he was an asthmatic who took medications [Marax, Actifed, and Sudafed] to treat the condition. Not once during the meeting was a red flag raised.

In Munich, the 400 freestyle was held midway through the competition, and it was regarded as the lesser of DeMont's two medal opportunities. The favorite was Australian Brad Cooper, a former world-record holder in the event, while DeMont's American teammates, Steve Genter and Tom McBreen, lurked. Also in the hunt for a medal was Aussie Graham Windeatt.

Missing from the event was the world-record holder, American Kurt Krumpholz, who set the global standard of 4:00.11 during preliminaries at the United States Olympic Trials. Krumpholz, though, couldn't replicate that performance in the final and placed an astonishing sixth, locking him out of an Olympic berth.

It didn't take long for Cooper and DeMont to establish themselves as the main contenders for gold, and, as they turned for the final lap, the Australian had the lead. Down the last lap, DeMont turned to his greater endurance base, boosted by his preference for the 1,500 freestyle, and gradually cut into Cooper's advantage. As they touched the wall, the outcome was too close to call, and it wasn't until eyes turned to the scoreboard that DeMont realized he won by the slimmest of margins. Just off the world record, DeMont was timed in 4:00.26, with Cooper touching in 4:00.27. The bronze medal went to Genter in 4:01.94.

"I've been swimming come-from-behind style since I began," DeMont said of his late rally. "At the United States Olympic Trials, I was strictly thinking of the 1500 meters. Now, I love the 400, especially after tonight".

The thrill experienced by DeMont only figured to bolster his confidence for the 1,500 freestyle, scheduled for the last two days of the meet. But that thrill quickly morphed into a nightmare when DeMont was informed that his postrace doping test revealed trace amounts of ephedrine, a banned substance. While some drug testing was performed at the 1968 Olympics in Mexico City, the Munich Games marked the first time that widespread testing was instituted.

Through the years, many athletes have pleaded ignorance after failing a drug test, often proclaiming, "I don't know how that substance entered my body." DeMont didn't play that card. There was no mystery that the

At the 1972 Olympics, Rick DeMont was robbed of a gold medal in the 400 freestyle due to a positive doping test beyond his control. Peter H. Bick.

ephedrine was contained in his asthma medication. However, that presence should not have been a problem, as USOC officials, after meeting with DeMont during processing, were supposed to discuss such medical-use scenarios with the International Olympic Committee. If the IOC had a problem with the substance, it would have informed the USOC, which would have worked with DeMont to find an alternative medication to treat his asthma.

Ultimately, the USOC did not engage in a discussion with the IOC concerning DeMont's listed medications and, therefore, DeMont was in trouble.

"It was [the USOC's] responsibility to let me know there was an illegal substance in my prescription and either get it cleared or find an alternative," DeMont said. "They failed to do it. I was only 16 years old. I relied on those officials to tell me what I could take, but somehow I ended up paying the price. I guess it was easier to hang a 16-year-old kid out to dry than to tell the truth."

Days after his apparent triumph, DeMont was stripped of his gold medal, and Cooper and Genter were elevated to the gold and silver medals, with McBreen given the bronze medal. The process of stripping a gold medal from a teenager who took a prescription upon his doctor's orders was messy enough, but the days between DeMont's apparent victory and his disqualification were made uglier by politics and an unwillingness by those in power to step forward and defend a young man.

After DeMont's urine test revealed ephedrine in his system, U.S. team doctors confiscated the medication DeMont was taking for his asthma. More, at a hearing with IOC officials, DeMont was peppered with questions while Team USA doctors sat quiet, offering no assistance or defense. Simply, DeMont was abandoned.

"It's a gross injustice," said U.S. Men's Coach Peter Daland of the IOC's decision to strip DeMont of his gold medal. "Young De Mont was robbed, robbed because of the mistakes of adults. [USOC personnel] knew of the boy's medical record because he had it on paper. They said nothing to me or his head coach about it. The communications were atrocious. It's a young man being punished when he should be applauded. He overcame asthma to win a gold medal and took nothing more than his doctor ordered."

While the IOC weighed his case, DeMont raced the prelims of the 1,500 freestyle on the penultimate day of action and advanced to the final. The next day, DeMont was preparing for the final and the possibility of redemption, when U.S. assistant coach Don Gambril, with tears running down his cheeks, approached the teenager and told him the IOC ruled he was not allowed to compete.

Reports indicate that several scenarios were discussed in the DeMont case, including the potential for leniency. A lighter sentence could have upheld the stripping of his gold medal in the 400 freestyle but allowed him to compete in the 1,500 free, particularly because DeMont had stopped taking his asthma medication ahead of that race. Instead, the IOC dropped the hammer, saying any other decision would have provided a green light for doping.

"We were all in a very disagreeable position," said Belgium's Prince Alexandre de Merode, the head of the IOC's Medical Commission. "We met the boy and spoke with him and were under great emotional pressure while trying to decide on the facts. Now I feel I can see the decision more clearly, and it was right. If we had not done so, it would not have been necessary to have a medical committee."

Not surprising, DeMont left Munich devastated. In the minds of many, he hadn't committed an error but instead was let down by officials who were supposed to provide support. DeMont consistently felt he was viewed in a negative light and experienced loneliness. Yet, he also forged ahead and flourished the next summer.

At the inaugural World Championships in Belgrade, DeMont engaged in a rematch with Cooper in the 400 freestyle and became the first man to break the four-minute barrier. DeMont was timed in 3:58.18, with Cooper also cracking the four-minute barrier in 3:58.70. DeMont also went under the existing world record in the 1,500 freestyle but had to settle for the silver medal when Australian Stephen Holland blasted an even quicker time.

"The world championship is important, but I'm not trying to get revenge for the Olympics," DeMont said. "What happened in Belgrade has nothing to do with Munich."

DeMont competed at the 1976 Olympic Trials, but he failed to advance out of the preliminaries of the 400 freestyle and did not earn a second Olympic invitation. Eventually, DeMont went on to a highly successful coaching career, serving as Frank Busch's longtime assistant at the University of Arizona. DeMont served as Arizona's head coach from 2014 to 2017, when he stepped down.

During his coaching tenure at his alma mater, DeMont mentored a bevy of NCAA champions and became well known for establishing a pipeline between the program and South Africa. It is DeMont who is primarily credited for molding the South African 400 freestyle relay that won gold at the 2004 Olympic Games in Athens behind the efforts of Roland Schoeman, Lyndon Ferns, Darian Townsend, and Ryk Neethling. DeMont served as a South African coach in Athens and coached every member of that relay.

A highly regarded artist who focuses on painting with watercolors, DeMont has never let the events of Munich escape him. At the 2000 Olympics in Sydney, an article discussing the biggest cheats in Games' history had him at No. 2, behind only Ben Johnson, the disgraced sprinter from Canada. Seeing articles of that type fueled DeMont in his quest to clear his name. In 2001, a measure of vindication was provided when the USOC honored DeMont at its annual banquet and presented him with a black leather jacket that was given to all 1972 Olympians.

"This is the end of a long chapter. A good end to a long chapter," DeMont said. "It means a lot to get the support of the USOC. I'm hoping this might be a stepping stone toward getting something similar from the IOC someday—if I can stay alive long enough. This is a big step. I'm honored."

Over the years, the possibility of DeMont's Olympic title being restored has been discussed by IOC members. However, the idea has never gained traction and the likelihood of DeMont receiving his gold medal is slim.

And that's where the story of Thorpe and DeMont veers in different directions. Years after his medals were stripped, the IOC restored Thorpe's results and recognized him as a gold medalist in the decathlon and pentathlon. For DeMont, he'll forever be the man who touched the wall first in the 400 freestyle but has no memento for the effort.

"I don't need any ceremonies," DeMont said. "I don't need any hoopla. I just want the IOC to repair the historical record."

DREAMS TO NIGHTMARES

Thousands of miles from American soil, in late December 1979, Soviet tanks rolled into Afghanistan. The nightly news in the United States aired footage of the invasion, along with images of troops taking their positions in a foreign land. Under the guise of bringing peace to a nation dealing with political instability, the Soviet Union instituted a puppet government and initiated a nine-year war with Afghan guerillas looking to defend their country and its ways.

At the same time, American athletes—from swimming, track and field, gymnastics, and beyond—counted the days until the start of the 22nd Olympiad in Moscow. In the pool, Tracy Caulkins churned through countless laps of freestyle, breaststroke, butterfly, and backstroke. Brian Goodell, a reigning Olympic champion, targeted a repeat. Rowdy Gaines yearned for the chance to become the United States' latest Olympic titlist in the 100 freestyle, his sport's blue-ribbon event. For these athletes targeting Moscow, the payoff for years of hard work and dedication was just around the corner.

Sports and politics have long shared a toxic relationship. Years ago, heavyweight boxing champion Muhammad Ali declared himself a conscientious objector of the Vietnam War and refused induction into the U.S. Army. Ali was subsequently arrested and sentenced to five years in prison, although he remained free on bail. More, Ali was stripped of his world titles and prevented from fighting in the United States when none of the sport's commissions would provide Ali with a license to pursue his career.

In recent years, primarily in the National Football League, athletes have knelt during the playing of the National Anthem to register their beliefs that members of the African American community have suffered social injustices, including racial inequality and police brutality. When athletes started to kneel in greater number, President Donald Trump called for team owners to fire the players who knelt during the Star-Spangled Banner. San Francisco 49ers quarterback Colin Kaepernick was one of the leaders of the "Take a Knee" movement and has been out of the league since he opted out of his contract with the 49ers in 2017. Because the "Take a Knee" movement was controversial and sparked outrage from many members of the American public, NFL owners have shied away from signing

Although denied the opportunity to race at the 1980 Olympics due to the American boycott, Rowdy Gaines went on to win three gold medals at the 1984 Games. Peter H. Bick.

Kaepernick, leading to assessments that Kaepernick has been blackballed from earning a living in the NFL.

Simply, the adage that sports and politics do not mix has been uttered for years. In many instances, fans want their athletes to play. They want touchdowns. They want goals. They want baskets. More, citizens don't need their elected officials to infuse government policy into the games they follow. If only the relationship was that simple.

The decision of the Soviet Union to invade Afghanistan was as much a move to flex political muscle on a global basis as it was to impart its influence on a neighboring nation. In an era of intense Cold War tensions, the sense that Afghanistan might trade its loyalties to the West, including the United States, triggered the Soviet Union's actions. In turn, U.S. president Jimmy Carter felt the need to respond and declare American opposition.

On the morning of January 20, 1980, nearly a month after the Soviet invasion, Carter appeared on the television program *Meet the Press* and threatened a U.S. boycott of the 1980 Olympic Games in Moscow. Although startling, Carter's comments were personal in nature and did not immediately strike wholesale fear the United States would withhold its athletes from the next Olympiad.

"Neither I nor the American people would favor the sending of an American team to Moscow with Soviet invasion troops in Afghanistan," Carter said. "I've sent a message today to the United States Olympic Committee spelling out my own position that unless the Soviets withdraw their troops, within a month, from Afghanistan, that the Olympic Games be moved from Moscow to an alternate site, or multiple sites, or postponed, or canceled. If the Soviets do not withdraw their troops from Afghanistan, within a month, I would not support the sending of an American team to the Olympics."

> It's very important for the world to realize how serious a threat the Soviet's invasion of Afghanistan is. I do not want to inject politics into the Olympics, and I would personally favor the establishment of a permanent Olympic site for both the Summer and the Winter Games. In my opinion, the most appropriate permanent site for the Summer Games would be Greece. This will be my own position, and I have asked the U.S. Olympic Committee to take this position to the International Olympic Committee and I would hope that as many nations as possible would support this basic position. One hundred and four nations voted against the Soviet invasion and called for their immediate withdrawal from Afghanistan, in the United Nations, and I would hope that as many of those as possible would support the position I've just outlined to you.

Carter's assertion that he did not want to inject politics into sports was farcical. The president's words signified a direct cause–effect relationship between the Soviet Union's invasion and the threat to boycott the Moscow Games, which served as the proverbial low-hanging fruit in Carter's quest to provide an answer to Afghanistan's occupation. Had the impending Olympiad been scheduled for another locale, Carter would have had to design another response. In a way, the Moscow Games acted as a built-in justification.

Once Carter revealed his thoughts on *Meet the Press*, he shifted into recruitment mode and began a campaign within his presidency. Over the next several weeks, Carter discussed his boycott plan with senators and representatives, trying to convince them that his plan was the proper path to travel. Carter, too, spoke with high-ranking officials within the United States Olympic Committee, ensuring he would have the organization's support.

On March 21, 1980, Carter met with approximately 100 United States Olympic hopefuls and delivered the news that the United States would not send a delegation to the Moscow Games. Athletes who attended the announcement thought the visit with President Carter would provide an opportunity to discuss a potential boycott, not hear the decision was final. Obviously, there were mixed reactions, ranging from sadness, to anger, to understanding. What was not mixed was the impact of Carter's decision. In the few minutes it took the president to deliver a speech outlining his reasons for a boycott, dreams were crushed.

"It is absolutely imperative that we and other nations who believe in freedom and who believe in human rights and who believe in peace let our voices be heard in an absolutely clear way, and not add the imprimatur of approval to the Soviet Union and its government while they have 105,000 heavily armed invading forces in the freedom-loving and innocent and deeply religious country of Afghanistan," Carter said. "Thousands of people's lives have already been lost. Entire villages have been wiped out deliberately by the Soviet invading forces. And as you well know, the people in the Soviet Union don't even know it. They do not even realize that 104 nations in the United Nations condemned the Soviet Union for their invasion and called for their immediate withdrawal from Afghanistan. The people of the Soviet Union don't even know it.

"The Olympics are important to the Soviet Union. They have made massive investments in buildings, equipment, propaganda. As has probably already been pointed out to you, they have passed out hundreds of thousands of copies of an official Soviet document saying that the decision of the world community to hold the Olympics in Moscow is an acknowledgement of approval of the foreign policy of the Soviet Union, and proof to the world that the Soviets' policy results in international peace.

"I can't say at this moment what other nations will not go to the Summer Olympics in Moscow. Ours will not go. I say that not with any equivocation. The decision has been made. The American people are convinced that we should not go to the Summer Olympics. The Congress has voted overwhelmingly, almost unanimously, which is a very rare thing, that we will not go. And I can tell you that many of our major allies, particularly those democratic countries who believe in freedom, will not go.

"I understand how you feel, and I thought about it a lot as we approached this moment, when I would have to stand here in front of fine young Americans and dedicated coaches, who have labored sometimes for more than 10 years, in every instance for years, to become among the finest athletes in the world, knowing what the Olympics mean to you, to know that you would be disappointed. It's not a pleasant time for me.

"You occupy a special place in American life, not because of your talent or your dedication or your training or your commitment or your ability as an athlete, but because for American people, Olympic athletes represent something else. You represent the personification of the highest ideals of our country. You represent a special commitment to the value of a human life, and to the achievement of excellence within an environment of freedom, and a belief in truth and friendship and respect for others, and the elimination of discrimination, and the honoring of human rights, and peace.

"Even though many of you may not warrant or deserve that kind of esteem, because you haven't thought so deeply about these subjects, perhaps, the American people think you do, because you are characterized accurately as clean and decent and honest and dedicated."

While Carter's speech was accurate in its assessment of the Soviet invasion, his claim that he understood the feelings of the athletes was a considerable misfire. How could Carter truly know what the athletes felt? He had not endured the daily workouts adhered to by the athletes. He had not sacrificed time with family for training and competition. In pursuit of a lifelong goal, he had not delayed the next phase of his life to remain in the pool, on the track or in the gym.

Since Carter left office in early 1981, after being defeated in his reelection run by Ronald Reagan, he has been rightly lauded for his humanitarian efforts, namely, his work with a hammer on behalf of Habitat for Humanity. Yet, before he made an impact by helping to build homes for families in need, Carter used a hammer on the dreams of hundreds of Olympic hopefuls.

With the United States leading the way, more than 60 nations boycotted the 1980 Olympics. Among the most notable nations not sending a delegation to Moscow were Canada, China, Japan, and West Germany. Four years after the American-led boycott, when the United States played host to the Olympics in Los Angeles, the Soviet Union orchestrated a retaliatory boycott that featured the Eastern Bloc countries. In addition to the Soviet Union, nations not participating in the Los Angeles Games included East Germany, Hungary, Czechoslovakia, and Poland.

The pureeing of sports and politics in the same blender led to different outcomes for the affected athletes. For Brian Goodell, an Olympic

champion from the Montreal Games of 1976, the Moscow boycott signified the end of his international career and robbed Goodell of a showdown
that was among the sport's most anticipated clashes.

In Montreal, Goodell flourished as a member of a team regarded as
the finest the sport has seen. As the United States won all but one event, a
17-year-old Goodell set world records en route to gold medals in the 400-
meter freestyle and 1,500-meter freestyle. In 1980, Goodell would have
been in his prime, greater strength and experience part of his arsenal. He
also would have clashed with the Soviet Union's Vladimir Salnikov, a rising
star on the distance scene and the world champion from 1978 in Goodell's
Olympic title events.

"I was 17 in Montreal," Goodell said.

> In Moscow, I would have been 21 and in the prime of my career.
> And zippo. (Carter) screwed with everybody's lives. I could have made
> some pretty good coin. It really did screw me up. It totally derailed
> me and changed my life. I didn't know what to do with myself. My
> life took a totally different path than what I had expected. I was pretty
> clearly depressed. I couldn't get up in the morning. Never got help,
> but I should have. I've tried to forget it a zillion times, but I'm still
> disgusted.

With Goodell sidelined and heading into retirement, Salnikov went
on to strike gold in the 400-meter freestyle and 1,500-meter freestyle. The
Soviet standout broke Goodell's world record in the longer event and
became the first person to dip under the 15-minute barrier. Meanwhile,
fans were deprived of a head-to-head duel that was long desired.

Years removed from the boycott, Goodell still bristles at the mention
of Carter's name. He also knows his time in the spotlight was unnecessarily
cut short.

"I don't like seeing him. In person. On TV. In the newspaper,"
Goodell said. "He's always got something critical to say about somebody
else but when it comes to criticism of the boycott, he can't take it. He's the
victim. He can't take being criticized for the most hair-brained thing I've
ever heard of. I never got a chance to prove how good I was."

The boycott had different impacts on other athletes, their career arcs
determined by circumstances beyond their control. At the end of the 1978
World Championships, Cynthia Woodhead and Jesse Vassallo were pegged
as can't-miss headliners in Moscow. Woodhead, at just 14 years old, captured five medals at the World Champs, a world record in the 200 freestyle
her defining moment. For Vassallo, his momentum was built on the back

of world titles in the 400-meter individual medley [world record] and 200-meter backstroke, along with a silver medal in the 200-meter individual medley.

Of course, the predicted headlines of Moscow never materialized for Woodhead or Vassallo, who also faced a dilemma: Should they continue training for the 1984 Olympics, or retire? Ultimately, they both forged ahead, but their greatest chances at Olympic glory were in the rearview mirror. While Woodhead earned a silver medal in Los Angeles in the 200-meter freestyle, her time was more than a second slower than her career best. As for Vassallo, he finished just shy of the podium in the 400-meter individual medley, placing fourth.

"It was awful," Woodhead said. "Those four years (between Moscow and Los Angeles) felt like 10. It seemed like everything went wrong. But I felt I owed it to myself to compete in 1984, make the team, and actually go to an Olympics, so I pressed on. I enjoyed it, but I didn't. It felt like I was watching a movie and wishing I could have been there in my top form, at my peak. It certainly wasn't a highlight of my life".

The post-Moscow outcome was not as hurtful for Tracy Caulkins, Mary T. Meagher, or Rowdy Gaines. Like Woodhead and Vassallo, Caulkins, Meagher, and Gaines would have been in their prime at the 1980 Games. Caulkins was a six-time medalist at the 1978 World Championships and set three individual world records. She was also one of the few women in the world who could stand up and beat her foes from East Germany, which was a few years into the orchestration of a systematic doping program. Meagher, meanwhile, set three world records in the 200-meter butterfly during the 1979 season and took the butterfly events to new heights. As for Gaines, now the voice of USA Swimming for NBC Sports, he was a top contender for gold in the 100-meter freestyle and 200-meter freestyle and was a key relay link for Team USA.

"What really hits home to me about the boycott was the Soviets didn't pull out of Afghanistan for nine years," Caulkins said. "Did it put any pressure on them? No. It was just a missed opportunity for many athletes. It just doesn't seem fair."

Four years after Carter's decision concerning Moscow, Caulkins, Meagher, and Gaines enjoyed their moments of Olympic glory, albeit with a caveat. Due to the Eastern Bloc boycott, the competition level—as was the case in 1980—was not at its maximum. Still, the record book will always show Caulkins, Meagher, and Gaines as triple gold medalists in Los Angeles, Caulkins (200 I.M./400 I.M.) and Meagher (100 butterfly/200 butterfly) winning two solo events each, in addition to joining a triumphant

Mary T. Meagher dominated the butterfly events in the 1980s at a level that has never been seen before or since. Peter H. Bick.

relay. Gaines was the champion of the 100 freestyle and fueled a pair of American relays to gold.

"I felt physically at my peak in 1980—and mentally up, too," Gaines said. "It was tough, really tough. I had a chance for four golds. It was a long four years. There were a lot of peaks and valleys. I almost quit a few times. In fact, I actually did retire for six months in 1981 just after I finished college, but I couldn't stay away. I felt something was missing in my life. I looked back and realized it was the Olympics. Just to get a chance to compete. It was tugging at me."

Although several of his USA Swimming teammates eventually realized their Olympic dreams, the same could not be said for Craig Beardsley. In 1980, Beardsley was the unquestioned class of the 200-meter butterfly, a 1979 title in the event from the Pan American Games sending the American into the Olympic year with confidence. Then came Carter's decision, which Beardsley did not entirely oppose at the time the boycott was announced. It wasn't until years passed, and a perspective became available, that Beardsley saw the boycott as a pointless political maneuver.

"(In 1980), I don't want to say that I supported the boycott, but I wasn't against it, either," Beardsley said. "I tried to think there was some good in it. We were doing the right thing. I supported everything at that time. However, I began to realize that it was just another political movement. I became strongly opinionated about trying to separate sports and politics. It will never happen again. Sports, like music, is one of those great things that bind people together."

Beardsley didn't take a woe-is-me approach around the 1980 Games. Instead, he started grinding toward Los Angeles. Just days after the Soviet Union's Sergey Fesenko won gold in the 200-meter butterfly in Moscow, Beardsley broke the world record on American soil. A year later, Beardsley further lowered the global standard.

However, fate was not on Beardsley's side at the 1984 United States Olympic Trials. With just the first- and second-place finishers qualifying for the Olympics, Beardsley finished third at Trials and was left off the team that would compete at home. Making his miss more difficult to digest was the fact that 1984 marked the first year in which countries were limited to two entries per event. Previously, nations could send three athletes per event.

"The lesson I learned from that was actually a very good life lesson," Beardsley said. "Sometimes, you do everything in your power, you do everything you're supposed to do, but sometimes things are just out of your control. You've got to learn to put that behind you, let it roll off your shoulders, and just move on."

Moving on is how Salnikov handled the repercussions of the United States boycott. With the United States out of the fray, Salnikov's Moscow Games featured victories in the 400-meter freestyle and 1,500-meter freestyle, the events in which he was expected to duel with Goodell. What Salnikov could not envision at the time was his inability to defend those crowns by no fault of his own.

When the Soviet Union announced its retaliatory boycott of the 1984 Olympics, Salnikov figured his Olympic days were over. However, come the 1988 Games in Seoul, the 28-year-old veteran took to the blocks in his signature event, the 1,500 free, and walked away with an improbable gold medal. The effort was not lost on Salnikov's fellow Olympians. Hours after prevailing, Salnikov walked into the dining hall in the Athletes' Village and was greeted with a standing ovation, as competitors across various sports put down their silverware and rose to laud a man known as "The Monster of the Waves."

Despite his fairytale performance in Seoul, Salnikov has not forgotten the way politics interfered with his career. Like his American foes, he knows the boycotts of 1980 and 1984 achieved nothing, with the exception of penalizing the hard work and dedication of the athletes.

"They (political leaders) used us as pawns in their game," Salnikov said of the boycott which deprived him of a repeat opportunity in Los Angeles.

> I was shocked when I heard about the boycott. I felt emptiness inside me. My first desire was to quit, but after I thought about it, I realized that would only make me feel even worse. And I kept training more intensely than ever before so I could not think of anything else. If I had won in Los Angeles, I probably would have retired soon thereafter. But I stayed in the sport and won in 1988 when almost everyone had given up on me.

Sports have a unique power to forge bonds. Individuals from different backgrounds and beliefs often come together and cheer for the same team, forgetting their differences. But in 1980, and on a smaller scale in 1984, sports were used in a way that tore at athletes' dreams.

When President Jimmy Carter first hatched the idea of boycotting the 1980 Olympic Games in Moscow, he felt the move would be an appropriate response to the Soviet Union's invasion of Afghanistan. He knew the Soviet Union was eager to host the Olympic Games and if high-profile nations stayed away, they would not legitimize the Soviet Union as the focal point of a significant global event. Ultimately, the plan backfired, as the Soviet Union retained its presence in Afghanistan for nine years.

The athletes who trained and dreamed of competing in the Olympic Games were left with heartache to show for their efforts, and nothing more. As a door prize of sorts to those athletes who did not get to compete in Moscow, Carter offered an invitation to attend an event at the White House. It was during this gathering in which Carter may have truly realized the damage he inflicted on the careers and psyches of those affected. It may have been an epiphany that sports and politics, when mixed, form a toxic relationship.

"(Carter) reached out to shake my hand and he said 'How would you have done in Moscow?' " Vassallo recalled of his moment with Carter. "And I said, 'I would have won two golds and a silver.' And he just gave me this (pained) look. He didn't ask anybody else that question."

A HISTORIC FINISH

What's a hundredth of a second? In the career of Michael Phelps and the history of swimming, it rates as a most significant measure of time.

The 2008 Olympic Games, an epic spectacle that began with a grand Opening Ceremony, will be best remembered for what unfolded in Beijing's two premier venues. In the Bird's Nest, the nickname for Olympic Stadium, Jamaican track star Usain Bolt ushered in an era of sprinting not previously seen. Across the street in the Water Cube, the nickname for the Olympic Aquatics Center, Michael Phelps needed just eight days to bump Mark Spitz—for 36 years the king of the Olympic pool—to a silver-medal identity.

As was the case four years earlier, when he won eight medals (six gold/two bronze) in Athens, Phelps attracted the spotlight the moment the Beijing Games commenced. The obvious question: This time, would all eight medals be of the golden variety? If the question was simple, the answer was complicated.

There were a few certainties for Phelps, who was slated to race five individual events and three relays. Barring shocking upsets, the 400 individual medley, 200 freestyle, 200 butterfly, and 200 individual medley were locks. The same designation was applied to the 800 freestyle relay and the 400 medley relay, where the United States had no peer. Uncertainty, however, revolved around the 400 freestyle relay and the 100 butterfly.

It didn't take long for the difficulty of the task to reveal itself. After producing a dominating victory in his first event, the 400 medley, Phelps was thrown an early life preserver when the United States, on the strength of Jason Lezak's once-in-a-lifetime anchor leg, rallied for a comeback win over France. Meanwhile, Phelps endured a stroke of misfortune in the 200 butterfly, winning that event in world-record time despite racing the entirety of the fourth lengths with water-filled goggles.

Otherwise, Phelps' march toward history went smoothly and by the time he arrived at the 100 butterfly, he was 6-for-6. Instantly, all talk centered on Phelps equaling and surpassing the seven gold medals of Spitz from the 1972 Games in Munich. The problem, though, was that Phelps' most vulnerable final was next on the docket.

Even though Phelps was the reigning Olympic and world champion in the 100 fly, several factors were at play. By that point in the meet, Phelps had raced 15 times and the hectic nature of the week, both physically and mentally, was taking a toll. In addition to racing, Phelps was forced to deal with daily media obligations, regular doping-control visits, early wakeups for morning finals, and late-night dinners after evening preliminaries. More, with each victory, the pressure to match Spitz magnified, and even an athlete as focused and measured as Phelps is not immune to expectations and hopes.

"I'm exhausted," Phelps said after winning the 200 individual medley for his sixth gold. "I've got nothing left."

Although Phelps injected a bit of hyperbole into that statement, he knew his penultimate race would call for every ounce of energy he could muster. Why? As worn down as Phelps was from the first six days of action, his primary challengers in the 100 butterfly were fresh and—emblematic of life in the wild—eager to pounce on a wounded animal.

Acutely aware of Phelps' tiring body and mind, Serbia's Milorad Cavic sensed it was his moment to attack. After posting a pair of sub-51 times in the preliminaries and semifinals, Cavic affirmed his status as the biggest threat to Phelps. His front-end speed was the best in the field and, given Phelps' propensity for being a strong finisher, Cavic was in a position to place immense pressure on Phelps from the start. It was a scenario Cavic envisioned in the lead-up to Beijing and came to fruition.

"You definitely want to shoot for the gold," Cavic said two months before the Beijing Games. "As much as the world would like to be entertained to see Michael Phelps get eight gold medals, I don't want to give

At the 2008 Olympics in Beijing, Michael Phelps won the 100 butterfly by the slimmest of margins, 0.01, and then watched as controversy ensued after the race. Peter H. Bick.

it to him. I hope to stand in the way. I hope to slay the dragon. I don't know if I can say that, but I did just say it. And that's kind of what it is. Everyone has this idea that he's unbeatable, and he's not. I think I'm going to have a shot."

Cavic might have raced for an Eastern European country, but he was very much an American like Phelps. Born in Southern California to parents who immigrated to the United States from the former Yugoslavia, Cavic excelled as an age-group performer and emerged as an elite recruit during his days at Tustin High School. During his senior year, Cavic, who at that point went by "Mike," set a national high school record in the 50 freestyle and was named *Swimming World Magazine*'s High School Swimmer of the Year, an honor that generated considerable hype as he entered his freshman year at the University of California-Berkeley.

Cavic, who held dual citizenship between the United States and Serbia, enjoyed a strong career at Cal, helping the Golden Bears to several NCAA relay championships, along with collecting All-American accolades in the 50 freestyle, 100 freestyle, and 100 butterfly. Simultaneously, Cavic demonstrated respect for his heritage, choosing to represent Serbia in international competition. That decision was certainly the easier path than having to negotiate the more talented and deeper waters of the U.S. system, but it was also Cavic's way of expressing appreciation for his roots.

Although it cost him to be disqualified from the rest of the meet, Cavic made a political statement on the podium at the 2008 European Championships. After winning the 50 butterfly, Cavic wore a T-shirt to the awards ceremony that read, "Kosovo is Serbia." The commentary revolved around Kosovo's desire to gain its independence from Serbia, and Cavic's willingness to raise the issue prompted officials to send him home, citing the competition as "a place of sport, not political protest." The decision to disqualify Cavic prevented him from contesting the 100 butterfly, which would have allowed him to produce a pre-Olympic marker for Phelps to contemplate.

"I didn't do it to provoke anger. I didn't do it to provoke violence," Cavic said of his protest. "The country is torn apart and my goal was just to uplift them."

Cavic's political protest was not the only mistake he made during the Olympic year. Never one to shy away from providing an opinion, Cavic made the comment after the semifinals that it would be good for the sport if Phelps lost and did not go 8-for-8 at the Olympics. The moment those comments were uttered, Phelps' coach Bob Bowman presented them to his pupil, who logged the information for later use.

Cavic may have been Phelps' primary obstacle in Beijing, but a familiar face was also on the deck. From 2003 to 2007, Phelps and Ian Crocker regularly traded jabs in the pool, a friendly rivalry developing. While Crocker won world titles over Phelps in 2003 and 2005, Phelps claimed the Olympic crown in 2004 and the world championship in 2007.

In Beijing, though, questions surrounded Crocker's sharpness and whether he could replicate the excellence he had frequently shown. If nothing else, Crocker had experience on his side, and with retirement in his plans following the 2008 Olympiad, Beijing was a chance to leave the sport with a flourish.

Heading into the final of the 100 butterfly, Phelps' tiredness was countered by Cavic's freshness, as the Serbian only had three races under his belt. In addition to racing the opening two rounds of the fly, Cavic contested the preliminaries of the 100 freestyle. Despite qualifying for the semifinals, Cavic chose to scratch the remainder of the event, using his prelim swim as nothing more than a get-wet outing.

As was the case when the 400 freestyle relay was contested, tension filled the air in the Water Cube. If Phelps could find a way to gold in his seventh event, he would tie Spitz's Olympic record for most gold medals in a single Games, and an eighth in the 400 medley relay would be nothing more than a formality. If he couldn't keep his unbeaten streak going, a sense of disappointment would fill the air. At this point in the Games, athletes, spectators, and the media wanted to see history made.

As expected, Cavic surged into the lead from the start, using his early speed to make a come-and-get-me statement. At the turn, Cavic was timed in 23.42 and held a half-body length lead over Phelps, who was seventh at the wall in 24.04. Even for Phelps, who had a penchant for late rallies, this deficit seemed to be too much to overcome.

But coming off the wall, Phelps turned to one of his powerful turns and started to surge. With each stroke, Phelps seemed to cut into Cavic's advantage, but had he yielded too much of a margin over the first lap? As they neared the wall, there didn't appear to be enough room for Phelps to prevail, as he was only at Cavic's shoulders. However, Cavic opted for a gliding finish and Phelps, turning to instinct, decided to squeeze in an extra half-stroke, a move that made history.

At the touch, and to the shock of nearly everyone inside the Water Cube, Phelps found a way to win, his time of 50.58 the slightest bit quicker than the 50.59 of Cavic. For Phelps, it was his latest magic act and basically guaranteed a perfect week, one that was confirmed when the medley relay set a world record on the final night of competition.

"When I did chop the last stroke, I thought that had cost me the race," Phelps said. "But it was actually the opposite. If I had glided, I would have been way too long. I took short, faster strokes to try to get my hand on the wall. I ended up making the right decision."

An elated Phelps raised his fist and splashed the water, the significance of his latest win also understood in the context of what the week meant to his sport and the history of the Olympic Games. Meanwhile, Cavic couldn't believe his eyes, and neither could the Serbian delegation, which filed a protest contending that Cavic had touched the wall first. FINA, the international governing body for the sport, considered the protest and viewed footage of the finish before confirming Phelps as the winner. Crocker turned out to be a non-factor in the race for gold and agonizingly lost out on the bronze medal by a hundredth of a second.

Omega, the official timekeeping company for the Games, offered to make images of the finish available to the media after the race but had to renege on that gesture when FINA decided otherwise. The organizing body stated it did not want to feed into any form of controversy, but that is the scenario that unfolded when it forbid Omega from showing its images.

"We are not going to distribute footage," said Cornel Marculescu, FINA's executive director. "We are not doing these kinds of things. Everything is good. What are you going to do with the footage? See what the Serbians already saw? It is clarified for us beyond any doubt. (Phelps) is the winner in any way. He's the winner no doubt. Even if you could see the pictures, I don't know how you could use them."

Cavic tried to straddle the proverbial fence as he addressed the media. While he didn't fully support the Serbian Federation's decision to protest the outcome, he refused to buy into the official results and claimed a rematch would go his way.

"I'm stoked with what happened," Cavic said. "I don't want to fight this. People will be bringing this up for years and saying you won that race. If we got to do this again, I would win it."

Sports Illustrated photographer Heinz Kluetmeier, revered in his profession, had proof of Phelps' victory. Due to his status, Kluetmeier was one of a handful of photographers given access to the pool and allowed to install underwater remote equipment that could capture images during races. Ultimately, it was Kluetmeier's work that confirmed Phelps' win amid the arguing by Cavic and his camp.

"The photograph proved what happened," Kluetmeier said. "The fact that the photograph shows in a single image and in a single moment that Michael won, when everyone thought he lost, is so important. You look at the image and it shows that his hand is touching, and Cavic's hand is not. There is still some space between his fingertips and the wall. It took an hour to set up, but it was worth it."

At the next year's World Championships in Rome, Phelps and Cavic again engaged in a head-to-head duel, this time at the height of the tech-suit crisis in which apparel companies created swimsuits made of polyurethane that allowed swimmers to be more buoyant in the water and have greater energy in the latter stages of their races.

With the super suits leading to more than 40 world records in Rome, it was clear the sport was no longer based on pure talent but also based on technology. This concern was raised by Bowman, who noted he would keep Phelps out of international competition after the World Champs until FINA dealt with the problem. Given the chance to respond, Cavic basically told the Phelps camp to quiet down and also reiterated his belief that he defeated Phelps in Beijing.

In the final of the 100 fly at Rome, a fired-up Phelps once again got the best of Cavic, earning the gold medal in a world-record time of 49.82, with Cavic just behind in a European record of 49.95. Phelps celebrated his victory more boisterously than usual, splashing the water and tugging on his suit, which was deemed inferior to the brand worn by Cavic.

"You can tell by my celebration that satisfied me a little bit," Phelps said. "I set it up perfectly. That was exactly what I wanted to do. There are always things that fire me up and motivate me. Sometimes, it's a comment. Sometimes, it's what people do. That's just how I tick."

Cavic's words and antics should have served as a warning to others: Don't poke the bear. But South African Chad Le Clos apparently didn't get the memo ahead of the 2016 Olympic Games in Rio de Janeiro. Four years earlier, while paying homage to Phelps and calling him an inspiration, Le Clos did the unthinkable when he ran down Phelps in the closing meters to capture the gold medal in the 200 butterfly at the London Games. It was a stunning upset, as Phelps lost the event that launched his career, and in a manner that was quintessential Phelps.

For years, Phelps had been the guy who reeled in the opposition, often rallying for victory when defeat seemed imminent. Even before he stunned Cavic in Beijing, Phelps used a late flourish to complete a comeback triumph in the 100 butterfly over Crocker at the 2004 Olympics in Athens. Three years later, at the World Championships in Melbourne, Crocker once again watched Phelps clip him at the finish of the 100 fly. In London, Phelps tasted his own medicine.

As the reigning Olympic champion, Le Clos had no reason to antago-nize Phelps in Rio, but the South African foolishly chose to travel that road in Brazil. As Phelps and Le Clos awaited the start of the second semifinal of the 200 butterfly in Rio, Le Clos engaged in a shadow-boxing routine in front of a seated Phelps. The show took place just feet from Phelps and clearly was Le Clos' way of trying to distract, intimidate, or confuse the greatest Olympian in history. Phelps, with pursed lips and an irate look on his face, simply stared ahead.

While Phelps and Le Clos finished second and third, respectively, in that semifinal, Phelps had the additional motivation he needed for the next evening's final. The outcome was not a surprise, as Phelps reclaimed his throne and managed his third Olympic title in the event. Le Clos, mean-while, finished fourth and off the podium.

"I really wanted that one back," Phelps said in Rio. "That event has been my baby for a long time."

The lesson learned in Rio was simple: When facing an athlete with as much talent as the sport has ever seen, don't give him an extra reason to elevate his performance. Cavic learned that lesson the hard way.

"When Bob told me [what he said], I was like, O.K," Phelps said. "When people say things like that, it fires me up more than anything."

A DETRIMENTAL INNOVATION

Without innovation, there would be no progress. Through the years, forward-thinking approaches have led to faster times, better competition, and greater visibility for the sport. From improved equipment to enhanced training methods to technological advances, all have allowed the sport to grow.

But not all revolutions are positive, and for a two-year stretch from 2008 to 2009, there was more focus on what the athletes wore than on the skill they possessed. Thanks to the introduction of swimsuits that basically acted as motors, the record book was shredded, pure talent was neutralized, and meets—at all levels—featured circus atmospheres.

The day February 12, 2008, was supposed to be like many other com-pany shill sessions. With its sponsored athletes coordinated in four locales around the world—New York, London, Sydney, and Tokyo—Speedo revealed the swimsuit that would make competitors go faster. It wasn't an unusual statement. All athletic equipment companies hail their innovations as game-changing, hoping the public will buy into the claims.

In its reveal parties for the suit called the LZR Racer, which was constructed of 50 percent polyurethane, Speedo presented the invited media members and other guests with several superlatives designed to generate hype. Among the points that were highlighted:

- Research was conducted over a three-year period and included the input of NASA scientists who focused on creating a suit that minimized drag, maximized support to the muscles, and did not constrain motion.
- Speedo claimed the LZR Racer would reduce drag by more than 10 percent in comparison to its 2004 suit and would reduce drag by 5 percent in comparison to the suit it designed in 2007 and which accounted for 21 world records.
- Allowing athletes to perform with greater efficiency, Speedo argued the suit would provide swimmers with 5 percent more oxygen intake, consequently allowing them to swim stronger for a longer period.
- The use of ultrasonic welding created a suit with no seams and a compression system was designed to help swimmers remain in a streamlined position, leading to greater power in the water.

"When I hit the water, I feel like a rocket," said Michael Phelps, who was preparing for his eight gold-medal pursuit at the Olympic Games in Beijing. "I can't wait to race in it. This is going to take the sport of swimming to a new level."

It didn't take long after Speedo's launch events for the LZR Racer to show its power. Less than a week after the multi-city reveal and in the first days of the suit being introduced to competition, three world records were set by athletes wearing the new Speedo product. The first record went down on February 16 when Zimbabwe's Kirsty Coventry covered the 200-meter backstroke in 2:06.39 to break the 16-year-old world record of Hungarian Krisztina Egerszegi. The standard was set at USA Swimming's Grand Prix stop in Columbia, Missouri, a meet that typically serves as a midseason tune-up, and not as an event featuring swift times.

A day later, the record-breaking continued. While Australian Eamon Sullivan took 0.08 off the global standard in the 50 freestyle at the low-key New South Wales State Championships in Sydney, Natalie Coughlin broke the world record in the 100 backstroke by 0.23 at the Grand Prix meet in Columbia.

Peter Vanderkaay is shown wearing the Speedo LZR Racer, one of the tech suits that launched a controversial era in the sport. Peter H. Bick.

In short order, the impact of the LZR Racer was felt, and a Pandora's Box had been opened. Still, no one could truly predict what was to come. Simply, the sport—which lost its way over the next two years—was defined by technology and not by battles based sheerly on human talent.

Upon the release of the LZR Racer and the spate of records it yielded, controversy started to brew. Not only was talent neutralized to a degree, athletes sponsored by Speedo had a distinct advantage. With swimmers scrambling to gain possession of suits, especially ahead of the 2008 Olympics, an uneven playing ground had been created. In Japan, where most swimmers were sponsored by Mizuno, Asics, and Descente, the national federation had to intervene and give permission for its swimmers to race outside of their contracted swimwear. Any other decision would have left Japanese athletes well behind.

At the 2008 Games in Beijing, more than 90 percent of the medals awarded were won by swimmers wearing the LZR Racer, with 23 world records set in the Speedo creation. As Phelps won eight gold medals, to eclipse the seven-gold total of Mark Spitz from the 1972 Olympics in Munich, the American wore a variety of LZR Racer suits. Of his four individual world records set in Beijing, his 4:03.84 clocking in the 400 individual medley remains untouched.

While the LZR Racer ignited the swimsuit controversy, it was just the tip of the iceberg. With Speedo establishing a blueprint for an energy-conserving and buoyancy-supplying suit, other manufacturers quickly jumped into the marketplace and took the suit storm to another level. Companies such as Arena, Jaked, and BlueSeventy developed their own products and built on what they learned from Speedo's efforts.

In its creation of the LZR Racer, Speedo made a suit that featured polyurethane panels, with that material accounting for approximately half of the suit. Jaked and Arena went a few steps further, designing suits that were made entirely of polyurethane and provided increased buoyancy. During the 2009 season, nearly 150 world records were set, a sizable jump over the 108 marks established in 2008. Again, an uneven playing ground emerged, with Speedo athletes now possessing an inferior suit compared to the Jaked and Arena options. Demand for the suits was also difficult to meet, leaving those unable to gain possession at a significant deficit.

"The thing that's really hurt more than anything else is that the whole suit situation has devalued the athletes," said University of Southern California Coach Dave Salo, also a United States Olympic coach.

> They're standing in line for an hour to get a suit. How many companies are going to sponsor an athlete that's scrambling to pick up your suit because it's the latest thing? A lot of them are not sure what suits they should wear to create an even playing field. They're all complaining about the suits and it's out of control. When FINA didn't define the rules, it opened up this huge quagmire for all these companies to say, "Oh, there are no rules." It devalued athleticism. A lot of these kids who aren't in very good shape can put on one of these suits and they were streamlined like a seal. Seals don't have to be skinny.

Nowhere was the outlandish nature of the suits more evident than Rome, site of the 2009 World Championships. Over the course of eight days, the 40 events produced 43 world records, or more than one global mark per event. Additionally, 44 championship records were set, and hundreds of national records were wiped out. The ease with

France's Fred Bousquet is shown wearing a Jaked swimsuit, one of the fastest options of the controversial tech-suit era. Peter H. Bick.

which records were erased prompted the use of the term "technological doping".

Among the more outrageous performances in a collection of unbelievable efforts was the 7:32.12 showing of China's Zhang Lin in the 800 freestyle. That time is the equivalent of back-to-back 3:46.06 swims in the 400 freestyle and took more than six seconds off the previous world record. Meanwhile, American Ariana Kukors touched the wall in the 200 individual medley in 2:06.15 to take more than two seconds off the prior world mark. En route to silver and bronze medals, Australian Stephanie Rice and Hungary's Katinka Hosszu were also under the former world record.

"We've gone down a very dangerous road," Italian coach Alberto Castagnetti said during the suit crisis. "It removes the purely competitive aspect of the sport and puts outside factors into play. Swimming has always been based on ability. Now, there are other aspects. It's like technological doping. It's not in the spirit of the sport."

As the World Championships in Rome unfolded, FINA, the international governing body of the sport, recognized that the suits needed to be removed and called for all suits to be made of a textile material. However, the organization noted that it would take several months into 2010 for the ban to go into effect. Not long after making that statement, FINA was forced to reverse course, or risk losing its main attraction.

The final of the 200 freestyle served as the perfect example of the impact of shiny suits. When Germany's Paul Biedermann raced his four laps in 1:42.00, good for a world record, he also buried Phelps, the reigning Olympic and world champion who earned the silver medal in 1:43.22. More, he completed a progression that saw Biedermann go from a 1:46 performer in the event to 1:42-flat in only 11 months. That type of evolution is seen in the sport only at the age-group level or when performance-enhancing drugs are at work.

Agitated by the entire suit situation and the fact that his pupil had his natural gifts nullified by technology, Phelps' coach Bob Bowman went on the attack.

"Probably expect Michael not to swim until they are implemented," Bowman said of sanctions on the high-tech suits. "I'm done with this. [A ban] has to be implemented immediately. The sport is in shambles right now and they better do something or they're going to lose their guy who fills these seats. That would be my recommendation to him, to not swim internationally. He might swim locally, but who knows. The mess needs to be stopped right now. This can't go on any further."

Bowman's comments triggered immediate action by FINA, which took just a few days to move its ban on shiny suits to January 1, 2010. Discussion took place about what to do with the records set during the super-suit era, with some coaches suggesting listing two records and others calling for asterisks to sit beside the records that were set with the assistance of a polyurethane. Ultimately, the records stood, FINA preferring not to rewrite history.

Lauded by most for using his position as Phelps' coach to enact change, Bowman also caught heat for his comments in Rome. Serbian Milorad Cavic, who Phelps defeated by 0.01 for gold in the 100 butterfly at the 2008 Olympics, said Bowman was whining since Speedo's LZR Racer was no longer the most beneficial of the tech suits. Cavic even offered to loan Phelps one of his suits for their impending duel at the World Champs, a gesture that was rejected and only lit a fire in Phelps.

In the final of the 100 fly, Phelps set a world record of 49.82, with Cavic back in 49.95. After realizing his latest victory over Cavic, Phelps engaged in a boisterous celebration and tugged on his LZR Racer suit in a clear rebuke of Cavic's comments.

"I don't think I have ever been that emotional and fired up after a race," Phelps said. "You could tell by my reaction how much I wanted that."

In the five months following the circus in Rome, world records continued to go down with regularity, and some athletes were keen to get in their final shots at writing their names in the record book. But when the calendar flipped to 2010, the suits were relegated to history.

During the 22-month shiny-suit era, a description coined by veteran journalist Craig Lord, 255 world records were set, and they improved by an average of 1.8 percent across all events. This percentage represented a considerable drop, given the longtime tendency for records to be lowered by fractional margins, a hundredth here and, more infrequently, a tenth there.

Some events saw greater improvements than others, with the women's 200 butterfly improving by 2.9 percent from 2:05.40 to 2:01.81. That record is viewed as one of the most untouchable in the sport, and no woman has come within two seconds of the record since it was established more than a decade ago. Meanwhile, the super-suit days saw the world record in the men's 50 freestyle improve by 3.3 percent, moving from 21.64 to 20.91.

To put the impact of tech suits into perspective, the world record in the women's 200 butterfly improved by only 1.3 percent between the last time it was broken in 1979 and 2006, a span of 27 years. More, it took 15 years for the world record in the men's 50 free to improve by the same margin it shifted in super suits, with the record evolving from 22.40 in 1985 to 21.64 in 2000.

More than a decade after the super-suit era, their impression continues to be felt. In addition to several world records enduring from the 2008–2009 campaigns, including a few that have not been remotely challenged, most events have at least one mark in their top five remaining from the shiny-suit days. Truthfully, it could take decades for tech-suit times to be fully erased from top 100 lists.

"I'm just glad they are gone," Phelps said when the ban went into effect. "Now, the focus can return to the swimmers and not on what we're wearing."

Chapter 6

BIGGEST UPSETS

Fans typically love an upset, that moment when unpredictability runs wild. American Misty Hyman and Australian Duncan Armstrong delivered two of their sport's greatest upsets on the Olympic stage.

A STUNNING CONCLUSION

It was a week filled with frustration. A week of agony and pain. A week of what-if questions. As the 1976 Olympic Games in Montreal unfolded, little went the way of the U.S. women. It wasn't that the Team USA roster was weak or underperforming, either. The problem was a glaring issue out of the control of those in Red, White, and Blue.

Event after event, East Germany sent its women to the medals podium, often following a world-record performance. Those girls may have put in a significant work in the pool. They may have been talented. But they also benefited from another influence: The use of performance-enhancing drugs.

In what is considered one of the darkest hours in the sport's history, the Montreal Games—at least on the women's side—was a meet that matched skill versus illicit science. Not surprising, science came out on top, as East Germany ruled the medals table and repeatedly leveled the United States with a tainted hammer.

But for one instance during that dreadful week, the United States had a chance to celebrate as the foursome of Kim Peyton, Wendy Boglioli, Jill Sterkel, and Shirley Babashoff rose up in the 400-meter freestyle relay and pulled off a triumph that was impossible to foresee.

The domination of the East German women rivaled what the American men pulled off in Montreal. While Team USA won 12 of 13 gold medals in the men's competition, the East German Wundermadchen captured 11 of 12 gold medals heading into the 400 freestyle relay. More, they posted five gold-silver finishes and swept the podium in the 200 butterfly.

But unlike the American squad, which is considered the greatest in history, the East German success was the worst-kept secret in the sport. Their accomplishments came out of nowhere in the early 1970s and were complemented by deep voices, acne, and abnormal musculature—all indicators of steroid use.

To enhance its international sports presence, East Germany implemented a systematic doping program that took effect around the 1973 season. Run at the government level and precise in nature, the program provided athletes with combinations of injections and pills that enabled them to build muscle mass and endure longer training sessions. The primary prescription in the program was Oral-Turinabol, an anabolic steroid that came in the form of a blue pill.

Before and after workouts, coaches or East German sports officials, including Dr. Lothar Kipke, would provide swimmers with a cup of the pills or give injections. The medication was presented as vitamins to help with the recovery process and was non-negotiable. Either take what was ordered, or another teenage upstart would be brought in as a replacement.

"Before training, the coach would come in with a big pill box and distribute pills," said Renate Vogel, the 1973 world champion in the 100 and 200 breaststroke. "Each (swimmer) would hold out their hand and they told us it was so you didn't catch a cold. They were vitamin pills. And there were also other pills among them, and the coach would separate them and tell you to take this one in the first week three times, always at some interval. But they never told us what it was. Doping was shoved to the forefront. Who knows what could have happened to your health?"

The systematic program that was orchestrated even featured a safety net in which athletes were tested by East German officials to detect whether any would return positives for performance-enhancing drugs. Leading into the 1976 Games, Barbara Krause was expected to excel for East Germany, having broken the world record in the 400 freestyle on the road to Montreal. But when the Games opened, Krause was conspicuously absent, said to be suffering from an undisclosed illness. However, it was believed her unknown sickness was a cover for the fact that Krause was given an incorrect dosage of steroids and would have tested positive at the Games.

As much as steroid use was understood to be at work, no East German women tested positive for a banned substance. That scenario allowed the administrators of the sport—at least publicly—to turn a blind eye and deny the presence of performance-enhancing drugs as a factor for East Germany's dominance. In turn, East Germany felt it was untouchable and pushed its program further.

If silence was the predominant approach to East Germany's supremacy, Babashoff wasn't in the mood to take the politically correct path. A year before the Montreal Games, Babashoff was beaten at the World Championships by the East Germans on three occasions—once individually and twice in relay action. However, she also claimed victories in the 200 freestyle and 400 freestyle, so the notion her European foes were unbeatable had not been formulated.

But by the time the last event of the 1976 Olympics was set to begin, that narrative had changed. In the 200 freestyle, 400 freestyle, and 800 freestyle, Babashoff was the silver medalist, beaten by East Germans in all three events. Meanwhile, the U.S. 400 medley relay, of which she was a member, also won silver, suffering a six-plus-second setback to East Germany. The repeated losses and clear use of chemical means by the opposition was simply too much to take.

"She was the only one that had the guts to speak out back then," said Mark Schubert, Babashoff's coach. "If anybody had the right to speak out, it was her because she was the one that was cheated out of Olympic gold medals".

When she spoke out, Babashoff did not hold back. She straightforwardly accused the East Germans of using steroids and said she thought she was in a men's locker room when she first heard the low voices of her competition, the pitch a side effect of steroid use. Because she was a runner-up in several events and the East Germans had not testified positive for performance-enhancing drug use, Babashoff was viewed as a sore loser.

The media eviscerated Babashoff for the accusations she lobbed against the East Germans, dubbing her "Surly Shirley." It was a nickname that stung, particularly because Babashoff knew she was correct in her assessment, even if tests did not confirm her accuracy. In a way, Babashoff was not only unfairly beaten in the water but unfairly beaten out of the pool, too.

"It was horrendous for me," Babashoff said.

We knew something was going on, but no one was knowledgeable about steroids in sports. All these swimmers were coming out of this

Shirley Babashoff was part of the legendary 1976 U. S. women's 400 freestyle relay that upset heavily favored East Germany. Peter H. Bick.

little Communist country with a wall around it, so we couldn't see what was going on. They were telling us, we have new swimsuits, we train at high altitude. Never once did they say we are trying out a steroid program, you know? It was so obvious to me. That's why I said something. I felt cheated. You can see it when I'm on the podium getting my silver. I thought to myself, "Why is everyone turning their back on this huge thing that is happening?" Then I came home from Montreal and had to live with what I had said.

Kornelia Ender and Petra Thumer were the primary rivals of Babashoff, Ender having split with Babashoff in the 100 freestyle and 200 freestyle at the 1975 World Championships, and Ender winning those events at the 1976 Olympics. In the 400 freestyle and 800 freestyle in Montreal, Thumer beat Babashoff twice, by 1.02 seconds combined.

If there was a poster woman for East Germany's systematic doping program, it was Ender. In Montreal, the 17-year-old captured gold medals in the 100 freestyle, 200 freestyle, and 100 butterfly, all in world-record time. She also contributed to East Germany's gold-medal 400 medley relay and would have been the heavy favorite for gold in the 200 individual medley, if the event hadn't been eliminated from the Olympic program for the 1976 and 1980 Games. In 1972, as a mere 13-year-old, Ender was the silver medalist in the event.

Between 1973 and 1976, Ender set 23 world records in six individual events. In the 100 freestyle, she broke the world record on ten occasions, taking the mark from 58.25 to 55.65 in a span of three years. It took another 32 years for the world record in the event to drop by that margin, an indication of the potency of the steroids that fueled the East German machine.

"There was a discussion with my coach, my father and Dr. Kipke where (my father) said he heard doping was being done on young athletes," Ender said during the documentary *The Last Gold*, which focused on the 1976 women's 400 freestyle relay. "My father said, 'If you dope this child, I will take her immediately out of the sports school.' But I don't think my father had influence over any of the things that were done in the sports school. My father had to tolerate that, even though I was still a minor."

The spirit of the U.S. women had been broken multiple times during their week in Montreal. While Babashoff was denied gold in three events, some of her teammates were denied places on the podium, their fourth- and fifth-place finishes hardly registering a reading on the sport's Richter Scale. But when it was time for the meet to conclude with the 400 freestyle relay, a fire ignited in the ladies who would make one final chase for gold.

East Germany's march to a 12th gold medal seemed like a formality, its margin of victory the only question. After all, it featured a stacked lineup, highlighted by Ender and Petra Priemer, the gold and silver medalists in the 100 freestyle. Also on the relay were Claudia Hempel, who was sixth in the 100 free, and Andrea Pollack, who was the Olympic champion in the 200 butterfly and the silver medalist in the 100 butterfly.

Somehow, though, the United States convinced itself that an upset was possible. Knowing the U.S. relay order would be Peyton, Boglioli, Sterkel, and Babashoff, the athletes started to envision the race. They discussed split times, pictured perfect relay exchanges, and saw themselves ahead of the East Germans.

"We got together before the relay and sat there and did this mental thing where you swim the race over and over, see where you are and the time you want to do," Babashoff said. "We did the swim over and over in our head. This is how we're going to win. We're going to train our brains to make us win."

There was a slight surprise when it came time for the relay to begin. Rather than use Ender on the anchor leg, East Germany opted to lead off with its biggest star, who raced opposite Peyton. While Peyton went 56.95, a solid performance, Team USA found itself a body length behind after Ender touched in 55.79. Through the first leg, the race was unfolding according to expectations, and there was no reason to believe a change was coming.

But on the second leg, Boglioli produced the fastest split of her career by two seconds, going 55.81 to Priemer's 56.16 split. Although the United States still trailed, the anticipated larger deficit was negated. For Boglioli, who was the bronze medalist in the 100 butterfly earlier in the week, she wasn't about to let the United States leave Canada without a gold medal.

"At the end of that week, as a team, we said, 'This is not how this is going to end,'" Boglioli said.

A 15-year-old racing in her first of three Olympiads, Sterkel was given the chore of cutting into the East German lead further. The teenager accomplished her goal, and more, as she posted a split of 55.78, with Pollack going 56.99. Through 300 meters, the United States was in the lead by 0.40, with Babashoff facing off with Hempel on the anchor leg. Initially a dream, the potential of an American victory was real.

Dealing with a week of frustration and unfairness, Babashoff was not going to yield the lead. Producing a split of 56.28, against the 56.56 of Hempel, the United States beat East Germany by 0.68 and established a world record of 3:44.82, breaking the former mark by four seconds. A gold-medal shutout was averted, and a testing week ended on a positive note, thanks to one of the biggest upsets in Olympic history—then and now.

"What was so outstanding was that they won with their minds," said Jack Nelson, the 1976 U.S. Olympic coach. "They didn't worry about the East Germans. They were worried about America winning, and people went bonkers. They were truly great Americans and had no fear. No fear. A number of coaches would look away when they saw me because they, themselves, did not realize what these girls achieved. They did not realize these girls had been cheated to the limit."

Overall, the U.S. women set 15 American records during the 1976 Games, several of those marks faster than the previous world record. But because of the East German dominance, the effort by Team USA has gone overlooked and underappreciated, even with the passing of time.

Attempts to have the International Olympic Committee either nullify the East German results or reallocate medals have failed, an unfortunate development considering the release of Stasi (secret police) documents after the fall of the Berlin Wall confirmed a systematic doping program was at work. Although those who finished behind East Germans in Montreal, and at other points in the 1970s and the 1980s, were victims, so were the East German athletes who were treated like lab rats and suffered medical conditions from their steroid intake.

"What happened to the East German women was horrible," Sterkel said in *The Last Gold*.

> I don't want to see their medals taken away. I don't want to see them suffer anymore than they have already suffered. But I'm thankful and grateful that I'm an American athlete and I wasn't a victim who had to go through what they went through. The thing people have to wrap their head around is that there needs to be compassion for this group of (American women) who competed and did their best and were treated horribly by the press and by not recognizing what they did. It's hard. You can't go back. You have stolen something, the right to compete and see where you fall on an equal playing field is gone. And that's what sports is all about.

UNCAGING THE ANIMAL

One of the most used clichés in sports is the biblical David vs. Goliath comparison. It is a description utilized to describe a scenario in which a longshot challenger faces off with a heavy favorite. At the 1988 Olympic Games in Seoul, the final of the 200-meter freestyle fit the mold perfectly—and a little bit more.

Heading into the Games of the 24th Olympiad, Australian Duncan Armstrong possessed a modest resume. While he was the reigning Commonwealth Games champion in the 400 freestyle, he wasn't known for much else. As the 46th-ranked swimmer in the world in the 200 freestyle, a one-and-done showing in the event would not have surprised anyone.

The 200 freestyle was a stacked event in Seoul, featuring three world-record holders in American Matt Biondi, West Germany's Michael Gross, and Poland's Artur Wojdat. Because of the firepower that was present, the event was one of the can't-miss attractions of the week. If Armstrong was given the role of David, his small stone would have to take down three Goliaths.

In Biondi, Armstrong had to deal with a guy who was looking to match Mark Spitz's record of seven gold medals from the 1972 Olympics in Munich. Meanwhile, Gross was an Olympic and world champion and the defending Games titlist in the 200 freestyle. As for Wojdat, he was the world-record holder in the 400 freestyle. How could Armstrong possibly topple all, or even one, of these giants? And in the case of Gross and Biondi, they were literally giants, each standing 6-foot-7.

The answer was simple: Laurie Lawrence.

One of the most respected coaches in Australia, Lawrence had the ability to generate belief in his troops. He worked magic in that sense. A taskmaster while overseeing training sessions, Lawrence then shifted gears to psychologist, demonstrating a knack for building up confidence.

"He's a wonderful and enthusiastic person," Armstrong said of Lawrence.

> He just sells it. He sells passion. He's a wonderful man. In swimming, where you have to do hundreds and hundreds and hundreds of laps, passion and enthusiasm are very important. He really understood the Olympic equation that you only get one shot. The door of opportunity only opens once every four years. He gave you the tools of the trade to step on deck so the Olympic pressure would not crush you. You look down your lane and know you've done everything you possibly can and you're prepared for this race. Someone has got to win it. Why not me? You go out against great opposition and perform your best and not let the pressure cooker crush you.

So, when Armstrong strolled onto the deck for the start of the 200 freestyle, having qualified fourth in the preliminaries, the Aussie felt he belonged. Even after the arena's announcer read novel-length introductions for Gross and Biondi, compared with a snippet for Armstrong, Lawrence's pupil was undeterred. He was in Lane Six for an Olympic final, and that meant he had a chance.

To fully understand the significance of what Armstrong accomplished in Seoul, one must first examine the outcome of the 200 butterfly at the 1984 Olympics in Los Angeles. It was at those Games, which were boycotted by the Eastern Bloc nations in retaliation for the U.S. boycott of Moscow in 1980, in which Jon Sieben defied the odds and knocked off Gross in an epic upset.

Heading into the Los Angeles Games, Gross was the reigning world champion in the 200 freestyle and 200 butterfly and was expected to walk away from the McDonald's Swim Stadium with a fistful of medals.

Nicknamed the Albatross for his seven-foot wingspan, Gross was both powerful and elegant in the water. As for Sieben, whose 5-9 frame elicited the nickname "the shrimp," his top achievement was a bronze-medal effort in the 200 fly at the 1982 Commonwealth Games.

Once the swimmers were introduced to the crowd, Sieben took to his starting block in Lane Six and envisioned the best performance of his career. But even the most imaginative dream couldn't compare to what the 17-year-old Aussie actually produced, a world record of 1:57.04 that provided him with a 0.36 margin over Gross.

"This morning, I was looking at getting a medal. I didn't really think about winning," Sieben said. "I didn't let anything bother me or worry me. I felt comfortable. There wasn't any pressure on me. I felt completely relaxed before and during the race."

Leading Sieben to victory, through both physical and mental training, was someone Armstrong knew well: Lawrence. In addition to knowing what his athletes needed in terms of in-water preparation, Lawrence used his master motivator tactics to convince Sieben he could beat anyone, Poseidon included.

Lawrence's influence could be seen in Sieben's progression from his Commonwealth bronze medal and crowning moment. In the span of two years, Sieben dropped four seconds in the 200 fly and repelled the most intimidating swimmer on the planet. Only someone placing complete loyalty in his mentor could experience that type of growth in such a limited timeframe.

"We clipped the wings of the big fella," Lawrence said of Gross. "It's been fantastic. I knew Sieben could go (fast), but I didn't realize he could get the world record. I'm out of my tree."

It was coincidence that Armstrong raced the final of the 200 freestyle in Seoul in Lane Six, the lane Sieben occupied four years earlier in his moment of Olympic glory. But to Lawrence, the tie was meaningful. In prerace discussions with Armstrong, Lawrence convinced the 20-year-old that he had nothing to lose and was free to let loose against his better-known foes.

As expected, Biondi used his natural speed to bolt to the front of the field down the opening lap, and while Sweden's Anders Holmertz took the lead at the midway point, Armstrong was lurking and in a strong position. During the third lap, Biondi regained the lead and was in front when the swimmers made the turn for home.

With a superb final turn, Armstrong surged in front of Biondi off the final wall and managed to fend him off, along with the rest of the field, over the last 50 meters. At the finish, Armstrong was timed in 1:47.25, a world-record performance. Holmertz managed to edge in front of Biondi for the silver medal in 1:47.89, with Biondi setting an American record of 1:47.99 for the bronze medal. Wojdat placed fourth and Gross was fifth, the Goliaths dropped to their knees by Australia's David. Armstrong pumped his fist in the air several times, looked to the crowd on both sides of the arena and sat on the lane line before accepting congratulations from the men he raced against.

The race was a demonstration of tactical intelligence. Armstrong, off advice from Lawrence, had stayed close to Biondi's lane and drew a draft off the powerful American, allowing him to expend less energy than if he was racing in the middle of his lane and did not benefit from Biondi's wave. In one postrace interview, conducted by 1976 Olympic champion John Naber, Armstrong said he bodysurfed on Biondi's wave.

"The plan to ride Biondi's wave was based on the fact that he has a big kick," Armstrong said.

> I just sucked on the wave and stayed there early in the race. Maybe it helped me finish stronger. Who knows? I do know I turned for the last lap feeling a lot fresher than I usually do and I did not have to dig deep for that extra effort. I knew I was in with a big chance on the turn. Until the race was over, I didn't know the Swede was up there with us in Lane Eight. When I touched, I looked up and saw that no one else had touched so I knew I'd won. It didn't sink in straight away. I looked back at the results board and saw 1:47 flash up. I knew I had the record. That's when the emotion flooded over.

Lawrence never doubted the moment was possible. As Armstrong churned through the water, the veteran coach watched from the stands, unable to contain himself. With a rolled-up program in his hands, Lawrence alternated waving his hands in the air and slamming the program into his palm. Once Armstrong stopped the clock, revealing his triumph, Lawrence's true show began.

Overcome with emotion and excitement, Lawrence wandered up and down the steps in the stands, unsure what to do. He yelled Armstrong's name and called out, "Where's the animal?" He also repeatedly hollered, "Lucky Lane Six." The reference was to the fact that Sieben and Armstrong had both pulled off their upset wins out of the same lane. At one point, Lawrence started to shake a metal barricade with such ferocity that South Korean police approached him, prepared to escort him out of the venue, until Lawrence convinced them he was all right.

Lawrence's antics continued as Armstrong, Holmertz, and Biondi made their way to the medals ceremony. Looking down from the stands, the coach repeatedly called out, "Hey, Dunc, I know you." The behavior was so entertaining and erratic that Biondi asked Armstrong who the man was, prompting a sheepish Armstrong to explain his relationship. Lawrence's exuberance was also on display during an interview he gave to Australian television journalist Steven Quartermain. After Quartermain asked the typical, "How do you feel?" query, Lawrence summed up his feelings.

"Mate, we just beat three world-record holders," an elated Lawrence yelled at Quartermain. "How do you think I feel? What do you think we come for, mate? Silver? Stuff the silver. We come for the gold."

During the interview, Lawrence actually slapped Quartermain on the side of the face, gestures that were meant to be love taps. But in his excitement, Lawrence's slaps were stronger than intended and Quartermain suffered a broken jaw. Armstrong's success and Lawrence's antics are prominently featured in *Bud Greenspan's Favorite Stories of Olympic Glory*, one of the many superb documentaries put together by Greenspan, who was one of the foremost Olympic experts and documentarians before his death in 2010.

"To win at the Olympic Games you have to swim next year's time, this year," Lawrence said. "It was one of those incredible moments that I have been a part of in my sporting career. To have two kids (Sieben and Armstrong) go back-to-back with gold medals was incredible. When it comes to fruition, all that pent-up years of hard work, discipline with your young charge just gushes out."

For Biondi, his bronze medal ended his hopes of matching Spitz, but the race was one of the most challenging on his schedule and the fact that he was able to reach the podium enabled Biondi to win seven medals—five gold, a silver, and a bronze.

One of the greatest swimmers in the sport's history, Biondi was—in a way—the bridge between Spitz and Michael Phelps, who at the 2008 Olympics in Beijing won eight gold medals to break Spitz's record. Under considerable pressure, he excelled in Seoul, individual gold medals earned in the 50 freestyle and 100 freestyle. He was also a member of three winning relays and took silver in the 100 butterfly by a hundredth of a second.

"I finished third in a great 200 (freestyle) behind Holmertz and Duncan Armstrong of Australia, who broke Gross' world record with a 1:47.25," Biondi wrote in his *Sports Illustrated* diary. "I was happy. I swam the way I wanted to and beat the guys I thought I needed to, Gross and

Wojdat. Duncan just had a hell of a swim. I had the lead and he stayed right on my shoulder, right by the lane line. I think he should buy me a beer or something because he probably got a pretty good draft from me.

"The press always throws stuff at you. Like tonight I heard (NBC's) Bob Costas say on TV, 'Matt Biondi isn't going to win his seven gold medals. Today he had to settle for bronze.' But I feel good about the bronze."

As surprising as Armstrong's victory was, the Aussie was not done in Seoul. He returned to the 400 freestyle four days later and won the silver medal behind East Germany's Uwe Dassler, who set a world record of 3:46.95. Armstrong was also under the former world record, going 3:47.15, with Wojdat claiming the bronze medal.

To say it was a special week would be an understatement.

"It was (a feeling) of more relief than anything else because we had trained four or five years for that moment and the race takes less than two minutes," Armstrong said.

> You go two minutes on one day every four years. That's the clock. You do an enormous amount of training and then you get there and we had the perfect race. We had the great strategy and some good competition in the water. We had a world record. All my dreams and hopes in swimming came true in one touch of the wall. It was just wonderful. It was the perfect moment for us. It was the pinnacle of my swimming career.

Chapter 7

DARK DAYS OF DOPING

Athletes are always trying to find a way to enhance their performances. Unfortunately, it has been commonplace for some athletes to use illegal means to elevate themselves to the next level.

THE EAST GERMAN MACHINE

None of it made sense—at least naturally. In a sport defined by incremental improvement, what East Germany was suddenly producing was incomprehensible. Huge chunks of time were lopped off athletes' past performances and over short periods. The likelihood that these improvements were related to some innovative training program or a sudden influx of generational talent was minimal, for the sport—over many decades—had never seen anything similar.

Something was clearly wrong, and it wasn't difficult to ascertain the primary factor at work. The use of performance-enhancing drugs has been a staple in the sporting world, thanks to athletes' willingness to circumvent the rules—and integrity—to gain an edge on the competition. But what was seen in East Germany from the early 1970s through the late 1980s was an entirely different operation, as a systematic doping program was put in place at the government level. This adoption of a rogue movement, one which emphasized performance and results over everything else, changed lives and the history of the sport forever.

When serving as the host of an Olympic Games, most countries realize a boost in their medal counts. The desire to perform admirably on home soil, combined with greater funding to produce enhanced results, work collaboratively. But at the 1972 Games in Munich, East German women accounted for only five medals, none of them gold, and the total fell well short of the 17 medals collected by the United States.

This total, especially for an era in which medal distribution did not match the wider spread look of today, fell in line with what other nations achieved.

A year later, a different story was told.

In 1973, the World Championships were held for the first time, with Belgrade, Yugoslavia, awarded hosting duties. The schedule mimicked the Olympic program and, given its proximity to the Munich Games of the previous summer, the medals table should not have appeared much different. The United States, based on its decades of dominance, was expected to stand out, the likes of Australia, Hungary, and East Germany collecting modest amounts of hardware. Instead, there was a drastic change.

Of the 14 events contested, East German women emerged victorious in 10, the United States claiming titles in only three disciplines. Adding to the sudden dominance was the fact that East Germany complemented its gold-medal haul with five silver medals and three bronze medals. The outcome of 18 medals for East Germany to 13 for the United States turned the sport upside down and raised red flags concerning the German Democratic Republic's meteoric rise.

The podium dominance of East Germany, however, only told a portion of the story. Analysis of the results from the World Championships revealed margins of victory that were atypical for a stopwatch sport. In the 400 freestyle relay, East Germany beat the United States by more than three seconds, in the process taking nearly three seconds off the world record. The finish of the 400 medley relay was more startling, as East Germany defeated Team USA by almost nine seconds and slashed nearly four seconds off the world record.

Although the inaugural World Championships ushered in a new dominant force in women's swimming, public outcry did not yet manifest itself, no athlete or governing body wanting to be labeled as a sore loser. Within team circles, especially those of the United States, there were discussions about the undeniable use of performance-enhancing drugs by the East Germans.

Dubbed the Wundermadchen, or Wonder Women, the East Germans used 1973 as a springboard for a decade and a half of unmatched power in the pool. On the road to the 1976 Olympics in Montreal, East Germany won all 14 events at the 1974 European Championships, where they added 11 silver medals. More, at the 1975 World Championships, East

German women stood atop the podium in 10 of 14 events. As the Games in Montreal approached, there was no doubt what was about to unfold.

"Prior to the 1976 Olympics, the East Germans had just blown us away in the World Championships," said Jack Nelson, the coach of the U.S. women at the Games in Montreal. "And our girls were honestly bothered by the fact that they had been the greatest team in the world for a while and then suddenly the East Germans just are blowing us away. We knew while we were there that they were beating up on us with steroids and whatever and there was nothing we could do about it, right? Plus, we didn't want to be the nasty Americans at the Olympics."

The Montreal Games are largely remembered for the exploits of the American men, whose roster is considered the most dominant the sport has seen. Out of 13 events, the United States won gold on 12 occasions, with gold–silver finishes in nine events and sweeps of the podium in four events.

The East Germans managed similar success, as they won 11 of 13 events, Kornelia Ender the standout with world-record performances in the 100 freestyle and 200 freestyle, along with the 100 butterfly. For the Americans, Shirley Babashoff was relegated to silver medals in the 200 freestyle, 400 freestyle, and 800 freestyle. Coupled with past losses to East Germans at the World Championships, Babashoff had enough and spoke out, alleging doping use by her foes. In the media, Babashoff was vilified, identified as a sore loser, and dubbed with the unflattering moniker of "Surly Shirley."

"They had gotten so big, and when we heard their voices, we thought we were in a coed locker room," Babashoff said. "I don't know why it wasn't obvious to other people, too. I guess I was the scapegoat. Someone had to blame somebody. Something bad had to happen, and it had to happen to me. I didn't get the gold. I got the silver, so I was a loser."

Without any positive doping tests to point to as evidence, Babashoff merely hurled allegations in the minds of the sport's officials, and particularly in the view of East Germany. It didn't matter that the success of East Germany was sudden in nature and outside any trend the sport had previously witnessed. Consequently, through the late 1980s, except for the boycott of the 1984 Olympics in Los Angeles, East Germany remained an overwhelming force.

The individual progression of Ender in the 100 freestyle spoke loudly of the dominance by East Germany. Between the summer of 1973 and the summer of 1976, Ender set ten world records in the 100 free, lowering the record from 58.50 to 55.65 during that span. To put what Ender accomplished into perspective, it took 16 years for a similar jump to be made in the men's version of the event. The equivalent leap saw Mark Spitz's 1972 standard of 51.22 lowered to 48.42 by Matt Biondi in 1988.

The superlatives just start there. A journalist for the *Times of London*, Craig Lord has reported extensively through the years on East Germany and its dominance. Consider some of the statistics he collated that defined the East German reign:

- After holding zero world records at the conclusion of the 1972 season, East German women went on to set 127 world records between 1973 and 1989, including 110 individual global standards.
- During the three Olympiads in which East Germany competed during its doping era, it claimed 31 of a possible 40 gold medals and won more than half of the total medals available, 64 of 120.
- There were five World Championships contested between 1973 and 1989 and East Germany won 44 of the 72 gold medals available, accounting for 61 percent of the titles.
- At the seven editions of the European Championships conducted from 1973 to 1989, East Germany won 96 of a possible 104 titles, good for a success rate of 92.3 percent.

There is an adage that sports and politics do not mix, but it was a political development that turned allegations of doping against East Germany into confirmed beliefs. When the Berlin Wall fell in 1989, documents belonging to the Stasi, the East German Secret Police, were revealed. In these documents, it was found that an elaborate and systematic program, affecting as many as 10,000 athletes across multiple sports, was devised at the government level. The details of the program were alarming. Officials overseeing the program kept detailed documentation of the delivery of the performance-enhancing drugs, the amount that was administered, and when the athletes were taken off the drugs to ensure they would pass doping tests. Females who were barely teenagers were told they were taking vitamins to help them recover from training sessions, when in fact they were being supplied with steroids that may have boosted performances but also had detrimental side effects.

The primary drug administered to athletes, the Stasi paperwork revealed, was chlorodehydromethyltestosterone, better known by its brand name, Oral-Turinabol. An anabolic steroid most commonly found in the form of a little blue pill, Oral-Turinabol was produced by the Jenapharm pharmaceutical company and helped athletes build muscle mass quickly and endure longer training sessions. In the East German women, it also generated deeper voices and acne-covered bodies, with later side effects found to be worse.

"It was really exhausting," said Rica Reinisch, who won three gold medals at the 1980 Olympics and set four individual world records. "Sometimes you swam until you found your arms were dragging along the bottom of the pool. It was dreadful. We usually got the tablets after very hard water-training sessions. Vitamin C, Vitamin B, potassium, calcium, magnesium, all kinds of pills. It was a real cupful."

While the East German women were the primary targets of the systematic program, it expanded—in some instances—to men. For example, East German distance star Jorg Hoffman has admitted to being doped, that assistance helping him become a world champion and Olympic medalist. One of the few East Germans during the era to not be involved with the program at its height was Roland Matthes, widely considered the greatest backstroker in history. The Olympic champion in both backstroke events at the 1968 and 1972 Olympics, Matthes had proven his ability to excel without the assistance of chemical means, success that allowed his coach Marlies Grohe-Geissler to refuse involvement in the doping scheme.

The masterminds behind the systematic doping program, formally identified as State Plan 14:25, were Manfred Ewald and Manfred Hoeppner. Ewald served as East Germany's Minister of Sport from 1961 to 1989 and was the head of the East German Olympic Committee from 1973 to 1990. Ewald was the coordinator of the program across all sports and charged with identifying talented young athletes to be groomed for success.

Hoeppner, meanwhile, was East Germany's top sports doctor during the doping regime and in charge of the distribution of Oral-Turinabol and ensuring that procedures were followed to avoid detection by doping officials. Also involved was Dr. Lothar Kipke, whose role was to provide the performance-enhancing drugs through pill form or injections.

If the athletes initially believed they were indeed being given vitamin supplements, doubts quickly emerged. The deepening of voices and enhanced muscle mass that was gained were signs of steroid use. Still, none of the athletes would speak up, out of fear their careers would be instantly squashed.

"We had no knowledge, nor any way of knowing, that such a problem existed," Ender once told Lord. "There was no mention of it, and nobody spoke about it. It was possible that we were given things in our food and drink. We were fed by a special kitchen at the school, but we didn't know of anything. I was astonished that I had grown so much. I put on (about 18 pounds) in muscle."

"Now, after all this time, I still ask myself whether it could be possible they gave me things because I remember being given injections during training and competition, but this was explained to me as being substances to help me regenerate and recuperate," Ender said. "It was natural to think this way because the distance swimmers had more injections than we did as sprinters. It's very sad. The only losers in that are the athletes."

Reinisch has been one of the most outspoken athletes about what transpired in East Germany. She has spoken of a time in her career when she refused to be given an injection, only to be told by her personal coach, Uwe Neumann, that if she did not allow the injection, her career was over. It wasn't long after that Reinisch's mother burst into a practice one day, screamed at Neumann and removed her from the setting, effectively ending her daughter's career.

Reinisch has been joined in vehemently assailing the doping program by Petra Schneider, the 1980 Olympic champion in the 400 individual medley. Upon the revelation of the systematic program at work in her homeland, Schneider asked to have her records stricken, knowing they were not achieved through honest means.

However, denial is also a common theme of the East German doping era. While some athletes have readily admitted to knowing they were doped, others, like Ender, have indicated they weren't knowingly given performance-enhancing drugs. Also included in this group is Kristin Otto, who won six gold medals at the 1988 Olympic Games in Seoul. Otto has acknowledged that her name appears in Stasi documents and she likely was supplied with steroids, but she maintains it was without her knowledge.

After the Berlin Wall crumbled, a group of athletes filed suit against those who oversaw the systematic program, including Ewald, Hoeppner, and Kipke. The trials were nothing short of heart-wrenching, as the effects of Oral-Turinabol were revealed, and a lack of compassion permeated the courtroom.

During the trials, affected athletes testified about several of the side effects they experienced from their exposure to steroid use, ranging from enlarged ovaries to cancer to liver damage. Some athletes spoke of frequent miscarriages and deformities suffered by offspring.

In addition to the testimony of athletes, Dr. Dorit Rosler took the stand to discuss her complicity. Rosler provided an overview of the specificity of the program and admitted regret for her involvement.

"We documented all of this: The pills, the time of day, the training regimens," Rosler testified in court. "I was far too obedient. We were pressured into producing for the political leadership. We were tasked with creating champions in sport for the glory of the communist state. That was the same excuse used during the Third Reich, that if we didn't do as Hitler asked, another doctor would carry it out. I should have shown more courage."

While Ewald didn't show any remorse during his trial, Hoeppner apologized for his role but also attempted to justify his actions. Not surprisingly, the courtroom was in shock when Hoeppner made his statement.

"Many people pop pills in order to maintain their ability to work hard, so where is the real difference between sport and the real world?" Hoeppner said. "Doctors in the sports-medicine field don't have the opportunity to certify an athlete unfit to work, but the athletes nevertheless ask the doctors to help them maintain their competitive edge. So doctors should not shy away from this question. It is always like walking a tightrope."

"According to the 1987 pharmaceutical law, the proper use of drugs includes the prevention of damage. We did scientific studies in the East to prove that it was necessary to use these supporting means, these drugs, for performance. We justified our use of the drugs to prevent damage to the athletes. Even today we have an ongoing discussion about the ethics of using performance enhancement. If the court finds that I am wrong about the use of drugs, then I have to accept this, but 26 years ago, the situation was very different. The objective of supplying pills was to minimize injury and maximize training hours.

"I deeply regret that I was not able to protect all athletes from harm. I beg those athletes who suffered ill-health to accept my apologies for this."

Ultimately, Ewald, Hoeppner, and Kipke were found guilty for their transgressions, but their sentences of probation and limited fines were basically a slap on the wrist. In the meantime, the athletes they supplied with steroids have suffered. In early 2019, after Andrea Pollack lost her battle with cancer at just 57, several former teammates suggested her death was connected to her steroid use under the direction of State Plan 14:25.

Worse still, some of the athletes who were given performance-enhancing drugs were never intended to shine in international competition. Rather, they served as guinea pigs for the more talented athletes, used to determine proper dosage amounts and the correct timing for the administration of drugs. One of the swimmers serving this role was Catherine Menscher, who has endured seven miscarriages since being used as nothing more than a lab rat.

As much as the East German women were victims of their government's greed, Babashoff was also a victim, denied her rightful place in history. Between the 1973 and 1975 World Championships and the 1976 Olympics, Babashoff earned six individual silver medals, all behind East Germans.

Appeals have been made over the years, to the International Olympic Committee and to the United States Olympic Committee, to have the record books rewritten and for gold medals to be awarded to swimmers who finished behind East Germans. Those calls, however, have fallen on deaf ears, and the refusal to right the wrongs of the past is almost as difficult to accept as the doping that beat Babashoff and others.

"Everyone should be compensated somewhat or just acknowledged," Babashoff said.

> Even our own Olympic Committee should step up and have an event where they can invite those who are still alive and recognize them, perhaps with a commemorative medal . . . or at least say, "We know that this has been hard for you." They should at least acknowledge the women. Some people want to think that the issue is over. From our side of it, the whole issue has been shoved under the carpet. I think it is sad. So many women deserved their medals. They were cheated out of their medals at the Olympics. We would like to get what we earned. We were going for the medals, not the cash. We were amateurs. We worked so hard. We earned it and it was stolen right in front of everyone's face and no-one did anything about it. It was like watching a bank robbery where they just let the crooks go and then say, "It's okay."

For Reinisch and her compatriots, an additional layer to their story is the uncertainty of their skills. Without the assistance of steroids, could they have still medaled at the Olympics? The answer will never be known.

"We were guinea pigs, there to win Olympic gold, used like a taster in ancient Rome," Reinisch said. "The worst thing is they took away from me the opportunity to ever know if I could have won the gold medals without the steroids. That's the greatest betrayal of all."

DOMINANCE . . . AND DOUBTS

As he crossed the finish line, index finger raised, Canadian Ben Johnson was the most-celebrated athlete on the planet. He had just won the 1988 Olympic title in the 100-meter dash, his winning time of 9.79 difficult to comprehend. How could a human run that fast? It was a legitimate question, and one asked with a pointed undertone.

Within days, there was an answer, and the Seoul Games were sullied by controversy. Johnson, in what was an unsurprising revelation to those who raced against him, had tested positive for the use of an anabolic steroid and was stripped of his gold medal. Instantly, journalists feverishly worked to cover the story of Johnson's doping violation, while Johnson boarded a flight out of South Korea.

The news of Johnson's positive test coincided with the last days of the swimming competition, where two storylines stood out. On the male side, Matt Biondi's march to seven medals, including five gold, drew comparisons to what Mark Spitz accomplished at the 1972 Olympics in Munich. Although Biondi did not match Spitz's perfection, he became just the second swimmer to tally seven medals in a single Games.

Among the women, all eyes were focused on East Germany's Kristin Otto, who led her nation's dominant showing by setting an Olympic standard for individual success. Over the course of the eight-day meet, Otto was perfect, her four individual triumphs complemented by a pair of relay victories. If the program had included a women's 800 freestyle relay, as the men's schedule did, she almost certainly would have equaled Spitz's iconic effort from 16 years earlier. Still, her six gold medals set a record for female success at the Olympic Games, a standard that has gone unmatched.

But like Johnson, suspicions followed Otto, who was pegged at a young age to attend one of East Germany's prestigious sports schools. From the early 1970s through the late 1980s, East Germany was the dominant country in the pool, destroying the opposition at the European Championships, World Championships, and Olympic Games, and all other competitions in between. Even without official proof in the form of positive doping tests, there was little doubt unethical practices were at play.

Not only was East Germany's sudden and widespread success enough to activate prolonged skepticism, so were the physical characteristics of the athletes—abnormal musculature, deep voices, acne-covered skin. It was also said that the country's systematic doping program was so specific that athletes were monitored prior to competition and removed from action if there was the slightest risk they would test positive for a performance-enhancing substance.

Otto was accustomed to the doubts.

"I have never knowingly taken any banned substances," Otto said. "I have no knowledge of ever having taken something to help my performance."

There is a key word in Otto's statement—knowingly. Throughout the duration of East Germany's doping program, the teenage girls who were used as pharmaceutical guinea pigs and pin cushions simply did as they were told. Swallow this pill. Take this injection. Follow this workout. And . . . DO NOT ASK QUESTIONS.

It didn't take long for Otto to rise to the top of the sport after being identified as a potential future star. As a 16-year-old at the 1982 World Championships, Otto notched her first international success, capturing three gold medals—highlighted by a solo title in the 100 backstroke. The next year's European Championships brought three more medals, but the opportunity to shine on the biggest sporting stage had to wait.

In retaliation for the U.S.-led boycott of the 1980 Olympic Games in Moscow, 14 Eastern Bloc countries decided to skip the 1984 Games in Los Angeles. Leading this charge were the Soviet Union and East Germany, and the decision meant Otto had to wait an additional four years to chase Olympic glory.

Although 1984 was a loss for Otto on the Olympic front, she made the most of the campaign by setting a world record in the 200 freestyle and winning five medals at the Friendship Games, a replacement meet for the Olympics that provided boycotting nations the chance to experience some level of competition. In 1985, Otto was out of the pool for most of the year, sidelined by an injury that left her in a neck brace for nine months.

By the 1986 World Championships in Madrid, though, Otto was back to her pre-injury form and setting the foundation for two years in the future—the 1988 Games in Seoul. At the World Champs, Otto collected six medals, four of them gold, with individual titles earned in the 100 free-style and 200 individual medley. Her triumph in the 100 free arrived in world-record time and the mark endured as the global standard for more than five years.

A year later, Otto was equally impressive, evident in her five-gold exhibition at the European Championships that included solo wins in the 100 freestyle, 100 backstroke, and 100 butterfly. There was no doubt she was prepared to make her Olympic debut, and her ability to win international titles in a variety of events received considerable acclaim. Wolfgang Richter, East Germany's head coach in Seoul, admired Otto's mental side.

"She's the best because she works harder than the rest," Richter said. "She's tough (in the mind). She cannot stand to lose."

Her long Olympic wait over, Otto wasted little time jumping on the gold-medal wagon. In the first event of the meet, she won the 100 free-style by more than a half-second. That win was followed by comfortable victories in the 100 backstroke and as a member of the East German 400 freestyle relay. The last three days of action produced one gold medal per day, wins in the 100 butterfly and 50 freestyle sandwiching her contribution on the victorious 400 medley relay.

There it was, in a blink, six gold medals in as many events. There were no world records in Seoul, but Otto was an individual winner in three different strokes, an effort that prompted five-time United States Olympic coach Don Gambril to compare her to American legend Tracy Caulkins. It was an odd comparison for a U.S. coach to make considering how Team USA, particularly Shirley Babashoff, had long questioned the legitimacy of East Germany's success.

Otto simply took the end of her Olympiad in stride, noting that she had exceeded expectations and would fondly look back at the week. When asked about her involvement with doping, she pointed to the fact that she had never tested positive and was one of the most-tested athletes in the world.

"Personally, I never gave much thought to this because it would have been too much of a burden if you think of a gold in every event," Otto said. "I'm 22 and that is not so young anymore in this sport, so I have a very difficult decision to make (concerning retirement). I'm sure we will be very popular (back home). People will stop us in the street. But I'm also sure this will not change my life."

Indeed, Otto spurned retirement for a year after Seoul. In what proved to be her final international competition, she won four medals at the 1989 European Championships, including a gold in the 100 backstroke. She followed her career by pursuing a journalism degree and has been a longtime television journalist in Germany.

What Otto has not been able to avoid in her post-water days are links between her and performance-enhancing drugs. When the Berlin Wall fell, a plethora of East German secrets was revealed, among them the details of the country's systematic doping program, known formally as State Plan 14:25. In documents recovered from the Stasi, the East German Secret Police, Otto's name was listed among those supplied with anabolic steroids. Even when presented with this evidence, Otto denies her knowledge of the process. Yet, others have copped to the program of which they were part, including Rica Reinisch, a three-time gold medalist at the 1980 Olympics in Moscow. In addition to admitting that she was supplied with performance-enhancing drugs by her coaches and East German medical personnel, Reinisch has criticized Otto for not admitting the obvious and what is documented.

"When she claims she cleaned up in Seoul without taking anything, then I can only say she didn't win six golds by drinking buttermilk," Reinisch once said.

A 1993 inductee to the International Swimming Hall of Fame, Otto's exhibit now includes a doping disclaimer. The same disclaimer is attached to the displays of Kornelia Ender, Barbara Krause, Petra Thumer, and Ulrike Richter, among others. It reads: "In a German court of law, after this swimmer was inducted into the International Swimming Hall of Fame, team officials confessed to administering performance enhancing drugs to this swimmer, who therefore obtained an illegal and unfair advantage over other athletes."

From a pure performance standpoint, Otto will be remembered for turning in one of the greatest Olympic outings in history. In this age of enhanced depth, the notion of another female athlete winning six gold medals—four of them individually—is unlikely. Heck, when Michael Phelps won his eight gold medals in Beijing, he relied on two miracles to keep perfection alive.

Simultaneously, what Otto accomplished, before and in Seoul, will always be tarnished. How much did steroids aid her? What could she have achieved through only her innate talent? These are questions that will never be answered. Instead, she'll be forever connected to doping and will hedge her comments about the possibility. More, their Seoul link will keep Otto and Johnson inseparable, except that she got away and he did not.

"I've been facing [doping questions] for years," she said. "It is nothing new for me. Unfortunately, I can no longer rule [doping] out. However, I cannot imagine it because I was one of the most checked athletes in the world at the time."

Decide for yourself.

THE NOT-SO-INNOCENT IRISH LASS

The list of Ireland's Olympic medal winners in the pool starts and ends with Michelle Smith. The multi-event performer won three gold medals and a bronze medal at the 1996 Centennial Games in Atlanta. There was nothing before. There has been nothing since. And the fact that Smith stands as an anomaly can be linked to, perhaps, the most meteoric—and suspicious—rise the sport has seen.

Between the 1988 (Seoul) and 1992 (Barcelona) Olympics, Smith represented Ireland in seven individual events, never advancing out of the preliminary heats. A best finish of 17th in the 200-meter backstroke in 1988 defined Smith as nothing more than an also-ran, and her performances from 1992—which featured a top finish of 26th in the 400-meter individual medley—once again rendered Smith, then a 22-year-old, as inconsequential on the international stage.

Smith was an athlete who may have dedicated herself to her aquatic endeavors and put forth 100 percent during training sessions. But the sports world is made up of athletes who span the spectrum of talent, and Smith landed somewhere in the very good sector. She was gifted enough to earn coveted Olympic berths but not blessed with the skill to naturally appear on an international podium.

If Smith was an insignificant factor through the 1992 Olympics, the same could not be said of the Irishwoman by the time of the 1994 World Championships in Rome. By that point, Smith was training with Dutchman Erik de Bruin, a two-time Olympic discus thrower who had been handed a four-year ban in 1993 by the International Amateur Athletic Association (IAAF) for a failed doping test.

De Bruin, who Smith married in 1996, possessed a unique view of doping, and the advantages provided by the practice. The Dutchman identified disgraced Canadian sprinter Ben Johnson as an idol, despite Johnson being stripped of his gold medal in the 100-meter dash at the 1988 Seoul Olympics for a positive drug test. His words suggested a blind-eye approach to the potential boost of pharmaceutical assistance.

"Who says doping is unethical?" de Bruin once asked. "Who decides what is ethical? Is politics ethical? Is business ethical? Sport is, by definition, dishonest. Some people are naturally gifted, others have to work very hard. Some people are not going to make it without extra help."

Because Smith was not yet capturing medals on the global stage, the improvements she made between the 1992 Olympics and 1994 World Championships did not send the Irishwoman into an interrogation room.

They should have.

In the two years between Barcelona and Rome, Smith registered improvements that were highly unusual for a fledgling age-group swimmer, let alone a woman in her mid-twenties. In the 400-meter individual medley, Smith went from 26th out of 32 competitors in Barcelona to winning the consolation final in Rome. Her time in the event dropped by 11-plus seconds, an eternity in a sport where improvements are typically measured in fractions of a second. In the 200-meter individual medley, Smith notched a four-second improvement between 1992 and 1994, that jump enabling Smith to place 12th in prelims at the World Champs.

Perhaps the most startling of her performances at the 1994 World Championships arrived in the 200 butterfly, an event she didn't even contest at the Olympic Games two years earlier. Racing the 200 fly for the first time in international waters, Smith placed fifth in the final. The effort came on the heels of a bout of glandular fever that disrupted her training in the months ahead of Rome. There was also a change in Smith's physique, an alteration that could not be overlooked.

"It was a complete metamorphosis," said Gary O'Toole, a two-time Olympian for Ireland.

> The Michelle I remembered had been round and feminine and carried not a lot of excessive weight, but some. I looked at her and said, "My God, what have you been taking?" At the time, she was supposed to have had glandular fever. How could someone stay out of the water and be sick and show up at the world championships 3 1/2 months later looking like a lean, mean fighting machine? This was someone who had trained hard for 12 years and had never been able to shift any of that body fat. Something was going on. I said to her, "Well, whatever you're doing, be careful." She didn't say anything to me.

Smith's notable progressions from 1994 were followed by greater success at the 1995 European Championships, which served as her true breakout competition. The meet was also the precursor for what would unfold at the 1996 Olympic Games in Atlanta. Racing in Vienna, Austria, Smith left the European Champs with gold medals in the 200-meter butterfly and 200-meter individual medley, along with a silver medal in the 400-meter individual medley. Her times, just as they had in Rome, dipped considerably. Smith was a second quicker in the 200-meter butterfly and had improved by another four seconds in the 200-meter individual medley. In the 400-meter individual medley, Smith lopped five seconds off the time she managed in Rome.

With the 100th anniversary of the Modern Olympics approaching in 1996, there was no doubt that Smith would be a medal contender in multiple events. There was also little doubt among rival athletes that something was amiss. Competitors have a keen ability to sense anomalies in their foes, and Smith's performances were off the charts. Her time drops were complemented by a vast change in her physique, a change that mirrored what was seen in East Germany's swimmers during their country's systematic doping program of the 1970s and the 1980s.

It didn't take long in Atlanta for Smith to become one of the most-talked-about stories of the Games. On the opening night of action, Smith blew away the field in the 400-meter individual medley, her winning time of 4:39.18 almost three seconds faster than American silver medalist Allison Wagner, and just under 20 seconds quicker than what Smith posted in the previous Olympiad. Two days later, Smith won her second gold medal, taking the 400-meter freestyle in 4:07.25. The event was relatively new for Smith, whose best at the start of the year was a mere 4:26.

Aside from the 19-second improvement within the year, there was additional controversy tied to the 400 freestyle. Not originally entered in the 400-meter freestyle, officials allowed Smith to participate in the event despite the Olympic Council of Ireland (OCI) missing the entry deadline. It was argued, ultimately before the Court of Arbitration for Sport (CAS), that the Irish Olympic Committee was given incorrect entry information. With Smith entered, American distance legend Janet Evans finished ninth in the preliminary heats and failed to advance to the final. USA Swimming protested Smith's inclusion, but to no avail. Smith's late registration for the 400-meter freestyle was complemented by doping allegations against the Irishwoman.

"The Americans are jealous this swimmer from a little country like Ireland took a gold medal off them," said Pat Hickey, president of the OCI, referring to the 400 I.M. "They are doing all they can to get Michelle Smith thrown out. They couldn't win by appeal, so they are trying another direction with their suggestions about drug taking. There is nothing to justify it."

But there were black-and-white numbers, which, indeed, provided just cause for raised eyebrows. As Smith was congratulated by U.S. president Bill Clinton for her achievements, several athletes spoke freely about what they were witnessing. Included in that group was Evans, who was racing in her third Olympiad in Atlanta.

"Are you asking me if she's on drugs?" Evans said. "Any time someone has a dramatic improvement there's that question. I have heard that question posed in the last few weeks about that swimmer. If you're asking if the accusations are out there, I would say yes."

As allegations flew, Smith continued to flourish, winning her third gold medal in the 200-meter individual medley, and adding a bronze medal in the 200-meter butterfly in her final race. Not surprisingly, Smith became a national hero, citizens of her homeland hailing her accomplishments while ignoring the suspect circumstances surrounding her rise.

The next year, Smith starred at the 1997 European Championships in Seville, Spain. She won her prime event, the 400-meter individual medley, and claimed silver medals in the 400-meter freestyle and 200-meter butterfly. There was also a gold medal in the 200-meter freestyle, her first in that event in international competition.

For all the success Smith had experienced, she had proven to be difficult to monitor outside of the pool. On several occasions, drug testers had been unable to identify the whereabouts of Smith to perform doping-control tests, and Smith's unwillingness to cooperate with doping procedures triggered rebukes from FINA, the world governing body of swimming. Still, she remained eligible to compete and skirted the doping system.

Until the morning of January 10, 1998.

While the World Championships were unfolding in Perth, Australia, Smith was absent from the competition, having suffered injuries in a car accident a few months earlier. But doping officials decided to collect an out-of-competition test from Smith, which follows normal procedure. When the doping officials arrived at Smith's residence, they were forced to stop their car at a padlocked gate. Eventually, Smith walked down the driveway, unlocked the gate, and let the testers into her home.

Over the course of the morning, and with Smith's husband present, testers tried to obtain a urine sample from the athlete. Smith's husband initially indicated the couple was set to travel that morning and Smith did not have time to produce a sample. When testers noted they could travel with the couple and would wait until the athlete was ready, the trip was suddenly called off.

In two separate instances, Smith provided a urine sample, initially filling the testing vial shy of the necessary amount to be collected. When she came back the second time, the doping officials recognized the smell of whiskey emanating from the sample. The officials had Smith complete the appropriate paperwork and filed the sample. In April 1998, it was revealed that Smith faced suspension not for a failed doping test, but for tampering with a sample. The amount of whiskey found in Smith's sample was enough to cause human fatality.

In August 1998, Smith was banned by FINA for four years for tampering with a doping sample. Smith appealed the ban, but the Court of Arbitration for Sport upheld the penalty in 1999, although the ruling allowed Smith to retain her Olympic medals. To this day, Smith has maintained the innocence she proclaimed in her statement following the confirmation of her ban.

"I am deeply saddened by the decision of the court of Arbitration for Sport (CAS) and in particular their decision to prefer circumstantial evidence concerning the manipulation charge as distinct from direct evidence given by me at the hearing of my appeal," Smith said. "I today stand accused of having used banned substances over the course of my career and that was the motive found by the court as to why I would have attempted to manipulate the sample in question."

"I reaffirm what I have always told you, that I have never used any banned substances in the course of my career, nor have I ever been charged by FINA of using any banned substance in the course of my career. I am proud of what I have achieved and assure those who have supported me and believe in me, that my victories in Atlanta and Seville are not hollow and have been achieved without the use of any illegal performance enhancing substance.

"Both I and my husband have been publicly attacked and vilified by various sections of the media and public since I won my first gold medal at the Atlanta Olympics and that makes me deeply unhappy. I still believe that I have been targeted by FINA since my Olympic success and believe that I am, even today, correct in that view, having regard to the disclosures made for the first time by the *Irish Times* of the background to the Out of Competition Doping Control missions that were carried out on me in 1997 and 1998.

"I will forever cherish my moments of victory and hope that those who still believe in me will also cherish their memories of those times. I know that, in the dark days ahead, there will be moments when it will seem all too much to have to deal with. However, I am strong in the knowledge that I have not committed the offense with which I was charged or any other offense and to date no one has proven on a factual basis how the whiskey entered the sample which was tested by the laboratory in Barcelona.

"I would ask you in this difficult time to allow to allow me some privacy to try and come to grips with this decision and to make the necessary plans for my future."

The future for Smith following her ban included a life away from the spotlight she knew as an athlete, and a career as a barrister in Ireland. Her time, too, has been defined as being a poster girl for cheating, and by the willingness to cut corners and take advantage of performance-enhancing drug use to make the leap from an athlete of very good skill to one of elite status.

THE CHINESE CHARADE

The similarities could not be overlooked. Sudden, and massive, drops in time. A revolving cadre of new names. Deep voices. Extraordinary musculature. And, perhaps most important, whispers around the deck.

Just as the East German women emerged from obscurity in the early 1970s and embarked on a nearly two-decade-long reign, Chinese women surfaced in the 1990s to disrupt the hierarchy of the sport. It was eventually proven, through government-overseen documentation, that East Germany ran a systematic doping program in which teenage girls were fed and injected with steroids to build a superpower sports program.

There has never been concrete evidence of a systematic program in China, but spectacular individual improvements and specific periods of domination suggest the reliance on artificial support. Add in the numerous positive doping violations that were recorded during the decade, and only willful ignorance would deny that Chinese efforts in the 1990s were achieved through dishonest means.

At the 1988 Olympic Games in Seoul, China was largely an afterthought, as it captured four medals—three silver and a bronze. While that total did not attract widespread attention, it was a significant improvement over the previous two global championships in which China participated. At the 1984 Olympics, which featured a diluted field due to the Eastern Bloc boycott led by the Soviet Union, China did not earn a single medal in the pool.

Another empty performance was registered at the 1986 World Championships, but there was more to the story than the simple failure to miss the podium. In events in which the country had entries, Chinese athletes produced times that were far from world class and ranked near the bottom of the field. Yet, in two years, there was China with four Olympic medalists and finalists in several other events.

Early signs of a dirty operation had surfaced.

If the 1988 Olympics served as a breakout, the 1991 World Championships and 1992 Olympics confirmed that China was not going to fade away, but instead would become a presence in international waters. After China collected four gold medals, a silver, and a bronze at the World Champs, the Barcelona Olympics brought nine medals—four titles and five silver medals. More, world records started to fall to the nation's athletes.

Although suspicions over the Chinese performances were intensifying, the opposition was cautious to speak out publicly and levy accusations of performance-enhancing drug use. However, that timid approach changed at the 1994 World Championships, where China was unstoppable and looked every bit as unbeatable as the East Germans at the peak of their doping program. In Rome, China prevailed in 12 of the 16 events.

As China pummeled the competition, disgust built among coaches and athletes. One of the first big names to accuse China of orchestrating a systematic doping program was Dennis Pursley, the U.S. National Team director. Watching China sweep the women's relays and set multiple world records was too much for Pursley to take.

"I believe you have to be incredibly naive to ignore the circumstantial evidence," Pursley said.

> The current situation is an exact replica of [East Germany], and it is depriving deserving athletes of the attention and success they deserve. We can't put our heads in the sand again and pretend what we know is happening isn't happening. Our athletes just aren't buying it this time. Common sense tells you that our athletes aren't going to make the major sacrifices required to compete at this level when they know the deck is stacked against them. I have a high level of respect for the expertise of the Chinese coaches. I also have a lot of respect for the dedication of their athletes, but that alone cannot possibly explain how they could have a whole bunch of swimmers improve dramatically in waves, just like the East Germans. The ones here are different than in Barcelona, and we probably won't see the same [athletes] in Atlanta.

It wasn't surprising that China vehemently denied the doping allegations it faced, but the success the country enjoyed lied in the face of common sense. One of the primary defenses used by China and its supporters was the country's population and the statistical opportunity to find top-tier athletes in a land of more than a billion people.

But China long had a population that exceeded its rivals, so why wasn't there a history of success? Cheng Yun-Peng, the Chinese Swimming Association's national technical director, argued the nation featured superb coaches and elite training facilities that enabled its swimmers to excel. The reasoning wasn't accepted.

Ahead of the 1995 Pan Pacific Championships, the swimming federations of the United States, Australia, Japan, and Canada voted to exclude China from the competition. The unity demonstrated a concerted effort to shed light on the doping problems in sport and to specifically highlight the anomalies in China's performances.

"People are suspicious because we are getting stronger very quickly," Cheng said.

> The first thing is that maybe we haven't helped other people understand how hard we train. The second thing is maybe there are some sour grapes. The third thing is that for many years, there have been just Europe and America in swimming, no Chinese, and they can't stand that we caught up to them. Maybe it is a kind of racism, and it makes

us Chinese very angry. We learned from the Americans, the Australians, the Germans, the Hungarians, the Russians, everyone. And we developed a system we thought would work for us. Most of the swimmers I've seen here from other countries are not very strong. Speed depends on power, and power depends on a muscular body. The problem is that big muscles create misunderstandings. As soon as someone sees them, they think doping.

Cheng might have tried to divert suspicions with his words, but he couldn't alter the results of some doping tests that came back positive at the 1994 Asian Games, which were held a month after the World Championships. At the Asian Games, 11 positive tests were returned by Chinese athletes, including world-champion swimmers Lu Bin and Yang Aihua. If nothing else, the news confirmed the suspicions of Pursley and China's foes.

However, with the 1996 Olympic Games rapidly approaching, a leading member of the International Olympic Committee did not want to criticize China, even if clear evidence was at his disposal. Belgium's Prince Alexandre de Merode, the chairman of the IOC's Medica Commission, defended China's positive doping tests from the Asian Games as falling within typical guidelines.

"The Chinese had a delegation of 500 athletes at the Asian Games, and about 10 positive cases is not such a high percentage," de Merode said. "There are no more cases in China than anywhere else. These are epidemics that occur on occasion. There is no politics of systematic doping in China."

As the 1996 Olympics opened, there was major concern China would dominate at the same level it did at the 1994 World Championships. Ultimately, China won six medals in Atlanta, fueled by Le Jingyi capturing gold in the 100 freestyle and silver in the 50 freestyle. The huge drop-off in medal count from the 1994 World Champs to the 1996 Olympics likely resulted from China knowing it was being closely watched and not taking the same measures it did for Rome.

That careful approach was not adhered to a year later, though, as Wu Yanyan obliterated the world record in the 200 individual medley at the Chinese National Games. Wu took nearly two seconds off the previous world record, set by countrywoman Lin Li at the 1992 Olympics. Although Wu did not test positive during her prime days, a doping test in 2000 revealed the use of anabolic steroids.

With Wu's medley standard again raising questions, China arrived at the 1998 World Championships in Perth, Australia, under the microscope, and the country did nothing to convince the globe that it was competing fairly. During a customs check, the luggage of Yuan Yuan, a double medalist at the 1994 World Champs, was found to contain vials of human growth hormone (HGH). The amount of HGH seized from Yuan was enough to supply the entire Chinese roster for the duration of the World Championships. Meanwhile, four Chinese swimmers failed doping tests in Perth, their samples found to contain a masking agent often taken to cover up steroid use.

Although China is not dogged by the same questions it faced in the 1990s, when it had nearly 30 positive doping tests, it has not escaped frequent finger-pointing and positive tests. Before the 2012 Olympics in London, Li Zhesi was disqualified from the Games for a positive doping test. In London, Ye Shiwen won gold medals in the 200 individual medley and 400 individual medley, her performance in the longer event highly questioned when her last lap was faster than the last lap Ryan Lochte posted during his victory in the male version of the event.

Meanwhile, distance ace Sun Yang, a multi-time Olympic champion, was given an eight-year ban in early 2020 for tampering with a doping sample. That incident followed an earlier suspension of Sun for taking a banned medication that he claimed was to treat a heart condition.

Given its history of doping and the shrouded-in-secrecy nature of China, any time an athlete delivers a sensational performance or quickly emerges as a global star, questions are going to be asked and doubts will arise.

"History shows there have been issues," said John Leonard, the former executive director of the American Swimming Coaches Association. "When you have a history of doping like China has, there are going to be doubts."

WHEN THE SUN SET

A look at his competitive portfolio reveals an athlete who ranks among the greatest freestylers in history. Measured by sheer achievements, he ranks alongside the legendary middle-distance and distance names of Ian Thorpe, Vladimir Salnikov, and Don Schollander—all Hall of Fame inductees. Enshrinement was once considered a lock for him, too.

As an Olympian, he has the key to his own lounge, reserved for the only man to capture the distance-freestyle treble—titles in the 200, 400, and 1,500 distances. At the World Championships, he's been golden on 11 occasions, and again is the sole member of a unique club—freestyle champion in the 200, 400, 800, and 1,500 distances.

But Sun Yang is more than an elite athlete and a beloved figure in China. He is a pariah. He is a drug cheat. He's arrogant and unrepentant. He's the enemy of his fellow competitors. And, as of late February 2020, he was in exile, banned for an eight-year period after a second violation of the sport's anti-doping code.

In front of a home crowd at the 2011 World Championships in Shanghai, Sun rose to the top of the sport for the first time, winning the 1,500 freestyle in a word-record time. His closing speed over the final lap was spectacular and ushered in a new era in the middle- and distance-freestyle events. If Sun was within striking distance anywhere near the finish of one of those events, the Chinese star was likely to emerge ahead of the field.

As Sun clocked his first world record, it came with the assistance of Australian coach Denis Cotterell, long regarded as one of his country's top mentors. Interestingly, Cotterell was the longtime coach of Grant Hackett, the two-time Olympic champion in the 1,500 freestyle and world-record holder in the event before Sun's surge.

"I saw his potential, and it's my arena, and it's very reaffirming that you can work with that (skill) and you can produce a result that can interest the world," Cotterell said of Sun.

Whether his talent was too good to be true could have been called into question on the spot, particularly with China's checkered doping history and the nation's tendency to operate off the radar. It's never been unusual for China to conduct meets without the knowledge of the rest of the globe, world-class times often produced in the cover of dark.

Although a few doubts lingered about Sun and his prodigious closing speed, he was largely respected during the early part of his career as a surging youngster. A year after winning three medals at the 2011 World Champs, Sun was superb in his first Olympic Games. In London, he won gold medals in the 400 free and 1,500 free and earned a silver medal in the 200 free. By winning the longer events, Sun became the first man to complete the 400–1,500 double since Salnikov accomplished the feat at the boycotted 1980 Olympics in Moscow. At the previous Olympiad in Montreal, American Brian Goodell also managed the feat.

Sun continued his roll at the 2013 World Championships in Barcelona, where he won triple gold in the 400 free, 800 free, and 1,500 free. But it was also the last time he would compete free of doubt in international competition.

In May of 2014, Sun tested positive for the use of the stimulant trimetazidine, which he used to treat a heart condition. The drug was added to the list of banned substances only four months before Sun tested positive, but athletes are responsible for keeping abreast of changes to the anti-doping code. Consequently, Sun was handed a three-month penalty by the Chinese Swimming Association, but the suspension was not announced until it was served. The undercover penalty earned an admonishment from the World Anti-Doping Agency (WADA), but WADA also decided to not pursue further sanctions due to its belief that Sun did not intend to violate anti-doping rules.

"I have taken many doping tests during years of training and competition and I had never failed one before," Sun said of his 2014 violation. "I was shocked and depressed at that time, but at the same time, it made me cherish my sporting life even more. I will take it as a lesson and be more careful in the future."

Sun's fellow athletes did not see the violation as a minor incident. The mood toward his presence at the 2015 World Championships was sour, Sun receiving little fanfare and adulation for his repeat titles in the 400 freestyle and 800 freestyle, and his silver medal in the 200 freestyle. More, Sun was accused of making contact with Brazilian swimmer Larissa Oliveira in the warmup pool, an incident that triggered anger among Brazilian officials. However, the altercation was dismissed by FINA, the international governing body of the sport, as arising due to a crowded pool.

A tide was clearly building against the Chinese standout and that wave of disapproval came crashing down at the 2016 Olympic Games in Rio de Janeiro.

Before competition started in Rio, Sun got into another warmup pool altercation, this time with rival Mack Horton of Australia. As the men were completing laps, Sun splashed water in Horton's face, which the Aussie took as an attempt to intimidate and distract him. Rather than let the confrontation die down, Horton went on the offensive and publicly called Sun a "drug cheat," an accusation that drew anger from the Chinese Swimming Association and Sun supporters.

"He just kind of splashed me, but I ignored him because I don't have time or respect for drug cheats," Horton said. "He wasn't too happy about that, so he kept splashing me. I just got in and did my thing."

Horton's willingness to speak out against Sun was widely applauded by his fellow athletes, but his performance in the 400 freestyle was equally impactful. Despite being the underdog, Horton beat Sun in their head-to-head showdown, going 3:41.55 to the 3:41.68 of Sun. While Sun rebounded by winning gold in the 200 freestyle, Horton dealt his rival a surprise public setback.

"I don't know if it's a rivalry between me and him, just a rivalry between me and athletes who have tested positive," Horton said after his Olympic triumph.

At the 2017 World Championships, Sun reversed the Olympic outcome with Horton. While Sun won gold to Horton's silver, and took gold in the 200 freestyle, the atmosphere was not dominated by controversy. That quiet was short-lived, though, as the end of the 2018 campaign found Sun caught in the middle of another doping controversy.

In the late evening of September 4, 2018, testing officials from the International Doping Tests and Management company (IDTM) appeared at Sun's residence to obtain samples of the athlete's urine and blood as part of a routine out-of-competition doping test. Initially, Sun submitted to blood testing and a vial of his blood was collected. However, Sun eventually became combative with the testers and refused to supply a urine sample.

Over the course of several hours that bled into the early morning of September 5, Sun and the doping testers were at odds. Sun argued that the testers did not have the proper documentation to prove their status and called his personal doctor, Ba Zhen, to come to the residence. Despite repeated warnings from the testers that Sun's refusal to cooperate would be recorded as a missed doping test, Sun and his camp refused to budge.

Eventually, Sun obtained the vial containing his blood while his mother, who was also present, directed a member of Sun's security team to retrieve a hammer. When the security guard returned, he was directed to smash the blood vial with the hammer, thereby rendering the sample useless for testing.

When the details of the evening were reported to FINA, the governing body had its Doping Panel investigate the incident. The report from FINA found that there was a lack of accreditation with members of the testing team and, therefore, invalidated the sample and freed Sun from any wrongdoing.

> The blood that was initially collected (and subsequently destroyed) was not collected with proper authorization and thus was not properly a "sample." As a result, the sample collection session initiated by IDTM on September 4, 2018, is invalid and void. No FINA DC rule violations can result therefrom. The conduct on the part of the DCA (doping control assistant) is highly improper and extremely unprofessional. This should never happen. Ultimately, the BCA (Blood Collection Assistant) did not testify at the hearing or answer any questions from the athlete.

The Doping Panel is left with significant doubt whether the BCA was properly qualified to draw blood from an athlete.

When FINA released its ruling, there was immediate concern about the personal relationship between the governing body and Sun and whether the organization was protecting the athlete despite actions that violated doping-control protocol. One of the issues that raised concerns was Sun's relationship with FINA executive director Cornel Marculescu, who was seen hugging Sun at the Rio Olympics and had been called a "grandfather to me" by Sun.

Concerns were not limited to those within the sport as WADA chose to appeal the Doping Panel's decision to the Court of Arbitration for Sport (CAS). While the case awaited hearing in front of a three-person panel, the 2019 World Championships brought a revolt from several athletes against Sun's presence at the year's major international competition.

Racing at the World Champs in Gwangju, South Korea, Sun was embroiled in a pair of controversies, both involving the medals podium. After Sun beat Horton in the 400 freestyle, the Australian refused to stand with Sun on the podium during the Chinese National Anthem and refused to partake in the customary photos that take place after the medals ceremony.

"That was his idea to do that," said Australian head coach Jacco Verhaeren of Horton's protest. "Let's put it this way. I understand him very much. He has been very strong and vocal about (doping) in the past. You can only respect him for what he does."

Several days later, after Sun won the gold medal in the 200 freestyle, Great Britain's Duncan Scott followed Horton's podium protest with his own. This time, Sun vented his anger by approaching Scott, who was the bronze medalist, and pointing a finger in his face while yelling, "I'm a winner. You're a loser." Scott simply ignored Sun, allowing his actions to speak. FINA, in what was viewed by athletes as an affront to their push for clean sport, criticized Horton and Scott for making political statements and warned other athletes to not take similar action.

In November 2019, the appeal brought by WADA against Sun was finally heard by the CAS, and in an open forum. Multiple individuals testified, with the hearing lasting from morning into the evening. In late February 2020, the CAS rendered its verdict, which determined that Sun had tampered with a doping test and did not behave appropriately within a doping test. Because Sun had his previous violation from 2014, he was given an eight-year ban, which effectively ended his career.

"It is one thing, having provided a blood sample, to question the accreditation of the testing personnel while keeping the intact samples in the possession of the testing authorities," the CAS wrote in its verdict.

> It is quite another thing, after lengthy exchanges and warnings as to the consequences, to act in such a way that results in destroying the sample containers, thereby eliminating any chance of testing the sample at a later stage. It was striking that, in the course of his testimony, at no point did the athlete express any regret as to his actions, or indicate that, with the benefit of hindsight, it might have been preferable for him to have acted differently. Rather, as the proceedings unfolded, he dug his heels in and, eventually, sought to blame others for the manifest failings that occurred. At no point did he confront the possibility that he might have overreacted in his actions.

Sun's ban by CAS was widely lauded in the swimming community, the likes of Horton, Great Britain's Adam Peaty, South Africa's Chad Le Clos, and Australian Cate Campbell stating that justice was served, and there was an appreciation that clean sport was protected.

For his part, Sun indicated he would appeal the ruling to the Swiss Federal Tribunal and seek to have his eligibility restored.

"This is unfair. I firmly believe in my innocence," Sun said. "I will definitely appeal and let more people know about the truth."

Indeed, Sun followed the appeal process and in late December 2020, his eight-year ban by the CAS was overturned, with his case sent for retrial when it was learned a member of the CAS panel had made disparaging comments about China on social media.

Chapter 8

A RARITY IN THE SPORT

Swimming has long been a white-dominated sport, with black athletes rare to be seen even on the pool deck. But several swimmers have provided sterling moments and served as inspirations for their race.

BREAKING BARRIERS

How does history define the career of Enith Brigitha? The answer depends on the vantage point used to analyze what she accomplished while representing the Netherlands during the 1970s. Through one lens, Brigitha was a victim, robbed of her true achievements by the systematic doping program of East Germany. Through another lens, Brigitha was a barrier-breaker, flourishing as a black athlete in a white-dominated sport.

Emerging as a youth star from the island nation of Curacao in the Netherlands Antilles, Brigitha etched herself as one of the world's most consistent performers during the 1970s, appearing in a pair of Olympic Games and three versions of the World Championships. More, she was a regular medalist at the European Championships.

It didn't take long for Brigitha to become a known entity in the pool; such was her talent in the freestyle and backstroke events. But there was another factor that made the Dutchwoman impossible to miss. On a deck filled with white athletes, Brigitha stood out as one of the few members of her race to step onto a starting block, let alone contend with the world's best.

In Montreal in 1976, Brigitha captured bronze medals in the 100 freestyle and 200 freestyle to become the first black swimmer to stand on the podium at the Olympic Games. The efforts delivered a breakthrough for racial diversity in the sport and arrived 12 years ahead of Anthony Nesty's historic performance. It was at the 1988 Games in Seoul in which Nesty, from Suriname, edged American Matt Biondi by 0.01 for gold in the 100 butterfly.

What Brigitha achieved in Montreal fit neatly with the progression she showed in the preceding years. After advancing to the finals of three events at the 1972 Olympic Games in Munich, Brigitha was a medalist in her next five international competitions. It was this consistency that eventually led to Brigitha's 2015 induction into the International Swimming Hall of Fame.

"(It meant a lot) to be told by a coach, 'We believe in you. You are going to reach the top,'" Brigitha said during her induction speech into the Hall of Fame. "It is so important that people express trust in you and your qualities when you are working on your career. I am very grateful to all the people who were there for me when I needed them the most."

Brigitha's first medals in international competition were claimed at the inaugural World Championships. In Belgrade, Yugoslavia, Brigitha earned a silver medal in the 200 backstroke and added a bronze medal in the 100 freestyle. That performance was followed a year later by a five-medal haul at the European Championships, with four of those medals earned in individual action. Aside from winning a silver medal in the 200 freestyle, Brigitha collected bronze medals in the 100 freestyle and both backstroke events.

Bronze medals were added at the 1975 World Championships in the 100 freestyle and 200 freestyle and carried Brigitha into her second Olympiad. A silver medal in the 100 freestyle marked her lone individual podium finish at the 1977 European Championships, while the 1978 World Champs did not yield a medal and led the Dutch star into retirement.

Despite her success, which twice led to Brigitha being named the Netherlands' Athlete of the Year, her career is also defined by what could have been. No two athletes were more wronged by East Germany's systematic doping program than Brigitha and the United States' Shirley Babashoff. At the 1976 Olympics, Babashoff won silver medals behind East Germans in three events, prompting the American to accuse—accurately, it was eventually proved—her East German rivals of steroid use. For her willingness to speak out, Babashoff was vilified in the press, called a sore loser, and tagged with the nickname "Surly Shirley."

Brigitha experienced similar misfortune while racing against the East German machine. Of the 11 individual medals won by the Dutchwoman in international action, she was beaten by at least one swimmer from the

German Democratic Republic in 10 of those events. Her bronze medal in the 100 freestyle is the performance that stands out.

In the final of the 100 free in Montreal, Brigitha placed behind East Germany's Kornelia Ender and Petra Priemer. Upon the fall of the Berlin Wall and the release of thousands of documents of the East German Secret Police, known as the Stasi, it was revealed that Ender and Priemer were part of a systematic doping program that spanned the early 1970s into the late 1980s and provided countless East German athletes with enhanced support, primarily in the form of the anabolic steroid Oral-Turinabol.

Had Ender and Priemer not been steroid-fueled foes or been disqualified for their use of performance-enhancing drugs, Brigitha would have been the first black swimmer to win an Olympic gold medal, and her Hall of Fame induction would have come much earlier. Ender was a particular hurdle for Brigitha, as she won gold medals in six of the events in which Brigitha medaled on the international stage.

"Some gold medals didn't come my way for reasons that are now well-known, namely the use of drugs by my rivals," Brigitha said. "That gold has come my way [through induction into] the Hall of Fame. I thank the women who set an example and those who crossed the line with confidence and respect, but without the use of drugs."

Calls have frequently been made for East German medals—Olympic, World Championships, and European Champs—to be stripped and reallocated to the athletes who followed in the official results. However, officials from the International Olympic Committee and FINA, swimming's global governing body, have refused to meet these demands.

Babashoff has been a vocal proponent of reallocation, citing the need to right a confirmed wrong. If nothing else, she has sought recognition from the IOC and FINA that an illicit program was at work and damaged careers. Those pleas, however, have fallen short of triggering change, the IOC unwilling to edit the record book.

"Every once in a while, we've looked at the issue hypothetically," once stated Canadian Dick Pound, a 1960 Olympic swimmer and former vice president of the International Olympic Committee. "But it's just a nightmare when you try to rejigger what you think might have been history. For the IOC to step in and make these God-like decisions as to who should have gotten what . . . It's just a bottomless swamp."

Even without an Olympic gold medal that can be considered her right, Brigitha shines as a pioneer. In a sport in which black athletes were rare participants, Brigitha compiled an exquisite portfolio and proudly carried her race to heights that had never before been realized.

NEW TERRITORY

In any stopwatch sport, a hundredth of a second can define history. It's less than the blink of an eye. But it can be the difference between gold and silver. It might be the edge that awards an individual icon status. That miniscule measure of time could be the margin that—for better or worse—occupies an athlete's mind to the grave.

In the career of Anthony Nesty, a hundredth of a second built a legacy.

To be the first person to accomplish any task is a monumental feat. Neil Armstrong has his legacy. So does Charles Lindbergh. Edmund Hillary and Mount Everest will forever be linked. Roger Bannister is also known as a legend.

In the sport of swimming, Nesty registered one of the biggest cultural breakthroughs ever seen, as he became the first black swimmer to win an Olympic gold medal, managing the accomplishment at the 1988 Games in Seoul. In dramatic fashion, Nesty rallied in the final strokes to overcome American Matt Biondi, the heavy favorite.

Born in Trinidad, Nesty and his family moved to the small South American nation of Suriname before his first birthday. With a population of only 500,000, Suriname was hardly known for producing standout athletes. Yet, Nesty showed a gift in the water, as he rapidly became one of the world's premier butterfly specialists. By the age of 15, he had competed at the Pan American Games, and as a 16-year-old, he was an Olympian, having placed 21st in the 100-meter butterfly at the 1984 Games in Los Angeles.

The potential for greatness prompted Nesty to move to the United States following his first Olympiad and enroll at the Bolles School in Florida, where he was trained by Gregg Troy and molded into an Olympic title contender. The gold medalist in the 100 butterfly at the 1987 Pan American Games, Nesty carried momentum into Seoul, even if he wasn't the top contender for gold.

As the Seoul Games approached, Biondi was hyped as much as the impending sprint duel between track stars Ben Johnson of Canada and American Carl Lewis. Biondi was the most dominant U.S. star in years and his seven-event schedule prompted speculation whether he could challenge the seven gold medals won by countryman Mark Spitz at the 1972 Olympics in Munich.

Ultimately, Biondi won five golds, a silver, and a bronze in his second Olympiad, with Nesty denying Biondi by the slimmest of margins in the 100 fly. Bolting to the lead off the start, Biondi was in command throughout the race. But as the swimmers neared the finish, Biondi was caught between strokes and glided into the wall. Nesty, meanwhile, perfectly timed his finish, and when the scoreboard flashed the results, Nesty's mark of 53.00 clipped the 53.01 of the American stalwart.

"At the [75-meter mark], I knew I was top three and my goal at that point and time was to get a medal," Nesty said.

> So I just charged the last 25, put my head down and kept my strokes long. For me, I saw [Biondi] out of the corner of my right eye and he was way ahead, so there was no way I could have caught him. But obviously he glided in the last two meters and thought he had the race won, and fortunately for me, my stroke count was right on that day. It was pretty lucky, but sometimes it's good to have a little luck. It's the old cliché that the race is never over until you touch the wall, and that held true. It was a very special moment and a big deal back home in Suriname.

The gold medalist in the 100 butterfly at the 1988 Olympics, Anthony Nesty, is now the head coach of the men's program at the University of Florida. Peter H. Bick.

It was also a big deal for the sport. Only once before had a black athlete earned a medal in Olympic competition, as the Netherlands' Enith Brigitha won a pair of bronze medals at the 1976 Games in Montreal. Thanks to his perfectly executed race, Nesty was even better and ended nearly 100 years of futility for his race atop the Olympic medals podium.

Nesty was relatively subdued at the finish, and he was soft-spoken during a deckside interview with CBS Sports' John Naber, a 1976 Olympic champion in multiple events who ventured into the broadcast field. Conversely, Biondi did not struggle for words.

"I swam 99 meters like an Olympic champion but couldn't fit in another stroke in the 100th meter," Biondi wrote in a diary he kept for *Sports Illustrated* during the 1988 Olympics. "I was too close to the wall. I had to glide in, and Anthony Nesty of Suriname out-touched me. I had been winning the race easily the whole way. It's been eating me up. After all, what's a 100th of a second? Could I have won with longer fingernails? A slightly quicker start? Looking at the tape of the race just makes me sick to my stomach."

The showdown between Nesty and Biondi was mimicked two decades later by American Michael Phelps and Serbia's Milorad Cavic. At the 2008 Olympics in Beijing, Phelps finished ahead of Cavic by 0.01 in the 100 butterfly. In the more recent duel, Cavic glided into the wall at the finish while Phelps took an extra half-stroke just before the wall to narrowly prevail.

Nesty's upset victory over Biondi brought him instant star status. He was mobbed by crowds in the street, hailed with a parade, and had a plane named after him by Suriname Airlines. If that attention wasn't enough, Nesty's image was slapped on commemorative stamps and coins, and an image of him flying through the water even adorned the 25-guilder bank note.

"Going into the Olympics, I always felt I could make the finals," Nesty said. "Any time you make the top eight, you have a chance. You have to put yourself in position to do well. My dad was there, and it was a special moment. It was my second Olympics, and the first one didn't go so well. I was more prepared and fortunate enough to touch the wall first."

"It was an awesome experience. Any time you go to the Olympics and compete for your country, it's an honor and something you have for the rest of your life. In my case, I was fortunate enough to touch the wall first. Growing up in Suriname and as [a] little kid going to all these Caribbean meets, you always dream of being the best in the world."

If Nesty's success was expected to open the door to a greater number of black athletes reaching the podium at major international competitions, that was not the case. Since Nesty's title-winning effort, only two other black athletes have won individual gold at the Olympic Games: the United States' Anthony Ervin and Simone Manuel. While Ervin won gold medals in the 50 freestyle at the 2000 and 2016 Olympics, Manuel was the Olympic champ in the 100 free at the 2016 Games in Rio de Janeiro.

The Seoul Games only accounted for a portion of Nesty's success, as he went on to win the gold medal in the 100 butterfly at the 1989 Pan Pacific Championships and at the 1991 World Championships. Those victories were complemented by a bronze medal in the event at the 1992 Olympics in Barcelona. Inducted into the International Swimming Hall of Fame in 1998, Nesty served as an assistant coach at his alma mater, the University of Florida, from 1998 to 2018, when he was named the head coach of the school's men's team.

Although he is now known for developing the next legion of standout swimmers, Nesty will always be remembered for his breakthrough triumph in Seoul.

"I don't think of it much, but I know my place in history," he said.

> My philosophy is that I had a great career as an athlete, but my goal now is to be the best coach I can be for the athletes (at the University of Florida). That said, it's obviously a great honor, especially when I go to Suriname. They're still celebrating after 25 years and it's such a sense of pride for a small country like Suriname, and everyone who had a hand in my success should feel a sense of pride.

A UNIQUE ROAD TRAVELED

Enshrinement into the International Swimming Hall of Fame awaits Anthony Ervin. The date just needs to be determined. It's the type of honor appropriate for a two-time individual Olympic champion. Yet, no matter what Ervin has achieved in the sport, the sprint star will always be followed by a simple question: How good could he have been?

One of the iconic lines from the 1993 film *A Bronx Tale* goes like this: "The saddest thing in life is wasted talent." The quotation in the movie was initially spoken by Hollywood legend Robert De Niro and identified unfulfilled potential as an unfortunate characteristic of some lives. In a way, Ervin fits the quote almost perfectly, but with a happy ending written into the epilogue.

Coming out of high school and entering the storied program of the University of California-Berkeley, Ervin was viewed as a savant, much like a youthful piano genius or art prodigy. He was pure talent and raw speed, and his sprint future was filled with possibility. It wasn't a matter of if Ervin would excel at the highest level. It was a matter of when.

"Anthony's got the most efficient freestyle I've ever seen," said United States Olympic coach David Marsh, who coached Ervin on the road to Rio. "That's been the case since he was young. He's just a barracuda in the water."

Barracudas are described as being ferocious predators, and given Ervin's cerebral approach and predominantly reserved demeanor, the comparison seems off. But barracudas are also known for being opportunistic, full of surprise, and rely on bursts of speed to take down their prey. In this manner, the description was appropriate, matching Ervin's sprint prowess and ability to surprise his rivals by rekindling the talent he displayed early in his career.

Upon arrival in Berkeley, Ervin didn't waste any time establishing himself as a sprint phenom, as he captured NCAA titles in the 50 freestyle and 100 freestyle during his freshman year. Those victories not only confirmed Ervin's precocious talent but sent him into preparation for the 2000 Olympic campaign with considerable momentum.

Sixteen years, from 2000 to 2016, separated Anthony Ervin's Olympic victories in the fifty freestyle. Peter H. Bick.

Ervin was in the perfect atmosphere as he readied for the 2000 Olympic Trials. In addition to working with sprint guru Mike Bottom, his assistant coach at Cal, Ervin trained in a setting that was stacked with standouts. Following the collegiate season, Bottom oversaw The Race Club, a training group that included Ervin, American star Gary Hall Jr., and Poland's Bart Kizierowski, a European sprint champion. Each day, the men battled across the pool, sharpening their skills with the support of one another.

In Hall, Ervin found himself in a balancing-act situation. Although they pushed each other as teammates, they were also chasing the same goal: Olympic gold. Under those circumstances, maintaining a healthy environment is not always an easy task and one that Bottom had to delicately manage. At the Olympic Trials, the difficulty of the scenario revealed itself.

"There was an uncomfortable flare-up at the Olympic Trials," Hall said. "It was basically a brief snarling thing where we growled at each other. I forget what exactly it was over. I immediately wrote it off as the tensions of Trials. We both got over it immediately. Other than that one inconsequential exchange, I have always gotten on well with Anthony."

Indeed, Hall and Ervin deftly maneuvered through their brief blowup, with Hall setting an American record and Ervin following in second place in the 50 freestyle at Trials to earn berths to the 2000 Olympic Games in Sydney. That finish was merely a precursor of what was to come on a bigger stage.

At the Sydney Games, Hall and Ervin were viewed as medal contenders, along with reigning Olympic champion Alexander Popov of Russia and the Netherlands' Pieter van den Hoogenband. In the final, it was Hall and Ervin who best handled the pressure of the moment. At the wall, Hall and Ervin looked to the scoreboard and saw matching times of 21.98 next to their names. It took a few seconds for the tandem to process the outcome, with Hall and Ervin eventually realizing they tied for the gold medal, their months of head-to-head practices delivering a shared honor.

In that moment, Ervin became the first American swimmer of black heritage to win a gold medal. Born to a Jewish mother and African American father, Ervin also followed Suriname's Anthony Nesty (1988) as just the second black swimmer to win an Olympic title. For the 19-year-old Ervin, however, the cultural significance wasn't something he felt should be headline worthy.

"I have always been proud of my heritage," Ervin said. "But I don't think of it in terms of first of this, first of that. It is like people are trying to pin it down to one definitive thing. I never thought about it. In the nature of American society today, I would think having diverse blood would not be a big deal."

Ervin also left Sydney with a silver medal as a member of the U.S. 400 freestyle relay and pegged as a future star in sprinting. By the next year, he was the world champion in both the 50 freestyle and 100 freestyle, his trajectory exactly where it was anticipated. But by the 2003 World Championships, Ervin's passion had started to wane, and he was out of the sport shortly after.

For the next seven years, Ervin was away from the sport on a competitive level, his vast potential wasting away. While he occasionally gave lessons to young swimmers, Ervin was a traveling soul. He bounced around to various locations, slept on friends' couches, and played guitar in several bands. He also smoked cigarettes and used illegal drugs, not exactly habits typical of a former world-class athlete. Ervin also auctioned off his Olympic gold medal for a little more than $17,000, the proceeds donated to relief efforts following the 2004 Indian Ocean tsunami that claimed the lives of thousands.

"During eight years of retirement, Tony went through what is too often common to the highest-level athletes who retire," Marsh said. "He was a lost soul without a grip on a routine or pillar that would help him gain clarity for his next steps."

Eventually, Ervin arrived at a point where he yearned to find a more settled place in life, and he saw that opportunity via a comeback to the sport in which he once excelled. In 2011, Ervin started training with modest goals, uncertain where this comeback was headed. He quickly learned it would lead him back to the spotlight.

"I really felt like I had accomplished every goal I had set out to," Ervin said of leaving the pool behind.

> It became time to go back and reclaim some of the stuff I had sacrificed along the way. I was kind of shot down this tunnel. As a youth, as most people are, you're not really given a ton of options for a variety of reasons. When something sticks, people often stay with it. For whatever reason, I couldn't do that. I was convinced the grass would be greener somewhere else. Or, at the least, if I did make the journey that I would see the other side of that horizon, whatever was there. I think everybody's got that to a certain degree. But I certainly had a lot of angst and resistance toward being pushed in the direction I had always been going. I really just needed freedom, so I took it.

If Ervin's absence was necessary to find inner peace, it also acted as a chance for Ervin to find a renewed hunger.

At the 2012 Olympic Trials, Ervin earned an invitation to the London Games, where he finished fifth in the 50 freestyle and embarked on a path that would produce greater achievements in the years ahead. He followed with a sixth-place effort in the 50 freestyle at the 2013 World Champs and while he missed the final of the 50 free at the 2015 World Champs, Ervin was still producing fast times and enjoying his second life in the sport.

"For me, it's the best job in the world," Ervin said. "I get to work out and take care of my body. I enjoy the company of younger people. They keep you young. Although my own success is a vanity, I never said sport itself was meaningless, just my own success. I think sport is great. It's a beautiful thing and it leads to beautiful lives."

With a rekindled love for the pool and a new perspective on his life, Ervin made 2016 a banner year. For the third time, Ervin was the runner-up in the 50 freestyle at the United States Olympic Trials, but he turned that finish into greater gains at the Games in Rio de Janeiro. Advancing through the prelims and semifinals comfortably, Ervin saved his best effort for the final, where he churned out a career-best time of 21.40 to edge France's Florent Manaudou, the defending Olympic champion, by a hundredth of a second.

At 35 years old, Ervin became the oldest male champion in Olympic swimming history and wrote the latest chapter in a career of ups and downs. More, the 16-year gap between Ervin's first Olympic crown and his second gold medal served as further proof of his sheer skill.

"When I touched the wall, I saw a one," Ervin said of his triumph in Rio. "There was kind of an absurdity, a surrealness to it all. I smiled and laughed. It just seems so unlikely. What happened (in my life) is what happened. It's all contributed to what I've done—the good things, the bad things, the difficult things, the highs, the lows. It all stacks into building me into who I am now".

During the opening act of his career, Ervin hesitated to discuss his heritage and the dearth of black swimmers in the sport. But with more life experience, Ervin used his platform following the 2016 Olympics to focus on issues beyond what transpired between the lane lines. At one point, Ervin knelt during the playing of the National Anthem during a 2017 meet. That gesture followed the decision of NFL quarterback Colin Kaepernick to kneel during the Star-Spangled Banner to raise awareness of racial inequality.

Ervin also paid tribute to his mother's heritage by competing in the 2017 Maccabiah Games, a global sports competition featuring Jewish athletes. The combination of recognizing both his African American and Jewish roots was an illustration of Ervin seeing the big picture and not just

Anthony Ervin is frequently called the most gifted sprinter to step on the blocks. Peter H. Bick.

focusing on the outcomes of races. Ervin has also emphasized the importance of opportunity for all, having a strong support system, and understanding the meaning of family and friends.

"The American dream is for anyone, without exception, whether you're a boy or a girl, no matter what the shade of your skin or the shape of your eye, with no regard to who you love nor the beliefs you hold that give you peace, and for that matter where you come from," Ervin said. "If you want to pursue the American dream, the strength of those people around you will always overcome those who would attempt to limit or destroy it."

In sports, the outcomes of games and races are stressed above all else. In the case of most athletes, how they perform carries the greatest weight and defines who they are. Ervin, though, is an anomaly. Although he has risen to the top of his sport in two Olympiads, Ervin's approach has placed equal emphasis on the journey traveled.

"He was the special sauce to our group," Marsh said of Ervin's impact on his teammates. "He was the guy who came in and just added that extra context to what we were doing. His context was, 'Guys, this is just a piece of your life and it's part of your process.' When you've done everything from living on the streets of New York to contemplating suicide, you get that this is (just) swimming."

MAKING AN IMPACT

Ask a fan to recall the greatest memory from Cullen Jones' career, and two options will be presented. One choice is Jones' third-leg contribution on the U.S. 400-meter freestyle relay that won gold at the 2008 Olympic Games in Beijing. The second option is Jones capturing the silver medal in the 50 freestyle at the 2012 Games in London.

Ask a fan to recall the greatest memory from Simone Manuel's career, and a single option comes to mind. Until the day she is inducted into the International Swimming Hall of Fame, Manuel will be recalled for becoming the first African American female swimmer to claim Olympic gold when she tied for the 100 freestyle title at the 2016 Games in Rio de Janeiro.

Together, Jones and Manuel will also be remembered—and more importantly from a societal standpoint—for the impact they have had on fostering growth within their sport in the black community.

It is not a mystery that swimming has long been a lily-white sport, with African American participation overwhelmed by the enrollment of white athletes. Segregation no doubt played a role in few blacks getting involved in the middle of the twentieth century, as many pools were deemed "white only." But it is also the truth that other sports—namely, basketball and football—were so ingrained in black athletic culture that swimming was an afterthought.

Jones and Manuel have set out to change that dynamic.

"If you line up 10 African-American kids, seven of those 10 won't know how to swim," Jones said.

> It's harsh to put it that way, but it's the truth. It's so staggering, and when you put that image in people's minds, it's a big deal and it's a big problem. I think the reason is because we don't see swimming as a life skill in the U.S. and we need to change that. Fortunately, we're trying to do this before an unfortunate incident happens. People understand how important swimming is after something has already happened. What we need to do is get ahead of that, and it's simple. It's just swim lessons.

To emerge in a place where their voices held sway, Jones and Manuel had to first overcome the odds stacked against them. As they rose through the age-group ranks, black role models in the sport were not readily available. But Jones and Manuel let their skill sets speak for themselves, and as

Olympic champion Cullen Jones has been on a mission to promote water safety within the African American community. Peter H. Bick.

much as they did not fit the swimmer mold from a historical race perspective, their talent could not be overlooked.

From 2003 to 2006, Jones established himself as an up-and-coming sprint star at North Carolina State University, with his senior year producing an NCAA title in the 50-yard freestyle. What Jones showed during his collegiate years could not be missed, and by the summer after his graduation, he had the opportunity to prove his worth on the international stage.

At the 2006 Pan Pacific Championships, Jones officially introduced himself to the world by winning the 50 freestyle, an effort that launched him toward a silver medal at the next year's World Championships. In a matter of five years, Jones went from mid-level recruit to one of the world's premier sprinters.

The medals won by Jones on the global scene also put him within striking distance of joining a select group of black athletes as Olympic medalists in the pool. As Jones prepared for the United States Olympic Trials in 2008, he had only a few places to look for inspiration within his own race. While Dutchwoman Enith Brigitha won bronze medals in the 100 freestyle and 200 freestyle at the 1976 Olympics, Suriname's Anthony Nesty won gold in the 100 butterfly at the 1988 Games in Seoul.

From the United States, there were only two names that jumped out. In 2000, Anthony Ervin, born to a Jewish mother and African American father, shared the gold medal in the 50 freestyle at the 2000 Olympics in Sydney. Meanwhile, Maritza Correia earned a silver medal as a prelim swimmer in the 400 freestyle relay at the 2004 Games in Athens.

Although his goal for the 2008 Olympics in Beijing was to challenge for the gold medal in the 50 freestyle, Jones produced mixed results at the United States Trials. The positive from the competition was Jones' qualification for 400 freestyle relay duty. The negative was a pair of third-place finishes in the sprint-freestyle events relegated Jones to spectator status.

If his individual whiff bothered Jones in his Olympic debut, it wasn't obvious when he joined Michael Phelps, Garrett Weber-Gale, and Jason Lezak for the 400 freestyle relay. The United States entered that race as an underdog to France but emerged with its first Olympic title in the event since 1996 when Lezak, on the strength of the fastest 100-meter split in history, ran down French anchor Alain Bernard. Handling the third leg, Jones contributed a split of 47.65.

"I've been on Cloud Nine since we won the gold," Jones said. "I was shaking behind the blocks. I was so nervous. It was my first Olympics, and I wanted to really perform well because I had three other guys that were depending on me to swim fast. All the preparation, all the training that I'd done prepared me for it."

The success in Beijing made Jones a familiar name in the sport and provided him with a platform to discuss issues that were personally meaningful and important for the black community. Following his Olympic experience, Jones started to discuss a life-threatening event that took place when he was five years old. Enjoying a day with his family at a water park, the inner tube in which Jones was riding down a slide flipped over and Jones, unable to swim, was caught underwater for 30 seconds. Losing consciousness, Jones had to be rescued by a lifeguard and resuscitated. Shortly thereafter, Jones was enrolled in swim lessons.

Jones has emphasized the importance of swim lessons for young children, and particularly for African American kids. As part of the USA Swimming Foundation's Make a Splash initiative, Jones has spread the word that 70 percent of African American children cannot swim, and their likelihood of drowning is three times higher than the risk for white

children. He has also conducted numerous clinics around the United States
to drive interest in the sport among minorities.

"There's no reason why every child shouldn't learn how to swim,"
Jones said.

> Kids love to be near water and just like you wouldn't allow your kids to
> ride in a car without a seatbelt or play football without pads, you can't
> send your children to the pool without proper lessons. The reason chil-
> dren are not swimming is because parents are not making it necessary
> that their child learns how to swim. Once parents learn how important
> it is to learn to swim, we can start dropping drowning rates.

In conjunction with his push to bring greater awareness about water
safety in the black community, Jones continued to seek that elusive
individual medal from the Olympic Games. The 2010 and 2011 campaigns, however, did not do anything to promote confidence he would
be able to reach his target. After finishing sixth in the 50 free at the Pan
Pacific Championships in 2010, Jones bombed at the next year's World
Championships, failing to advance out of the preliminaries.

The Olympic year brought different results. Riding the momentum
he generated by successfully navigating the gauntlet that is the United States
Trials, Jones captured the silver medal in the 50 freestyle for the biggest
individual effort of his career. For good measure, he added a silver medal
as a member of the American 400 freestyle relay.

A third Olympic berth was not to be in 2016, but Jones remained a
factor in the aquatic world through his dedication to a cause that has grown
in meaning during his involvement.

"We started this initiative in 2009, and we've reached nearly four million kids," Jones said. "I would say that I'm as proud with the work that
I've done with Make A Splash as I am with my own career. We're really
breaking the cycle. We have to make swimming a life skill in this country."

The proof of Jones' influence can be seen in what Manuel has
accomplished. Making her Team USA debut at the 2014 Pan Pacific
Championships, where she earned a bronze medal in the 100 freestyle,
Manuel has called Jones an inspiration, citing his career as a blueprint for
her development.

Growing up in Texas, Manuel was one of the few African American
athletes on deck as she moved through the age-group system and, eventually, started to attend more significant competitions. The way Jones spoke of
his experiences provided Manuel with confidence she would find her niche

Although she was off the radar as a title contender in the 100 freestyle
at the 2016 Olympics, Manuel possessed an inner belief she could beat the

best in the sport. She proved her faith accurate when she tied for gold in Rio with Canadian teenager Penny Oleksiak, both women touching the wall in 52.70. The effort made Manuel the first black female swimmer to win Olympic gold and the first woman of her race to win an individual medal since Enith Brigitha 40 years earlier.

"It can only be positive," Jones said of Manuel's gold-medal effort. "I know that when she comes home, that's when I think everything's going to hit her. What she's actually done is change the face of swimming. She's an instant icon. There are going to be young girls that look at their parents and say, 'I want to be like her,' and that's an amazing, beautiful thing. It's something special that Simone did."

Manuel went on to add a silver medal in 50 freestyle and gold and silver medals in relay action. During her press conferences in Rio, she was repeatedly asked about being a barrier-breaker, and Manuel spoke of the desire to—one day—not have to answer those types of questions, as she wanted to be recognized only as "Simone, the swimmer, and not, Simone, the black swimmer." But she also embraced her identity and her ability to influence young African American girls who may not have sought out the pool if they hadn't watched Manuel excel at the Olympics. Manuel, too, focused on bringing Americans together, particularly with several cases in the news revolving around police brutality against black men.

"I definitely struggled with it a lot coming into the race tonight," Manuel said after winning her gold.

> I tried to take the weight of the black community off my shoulders. It's something I carry with me being in this position. This medal is not just for me but for the African-Americans who came before me . . . and for the people who come behind me. I would like one day for there to be more of us. I'm hoping I can give some people hope that even though there are some tough things going on in the world, you just have to keep fighting. Our ancestors did. What we do [now] is a reflection of what they have done for us. It's also a platform for what will happen in the future. We just have to keep fighting and persevering to try to make change.

Since Rio, Manuel has established herself as one of her sport's most-clutch performers. Despite her status as an Olympic champion, Manuel was not viewed as a gold-medal challenger in the sprints at the 2017 World Championships. All she did was win the title in the 100 freestyle, add a bronze in the 50 freestyle, and anchor a pair of triumphant American relays.

Two years later, she was in the underdog position again, only to rise to the occasion and win world crowns in the 50 free and 100 free, the

Simone Manuel shared gold in the 100 freestyle at the 2016 Olympics, marking the first time an African American woman won an individual Olympic title in swimming. Peter H. Bick.

longer distance in an American-record time. With an expanded schedule, she added five relay medals and elevated her status as an athlete who thrives under pressure.

"I feel like every time I step on the blocks, I have a chance to win," Manuel said. "I think it would be a waste of time to step up on the blocks shooting for second or third or fourth, or whatever place besides first. Every time I step up on the blocks, I'm there to win. I don't get distracted by what other people are doing or what people are saying. I focus on myself, stay on my path and keep pressing forward."

Forging forward is what Manuel and Jones will continue to do in terms of raising awareness about drowning rates in the black community. Through speaking engagements and clinics, they will publicize the importance of water safety for young children and serve as role models for African American athletes looking to replicate their success in the pool.

"When I was 12 years old, I came home from swim practice, and I asked my mom why there weren't many people that looked like me in the sport of swimming," Manuel said. "We did some research, and we looked up African-American swimmers. If you start showing some models with African-American children or Asian children or Indian children, then you're showing people that the demographic is different than just white people swim."

Chapter 9

GREATEST COACHES

Without a certain level of pure talent, athletes will not reach the top of their sport. Yet, they will also not reach the top of the mountain without elite coaching and guidance from an individual who maps their preparation.

BOB BOWMAN

It's not unusual for parents, fans, or even some journalists, to predict greatness for an athlete at a young age. It's easy to get caught up in early success and allow the mind to run away with a combination of hopes and expectations. It's an entirely different scenario for a coach to make grandiose predictions and establish a carefully designed pathway to Olympic success for a boy whose voice has yet to change.

Then again, Michael Phelps—ultimately with 28 Olympic medals—was anything but an ordinary youngster. Rather, he possessed generational talent, and it was Bob Bowman who recognized this rare skill set at the North Baltimore Aquatic Club and was willing to utter a few words that may have sounded premature—if not crazed.

A little more than a year after he started to coach Phelps, Bowman knew he had to have a critical conversation with his protégé's mother, Debbie. It was not going to be a simple chat, either. No, this talk was about much more than attending Sectionals or Junior Nationals. It was about a then-12-year-old competing on the biggest of stages.

"I told her that things are going to change, and they'll never be the same," Bowman said. "I wanted everyone to be ready for 2000. Debbie

Bob Bowman is the man who molded Michael Phelps into the most decorated Olympian of all time. Peter H. Bick.

said, 'Oh, no, not Michael. He's too young.' But I told her, 'What are we going to do to stop it? When he's ready to go, he's got to let it go.' "

As the cliché goes, the rest is history.

One day, Bowman will be enshrined in the International Swimming Hall of Fame, and his display will undoubtedly highlight his relationship with Phelps. From Sydney to Athens, from Beijing to London and Rio de Janeiro serving as the cherry topping, Phelps and Bowman crafted a masterpiece of a career.

Nothing Bowman did as the architect was put into action without deep thought and consideration. Heck, ahead of the 2004 Olympics in Athens, time was set aside to have Phelps' wisdom teeth removed, just in case they would prove problematic at an inopportune time in training, at the Olympic Trials or at the Games.

Bowman and Phelps first made their presence known—as Bowman foresaw—at the 2000 Olympic Games in Sydney. One month after Phelps became the youngest American male swimmer to qualify for the Olympics since 1932, the 15-year-old finished fifth in the 200 butterfly at the Games. Bowman saw the moment as an opportunity to motivate his pupil for the following year.

"Michael and I left Sydney hungry for more success," Bowman said.

> While a fifth-place showing at 15 was respectable, we both knew he was capable of much more. I remember giving him his training set the

day after his 200 final, and on the corner of the page, I wrote: "WR Austin." I didn't have to explain it. He already knew it meant world record. His next chance to do it would be in Austin the next April at the World Championship Trials. It was a way of refocusing and resetting our goals. Of course, he came through that April with his first world record in the 200 fly. Sydney inspired us to keep working and to really ask what was possible in the sport of swimming.

As the ensuing years showed, much was achievable for the pair—so much, in fact, that it is best to organize the highlights in the following list:

- At 15, in March 2001, Phelps delivered on Bowman's aforementioned written instruction. The performance made Phelps the youngest male swimmer to set an individual world record. He followed that summer by winning his first world title.
- At the 2003 World Championships, his first global titles featuring a multi-event schedule, Phelps captured gold medals and set world records in the 200 butterfly, 200 individual medley, and 400 individual medley.
- Phelps' first Olympic crown arrived in his first event of the 2004 Games in Athens, the 400 individual medley. Phelps went on to win a record eight medals in the home of the Olympics, including six gold.
- The next Olympiad was the crowning moment for Bowman and Phelps, with Phelps winning eight gold medals and setting seven world records in Beijing in 2008. The performance is considered the greatest showing in Olympic history and one of the greatest achievements in sporting lore.
- Phelps went on to excel in two more Games—London and Rio—capturing six medals in each Olympiad to bring his career total to an untouchable 28 Olympic medals, 10 more than the next-highest total. More, his 23 gold medals stand well clear of the next-highest total of nine.
- For his career, Phelps set 29 individual world records, won 26 world championships, and claimed 83 medals in international competition, including 61 between the Olympics and the World Champs.

"He's a father figure to me," Phelps said of Bowman. "He knew how to get the most out of me in the water, but he's helped me through some of the worst times in my life. He's been there every step of the way, and I'm forever thankful. I've said this all along. I don't think I could have accomplished what I did with any other coach."

Although Bowman will always be initially linked to Phelps, his success goes beyond molding the career of the greatest swimmer in history. Bowman has also crafted the career of Allison Schmitt, an eight-time Olympic medalist who won five medals at the 2012 Games. In London, Schmitt was the champion in the 200 freestyle and added a silver medal in the 400 freestyle.

Bowman has also played a role in the development of Olympic medalists Peter Vanderkaay, Klete Keller, Chase Kalisz, and Conor Dwyer. He was the U.S. men's coach for the 2016 Olympic Games and has served as an Olympic assistant on three occasions, while serving as the men's head coach at three editions of the World Championships.

After his success with NBAC, Bowman coached the University of Michigan men's program from 2005 to 2008 before returning to NBAC. Since 2015, he has been the head coach of the men's and women's programs at Arizona State University. Still, for all he has achieved at the pinnacle of the sport, Bowman frequently alludes to the early years of his career, when he bounced around to various locales, including the Cincinnati Marlins, Las Vegas Gold Swim Team, and the Napa Valley Swim Club, and fought through self-doubt before landing at NBAC.

"My advice is to work with the best program possible and learn from those who do the job well. I think joining a program is better than starting your own from scratch. I encourage working at the grassroots level, which is the best place to work on problem-solving skills. It's important to take something from everyone you work with. My style is a mix of the individuals I learned from."

FORBES CARLILE

A trawl through history can be beneficial in connecting specific individuals with the various advances brought to the sport. Usually, one name is linked to each revolution. Then the name of Forbes Carlile surfaces, and it becomes clear just how influential the legendary Australian coach was in launching the sport forward.

In any sport, arguments always surface when putting together lists of all-time greats. But when considering the finest coaches in the history of swimming, Carlile is a lock for inclusion. For 70 years, Carlile was a cutting-edge coach, never satisfied with the status quo, but instead eager to find the next breakthrough that would help his athletes go faster.

As athletes maneuver through their daily practices and prepare for competition, there is a tendency to take certain elements of their training for granted. Pace clocks. Interval training. Heart-rate monitoring. Warmup sets. The two-beat kick. Tapering. All of these innovations are commonplace in the sport, and all were pioneered by Carlile, as much a scientist as he was a coach.

"He was very innovative, down to the simple things like wearing swim goggles, using the pace clock, swimmers' log books, filming swimmers to observe their technique, position in the water, interval training and lane ropes so multiple swimmers could be in lanes," said former Australian National Team coach Alan Thompson. "He was a mentor to me and so many other people. Anyone who showed an interest in coaching or swimming, Forbes was there to inspire you, to take you under his wing."

From the mid-1940s through his death at the age of 95 in 2016, Carlile was a giant in the aquatic world. He received his first Olympic nod as the head coach for Australia at the 1948 Games in London and repeated that role at the 1956 Olympics in Melbourne. In between, he exhibited his own athletic talent by representing Australia in the modern pentathlon at the 1952 Olympics in Helsinki. In 1964, he was the coach for the Netherlands at the Tokyo Games, but he returned to his homeland afterward and was a constant presence on deck in a country that has long possessed a deep passion for swimming.

Carlile had the luxury of coaching for most of his career alongside his wife, Ursula. The couple never had children, but instead was dedicated to helping the athletes who came under their guidance reach their goals. While Forbes Carlile was inducted into the International Swimming Hall of Fame in 1976, his wife finally received her proper due with selection in 2020.

In assessing potential standouts, Carlile was not one to sugarcoat or mislead. He firmly believed in the need for a certain amount of innate talent and skill. If that ability was present, he would complement the physical workouts he drafted with psychological assistance. But the physiological side of the sport was always his primary focus.

"A swimmer has got to have attributes—body build, the right type of muscles," Carlile said. "You use psychological techniques, yes, but they are mostly intuitive. They're not programmed. Physiological and anatomic makeup are primary in a young swimmer. Psychology is secondary. Swimming is an endurance-type sport. If you don't have it physically, psychology doesn't matter."

Before implementing new strategies and training methods, Carlile frequently used himself as a guinea pig. If his practice runs were successful, he would introduce the concept into his athletes' training. If his tests proved unsuccessful, at least the time was not wasted on his swimmers. One approach that Carlile tested on himself was the benefit of hot showers before a race. While other coaches felt the heat would drain their swimmers of energy, Carlile found that his swims improved by 1.5 percent after taking a shower at the maximum temperature he could stand. He then applied this strategy to 16 of his swimmers, with 13 of them improving by 1 percent, a significant amount of time in a sport measured by fractions of a second.

In Shane Gould, Carlile unearthed the brightest gem of his coaching career. Between 1971 and early 1973, Gould set 11 world records, and at the end of the 1971 season, Gould held every freestyle world record from 100 meters through 1,500 meters. At the 1972 Olympics in Munich, Gould became the first swimmer to win five individual medals in a single Olympiad, capturing three gold, a silver, and a bronze. Although American superstar Michael Phelps matched Gould's solo medal count at the 2004 and 2008 Olympics, no female has equaled Gould's achievement.

Carlile and Gould enjoyed a give-and-take relationship in which they regularly shared information and provided honest feedback. During training, Carlile had Gould fill out a diary about her workouts, which was then collected, analyzed, and returned.

"At the end of the week, I'd hand my [notebook] into Forbes," Gould said. "He would spend Sunday afternoons going through those notes. He would put comments in it and hand it back on Monday morning. He wrote some fabulous comments. Not only encouraging but some rebuking as well. But it was all good feedback and I really enjoyed that."

While Gould was Carlile's star pupil, he also mentored the likes of world-record holders Karen Moras, Jenny Turrall, and Gail Neall. During his coaching days, Carlile guided 52 athletes to the Olympic Games, World Championships, or Commonwealth Games. More, his swimmers combined to set 31 world records and capture 12 Olympic medals, including five gold. In 1955, he opened the Carlile Swimming School, which continues to operate in various locales throughout Australia.

By conducting clinics and partaking in speaking engagements, often in front of global audiences, Carlile was able to give back to the sport. He was passionate about passing his knowledge on to new generations of coaches and enjoyed sharing his experiences, while contemplating new ideas that were brought to his attention. In 1963, he wrote *Forbes Carlile on Swimming*, a book renowned as one of the best works on the sport.

When Jacco Verhaeren left his home nation of the Netherlands in 2013 to take over as Australia's head coach, Carlile reached out and requested a meeting with the Dutchman. It was a flattering overture for Verhaeren, who guided Inge de Bruijn and Pieter van den Hoogenband to vast Olympic success. It was also an opportunity to pick the mind of a coaching legend.

"He was ahead of his time," Verhaeren said of Carlile.

> Until his last days, he was still talking about new training methods. If you do that at 95, I think that is very special. He contributed many training methods, but he invented the phenomenon of taper, resting up before competition. That was at a time, if you can imagine, when people said, "No, we need to work harder to get better results." To think the opposite and convince people to do things differently really made him special. For me, he is the best coach Australia has ever had in swimming. I was so honored to finally meet my swimming guru. After that, he sometimes sent me emails with recommendations about swimming and I know he did that with other coaches. He was incredibly sharp right until his last moments.

JAMES "DOC" COUNSILMAN

Some scientists work in a laboratory, using their time to study, analyze, and experiment. Although he did not wear a white coat or work in a conventional scientific setting, James "Doc" Counsilman was every bit a scientist, and the pool was his lab. It was there in which he tested new training methodologies, varied motivational techniques, and technological innovations.

Counsilman is widely viewed as the greatest coach in swimming history, his influence felt at both the collegiate and international levels. Ask a former athlete of Counsilman's for insight into his success, and the answer will almost certainly revolve around the man's ability to make an impact both physically and mentally.

Counsilman first made his mark in the sport as an NCAA champion swimmer at Ohio State University in the late 1940s. Shortly after his competitive career ended, the native of Birmingham, Alabama, ventured into coaching, his first jobs in that domain as an assistant at the University of Illinois and the University of Iowa. From 1952 through 1957, Counsilman served as the head coach at Cortland State University, a stretch that prepared him for the big-time role that came his way in 1957, when Indiana

University hired him and set in motion an era in which Indiana was a global force.

From 1957 to 1990, Counsilman guided the Hoosiers to immense success, his program capturing six NCAA team titles (1968–1973) and 23 Big Ten Conference crowns. During this time, Counsilman mentored some of the biggest names in the sport, including Mark Spitz, Jim Montgomery, Gary Hall Sr., Mike Troy, Charles Hickcox, George Breen, and Chet Jastremski, all world-record holders and Olympic medalists.

"He's the smartest guy I've ever known in my entire life," said Montgomery, who won Olympic gold in 1976 in the 100 freestyle. "Just sheer brain power. And he had a sense of humor."

Spitz was Counsilman's star pupil, and together they crafted what was—to that time—the greatest achievement in Olympic history. When Spitz arrived at Indiana in 1969, he was coming off a four-medal haul at the 1968 Olympics in Mexico City. Although Spitz was a member of two triumphant relays and won a silver medal in the 100 butterfly and a bronze medal in the 100 freestyle, the performance was viewed as a disappointment due to Spitz's status as a world-record holder.

It was Counsilman who rebuilt Spitz's mental toughness and provided his pupil with the confidence to rebound at the 1972 Olympics in Munich. Thanks to Counsilman's guidance, Spitz captured seven gold medals and set seven world records. The effort endured as the finest individual showing in Olympic history until 2008, when Michael Phelps collected eight gold medals and matched Spitz's seven world records.

"He was the most instrumental person in my career," Spitz said of Counsilman. "Especially because he was the one who gave me the self-confidence and belief in myself. He was a pillar of strength in regard to self-motivation. He was capable of making somebody rise to the occasion and get the most out of that person. He seemed to do that the best out of all the coaches I had, and it was at the most critical time of my life, when I was in college."

Counsilman's coaching greatness did not just influence the college scene, but reached the international stage, too. As the head coach of the U.S. men's squad at the 1964 Olympics in Tokyo, Counsilman led Team USA to gold medals in seven of 10 events and to 14 overall medals. But it was his job at the 1976 Games that was the defining moment of his career.

In Montreal, Counsilman guided the United States to victories in 12 of the 13 events, and to 10 silver medals and five bronze medals. More, Team USA swept the podium in four events and set 11 world records. While the squad was loaded with talent and is considered the greatest team in the sport's history, Counsilman didn't sit idly by as the team prepared for the Games. With Indiana and the University of Southern California fierce rivals on the college circuit, Counsilman found a way to generate camaraderie between the team members. He also generated a belief in the team that the most dominant showing of all time was within reach.

"(Counsilman) began the training camp with a pep talk to the team," said John Naber, a member of the 1976 squad who attended USC.

> He said, "Congratulations, gentlemen. I assume that each of you has a goal for your performances in Montreal. Allow me to share my goals for this team with you. In the 13 men's events on the program, I think we can win every one. I believe we can win more medals than the rest of the world combined, and I think we can win more medals than all the other U.S. sports teams combined." With those words, he magically lifted our sights from what each of us might do, to what we could accomplish as a team. The backstrokers began to encourage the butterfliers. The sprinters helped the distance men. Medley swimmers pulled for the relays. No one was left behind. Doc also ordered that all club and school T-shirts and jackets be shipped home.

As gifted as Counsilman was motivating athletes, he obviously possessed a knack for providing his athletes with the necessary training to excel at the highest level. Among the innovations that are credited to Counsilman include strength training, film analysis, underwater filming, altitude training, and hypoxic training. In an effort to spread his knowledge, Counsilman wrote *The Science of Swimming*, a book that is considered the bible of the sport and continues to be used today.

Counsilman was inducted into the International Swimming Hall of Fame in 1976, and his name adorns the aquatics center at Indiana University. Born in 1920, Counsilman died in 2004 while continuing to reside in Bloomington, Indiana, where Indiana University is located.

"What Doc had was this great ability to make you feel like the most important person in the pool," Spitz said. "Everyone came away with that feeling, whether he was a Mark Spitz or a walk-on."

PETER DALAND

Raised in a well-to-do Philadelphia suburb and educated at Harvard University and Swarthmore College, he was buttoned up and more proper than the familiar laid-back style of a West Coaster. But during a 35-year coaching stint at the University of Southern California, Peter Daland found a way to impart his influence on the athletes who came under his guidance, and he did so by imparting some of his East Coast personality.

As an assistant to legendary Yale coach Robert Kiphuth and the head coach of Rose Valley and Suburban Swim Club, Daland spent the early years of his coaching career in the East. However, in 1957, he accepted the head job at USC and changed the dynamic of the sport in the United States. By his third year in command of the Trojans, Daland had led the program to a national title, marking the first time a school West of Michigan had emerged on top at the NCAA Championships.

A dynasty was being built, and it was largely due to the mentality of Daland. The coach routinely said he was "eternally dissatisfied," and always expected more.

Over the next three-plus decades, Daland was a major influence on the American and worldwide swimming scene. He not only turned USC into a perennial power and attracted the top recruits in the country, but also played an influential role in the United States remaining the preeminent power on the international stage. Perhaps most important, Daland achieved his success with class and an eye toward preparing his mentees with a skill set to handle life's challenges.

"He was a rarity in college coaching because he was equally concerned with his team's academic and social growth as he was with his swimmers' athletic accomplishments," said John Naber, a five-time Olympic medalist who raced under Daland from 1973 to 1977.

> When Coach Daland was on deck, the pool at USC held no stars, only squad members. He made it a point to address each swimmer by name at least once per workout. He wanted his swimmers to be self-reliant, responsible, and as good as they could possibly be in all aspects of life. He challenged his teams to live up to the standards set by prior teams. He brought a wealth of knowledge and understanding on how to get the most out of his teams, and his swimmers repaid him with great admiration, loyalty and respect.

Daland churned out a who's who of stars from his Los Angeles base, that arsenal of talent leading to nine NCAA championships and 11 runner-up finishes. With 20 undefeated dual-meet seasons, Daland posted a career record of 318-31-1 and his athletes won 93 individual NCAA titles. Twice, from 1963 to 1966 and from 1974 to 1977, he led the Trojans to four straight NCAA championships.

In producing that type of success, Daland mentored numerous American Olympic medalists, including Roy Saari, Lance Larson, Bruce

During his coaching days, Peter Daland turned the University of Southern California into a national power. Peter H. Bick.

Furniss, Steve Furniss, Jeff Float, Dave Wharton, Mike O'Brien, and Joe Bottom. Meanwhile, Mike Bottom would have raced at the 1980 Olympics if not for the boycott of the Moscow Games.

Setting Daland apart was his willingness to also coach international stars. Australians Murray Rose, Jon Henricks, and John Konrads, all Olympic champions, competed collegiately for USC, as did Japan's Tsuyoshi Yamanaka, a four-time Olympic silver medalist. The depth of the roster at Southern Cal, particularly with its mix of American and international stars, created a rich training environment.

"Every time he spoke, everybody listened," said Bruce Furniss. "West Coast swimming was like a pimple on the ass of an elephant before Peter Daland came out here. He was to swimming what John Wooden was to basketball. He proved to be the bridge between the sport's pioneer coaches and today's modern-era coaches."

Collegiate excellence accounted for just a portion of Daland's success. In 1964, he served as the U.S. women's coach at the Tokyo Olympics, where Team USA won gold medals in six of the eight events, and tallied nine of the 16 minor medals available. Eight years later, Daland coached the American men at the 1972 Games in Munich, the site of Mark Spitz's seven gold medals. Overall, the United States won nine gold medals, nine silver medals, and eight bronze medals.

Although Southern Cal won its last NCAA title under Daland in 1977, the Trojans posted four runner-up finishes between 1979 and 1990. After the 1992 season, Daland surprised the USC faithful when he announced his retirement.

"I've been here 35 years, and I think that is enough," Daland said. "There is a time to come and a time to go. This is my time to go. Nothing lasts forever. Certainly, I don't. I've enjoyed coaching. I think it's been the greatest. One great truth about my experience: Anyone coaching the sport of swimming is working with the greatest people in the world. It is not how fast they swim but what kind of person they were and what kind of person they became."

While in charge of the USC program, Daland spent many years training athletes in a pool that was affectionately known as "The Dungeon." These days, the pool at the Uytengsu Aquatics Center is named after Daland, who was inducted into the International Swimming Hall of Fame in 1977, 15 years before his retirement. More, Daland was a co-founder of *Swimming World Magazine*, along with Kiphuth, the man he briefly assisted at Yale.

"I never looked at it like, 'These are all the great things I've done,' " Daland said upon his retirement.

What you do remember are the grievous losses. That keeps you from thinking too much about the past, because you remember the ones that got away in recruiting. Or the ones who didn't make it onto the Olympic team when they should have. Or the team that lost the NCAA championship when it should have won. Or the bad training you gave to someone that led to a bad result. The dissatisfaction from those things fades as things go on, and you get more involved in the present.

GEORGE HAINES

Of the greatest male swimmers produced by the United States, Mark Spitz and Don Schollander rank near the top of the list. They both excelled as freestylers during their careers and established themselves as Olympic champions. Another link between the men is the fact they were both guided by George Haines, a legend in the coaching ranks.

In 1950, Haines built the Santa Clara Swim Club from scratch, about ten athletes making up his initial roster. Like any program launching itself from nothing, it took several years for Santa Clara to grow into a force, but once its power was unleashed, there was no stopping what Haines had constructed.

During his tenure at Santa Clara, which spanned 1950 to 1974, Haines put together a resume that is difficult to comprehend. In addition to leading the club to 43 national championships, which stood as a record until Mission Viejo claimed a 44th title, Haines led his swimmers to 68 Olympic medals—44 gold, 14 silver and 10 bronze. To put that total in perspective, if Haines' athletes were considered a country, they would rank seventh in all-time medals won at the Olympic Games.

Haines was known for being a demanding taskmaster and infusing necessary humor into practices. It was a critical balance to strike due to Haines drawing up training sessions that required 10,000 to 15,000 meters of work. While he molded the careers of dozens of Olympians, Haines highlighted the team aspect of the sport, and had no trouble convincing his swimmers to buy into that thought process.

"We talked about team all the time," Haines said.

> When we went to a meet, and I did this as an Olympic coach, too, I made every kid on the team aware of the first event. That first event is the most important event in the meet. The team would be there to encourage those guys in the first event. And if they swam really well, then I could turn around to the others and say, "See that? Man, those guys were good. And if they can swim like that, look how ready you are." And it worked.

As much as Haines emphasized team success, he recognized the importance of designing training sets that fit the specific needs of his swimmers. Despite overseeing a pool filled with dozens of athletes, Haines was an expert at multitasking and was attentive to little details. In a sea of flailing arms and legs, he would call out corrections in the middle of a lap and get better results.

Schollander was among his first stars and tallied six Olympic medals between the 1964 and the 1968 Games. In his first Olympiad, Schollander won four gold medals, including individual titles in the 100 freestyle and 400 freestyle. As for Spitz, his first Olympiad was supposed to yield as many as five or six gold medals, but the eventual face of the 1972 Games settled for two relay golds and silver and bronze in his solo events. He also finished last in the final of the 200 butterfly, an event in which he was the world-record holder.

After the Games, tension rose between Haines and the Spitz family. Spitz and his father, Arnold, felt Haines overpacked the swimmer's schedule, which led to the poor results. As time passed, the relationship soured further, with Spitz refusing to race for Santa Clara in team competition. That decision prompted Haines to boot Spitz from his squad.

"I felt that the events were far enough apart that it wouldn't bother him," Haines said of Spitz's 1968 Olympic struggles. "Maybe we tried to do too much, but I don't think so. The only thing I worried about was him being so young and whether the pressure would get to him. I think it probably did. And I think any coach would have done the same thing [in regard to kicking him off the team]. In Mark's case, it was a matter of loyalty to his teammates."

Although Schollander and Spitz are the most prominent names coached by Haines, Haines' list of other Olympic champions reads on and on. Haines also developed Donna de Varona, Chris von Saltza, Claudia Kolb, Steve Clark, Lynn Burke, John Hencken, Dick Roth, and Pablo Morales. It's not surprising that *Swimming World Magazine* named Haines as the sport's top coach of the twentieth century.

Having reached the pinnacle of the sport at the club level, Haines sought a new challenge from 1974 to 1978, when he served as the men's coach at UCLA. He spent 1979–1981 back at the club level and then closed out his career as the women's coach at Stanford University from 1982 to 1988.

"George had the capacity to transform lives," von Saltza said. "If you met him halfway, you came away greatly enriched in all manner of living, even if you never reached Olympic heights under his tutelage. George has become part of me, and even now, he is in my heart encouraging me to go on, to embrace each day, and to keep a smile on my face."

Haines was a staple on Team USA coaching staffs, serving six consecutive stints as an Olympic coach from 1960 to 1980. He was the head coach of the 1960 women's team and the head coach of the 1968 men's squad. He was slated to be the head coach for both the men and the women at the 1980 Olympics until President Jimmy Carter announced the U.S. boycott of the Moscow Games.

Haines was inducted into the International Swimming Hall of Fame in 1977 and is accompanied in the Hall of Fame by 15 of the athletes he coached. On four occasions, he was named Coach of the Year by the American Swimming Coaches Association.

"He knows as much about training and mechanics as anyone," Schollander once said. "But he is truly great because he knows each swimmer. He can give himself to many people and in different ways. Whenever he says I can do a job, I know I can."

ROBERT KIPHUTH

Earning the title of pioneer requires significant contributions to a field. Albert Einstein and Marie Curie hold the distinction in science. Louis Pasteur owns the honor in medicine. In aviation, the Wright brothers were groundbreaking heroes.

Through the 100-plus years in which swimming has been an Olympic sport, several individuals have established themselves as coaching legends. But Robert J.H. Kiphuth is undoubtedly the one who can be called the sport's first deckside pioneer, a man who placed considerable emphasis on physical conditioning and the benefits it would reap in the pool.

Kiphuth took the reins at Yale University beginning in 1918, and until his retirement in 1959, he guided the Bulldogs to major success. Finishing his career with an almost unbelievable record of 528–12, Kiphuth led Yale to separate winning streaks of 175 and 169 meets and had a third unbeaten run of 63 meets. More, he paced the Bulldogs to four NCAA championships (1942, 1944, 1951, 1953) and eight runner-up finishes while Yale competed for the top spot on the collegiate scene with Michigan and Ohio State. For a brief stint, he also served as the university's athletic director.

Because the NCAA Championships did not debut until 1937, there is no telling how many years from 1918 until that season that Yale boasted the premier team in the country. What is known is that Kiphuth pushed his athletes to the maximum.

"Once the squad is in the pool, we don't stand for any loafing," Kiphuth said during a *Sports Illustrated* interview in 1956. "We have a saying around here: 'If you want to take a bath, get a cake of soap.' "

Kiphuth is credited for being an innovator in his sport, a major reason for his inclusion in the inaugural induction class to the International Swimming Hall of Fame. It was Kiphuth who introduced interval training to his athletes, and who recognized the advantages of his athletes enhancing their strength from weightlifting and other dryland workouts. For Kiphuth, top-flight conditioning could not be stressed enough.

Revered in the world of physical education, of which he was a professor at Yale, Kiphuth would call out his athletes if he felt they were cutting corners or not asking 100 percent of themselves—in the water or in the gym. Kiphuth felt the body could endure as much punishment as an individual could impart. It was this thought process that encouraged other swim coaches to increase the intensity levels of their training programs.

"We need to take special care of their bodies and train their muscles in order to overcome the enervating effects of present-day living, the softening that results from riding to school or a job instead of walking, from spending hours at sedentary work," Kiphuth once said. "You are given certain physical assets. Everyone has a certain neuromuscular pattern—a certain rhythm—they apply to swimming or any other sport. You probably can't change it, but you can help them get the most out of it."

As part of producing premier teams, Kiphuth churned out his share of elite individuals, headlined by Allen Stack and Alan Ford. At the 1948 Olympics Games in London, where Kiphuth served as the head coach for the American men, Stack captured the gold medal in the 100 backstroke while Ford was the silver medalist in the 100 freestyle. Meanwhile, Jeff Farrell won a pair of gold medals in relay action at the 1960 Games in Rome.

A five-time Olympic coach for the United States, Kiphuth also played a key role in the career of Australian John Marshall, who he met at the 1948 Olympics and convinced to attend Yale. Although Marshall owned Olympic silver and bronze medals by the time he joined Kiphuth's roster, the legendary coach helped the Aussie to a world record in the 400 freestyle.

Kiphuth didn't just focus on the physical aspect of the sport, but was keen to understand the mental side, too. He believed his swimmers should be able to handle a tough-minded coach with high expectations and felt some athletes did not meet their peak potential due to mental blocks.

"The boys of strong character and top-flight ability will like [a coach like me]," he said. "The shirkers and crybabies will not. This is as it should be. Once an athlete knows how to perform correctly and is in shape, the rest is in his mind. Take the four-minute mile. Once it had been done, the psychological barrier was removed, and four or five people did it soon afterward. The same is true of swimming. We have no idea how much we can take off our best times."

In 1968, USA Swimming named its high-point award at the national championships after Kiphuth, and in the early 1950s, Kiphuth became a co-founder of *Swimming World Magazine*. As today's swimmers put their bodies through grueling tests in the gym and pool, Kiphuth's influence can still be felt.

"More than any other coach, Kiphuth was responsible for adding dry-land exercises and cross-country running to swimming programs," reads his biography at the Hall of Fame. "His success changed the long-entrenched theories that swimming muscles had to be soft and trained only in the water. Kiphuth was accepted in physical education circles where his articles and several books made universal the knowledge and the techniques that had been kept secret in a few coaches' minds."

RICHARD QUICK

In the days after Richard Quick died in 2009, an inoperable brain tumor claiming his life at 66, many words were used to describe his decades-long influence. He was called a mentor. A motivator. An inspiration. He was lauded for his attention to detail and the genuine care he showed his athletes. He was remembered as one of the greatest coaches to ever stroll along a pool deck.

In the sports world, where the intensity can steer rivalries into nasty sagas, Quick was one of the most likable figures out there. Sure, there was some jealousy over his vast success, which was found equally on the international and collegiate stages. But respect was the prevailing theme for Quick, who spent four decades molding champions in the pool and in life.

Quick had head-coaching tenures at five schools during his college career, beginning with stops at Southern Methodist University and Iowa State. But it was stints at Auburn, Texas, and Stanford that launched him into the Hall of Fame and set the stage for Quick to be named a United States Olympic coach on six occasions.

After coaching the men's and women's programs at Auburn from 1978 to 1982, in which time he guided future Olympic champion Rowdy Gaines, Quick took over the women's program at Texas in 1982 and led the Longhorns to five NCAA championships before his departure after the 1988 season. Upon leaving Austin, Quick became the women's coach at Stanford and during his stay on The Farm, he guided the Cardinal to seven NCAA championships. His final years as a coach, from 2007 to 2009, brought a return to Auburn, his final season producing an NCAA crown for the men.

"I have so many memories, both at Stanford and in the coaching profession in general," Quick said. "I have been honored to have coached some of the finest athletes in the world, and we've competed at the very highest levels intercollegiately and internationally. But many of my memories simply revolve around the experience of working with student-athletes on a daily basis. That has been as big of a thrill as anything."

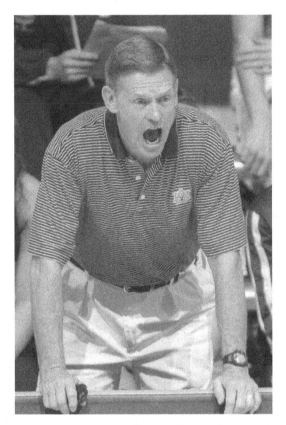

Richard Quick was a giant in the coaching world, excelling at Auburn, Texas, and Stanford. Peter H. Bick.

The number of Hall of Famers produced by Quick is eye-popping. At one stop or another, he developed Olympic champions Gaines, Jenny Thompson, Summer Sanders, Dara Torres, Janet Evans, and Misty Hyman. To his credit, Quick knew that each of his swimmers needed a different set of guidelines, and he would willingly adjust his schedule to ensure his athletes received the attention they needed.

On the road to the 2000 Olympic Games in Sydney, Quick started to train Thompson and Torres together, only to realize the arrangement would not work. Due to their win-at-all-times mentalities, practices devolved into head-to-head showdowns in which the atmosphere was unhealthy. Consequently, Quick separated Thompson and Torres. The decision proved beneficial when they returned from Sydney with a combined nine medals.

Quick was named to his first Olympic coaching staff as an assistant for the 1984 Games in Los Angeles, and his presence paid dividends for Gaines. Ahead of the final of the 100 freestyle, Quick approached Gaines and told him they had to rework his start due to the tendency of referee Francisco Silvestri to start the race quickly. Indeed, Silvestri hardly held the swimmers at the "set" position, and thanks to Quick's attention to detail, Gaines was prepared. Getting a superb start, Gaines led from start to finish and captured the gold medal in the sport's signature event.

"Part of me feels like it was yesterday," Gaines said. "I can remember specific details of the race. But another part of me feels like that was another person. I'm not sure how I did all that. It would have been impossible without Richard Quick. He had such a knack for picking up things to help his athletes, and that's what he did with the start. But more than a coach, he was always a confidant and friend."

Quick followed his initial Olympic nod with five more selections, including the position of head coach at the 1988, 1996, and 2000 Games. In addition to 1984, he was an assistant coach at the 1992 and 2004 Olympics.

In addition to his skills as a technician, Quick could get his athletes to buy into his beliefs. That aspect of his personality was on display at the 2000 Games, where Hyman registered one of the biggest upsets in history, beating Australian Susie O'Neill in the 200 butterfly. Heading into the final, O'Neill was the reigning Olympic and world champion, and was the world-record holder. More, she had destroyed Hyman in previous matchups. Still, Quick convinced Hyman that she could pull off a miracle, and she wasn't the only swimmer who Quick could influence mentally.

"Richard was in a league of his own when it came to making people believe they can do the impossible," said Sanders, the 1992 Olympic champion in the 200 butterfly. "I had goal times that were ridiculous. I don't know if people have gone that fast yet."

In late 2008, Quick was diagnosed with a brain tumor, but opted to continue coaching at Auburn. In March of 2009, Auburn captured the NCAA men's championship, giving Quick college crowns for both genders. He died three months later, but not without putting his situation into perspective.

"All I know is that I have been blessed to be associated with a lot of wonderful people during my coaching career," Quick said toward the end of his life. "I feel like I have gotten a lot more out of those relationships than the other way around. I feel really blessed."

EDDIE REESE

Not the kind of guy who enjoys speaking about himself, or dwelling on his achievements, Eddie Reese has a familiar defense when placed in the spotlight. He goes to his joke book. Never mind that his athletes and other acquaintances have heard some of these cracks a dozen times, Reese's one-liners or jokes buy just enough time to deflect attention away.

But if Reese isn't going to discuss his high level of success as the men's coach at the University of Texas, there are plenty of individuals who are willing to pay tribute to a guy who is simply known as Eddie. Former athletes. Assistant coaches. Opposing coaches. University administrators. Parents. Officials. Media members. All speak highly of Reese, who has been a mentor in the sport for more than a half-century.

"Here's the thing about Eddie," said Brendan Hansen, a six-time Olympic medalist who was coached by Reese from 2000 to 2012. "He cares about every one of his swimmers as people. He wants to teach them life lessons that can be used beyond swimming. In the pool, he gives each guy what will help him. He doesn't try to fit everyone into one mold. He pays attention to the little things and knows how to provide everyone with what they need".

As the headman at the University of Texas and a multi-time U. S. Olympic coach, Eddie Reese is considered one of the greatest coaches in history. Peter H. Bick.

Arriving in Austin for the 1979 season, Reese wasted little time building a dynasty at the University of Texas. He led the Longhorns to their first NCAA title in 1981 and 13 more national crowns have been added, the total of 14 NCAA championships a record for one coach in the sport. But the national titles account for only a portion of Reese's success. Consider:

- In 42 years at the Texas helm, Reese has led the Longhorns to 41 consecutive conference championships—every year but his inaugural campaign.
- Under Reese's guidance, Texas has been runner-up at the NCAA Championships on 12 occasions and his teams have finished in the top three in 33 of his 41 seasons.
- Following a 21st-place showing in Reese's first season as coach, Texas has never placed lower than seventh at the NCAA Championships during Reese's tenure.
- Through 2020, Reese's swimmers had won 73 individual NCAA titles and 50 relay crowns.

The above accolades paint the picture of a program that annually contends for the national championship, but there is irony in the way Reese operates. As the Longhorns maneuver through practices and their dual-meet season, Reese never points to winning the NCAA championship as a goal. Instead, he focuses on growth and figures if his athletes demonstrate improvement, the by-product will be championships.

"I've always worried about the individual first," Reese said. "We don't talk about winning the NCAA championship. We talk about what it takes for each individual to get better. What satisfies me as a coach is seeing people go faster than they ever have before. With that focus, we are in a battle for the championship every year."

Before Reese turned the University of Texas into a power program, he had proven himself at other stops. A high school state champion in Florida, he went on to become a multi-time Southeastern Conference (SEC) champion for the University of Florida. After serving as an assistant coach at his college alma mater from 1967 to 1972, Reese accepted the head-coaching job at Auburn University, which he turned into a nationally recognized program.

The year prior to Reese taking the reins, Auburn didn't advance one swimmer to the finals or consolation finals of the SEC Championships. But in his last four years with the program, Auburn had four top-ten finishes at the NCAA Championships, including a runner-up effort during the 1978 season, his final year with the Tigers.

As much as Reese is known for his sense of humor and genuine care for his athletes, his program is built on intense training sessions, which push his swimmers to limits they didn't know were reachable. Former Longhorns note they cannot remember repeating a practice; such is Reese's dedication to providing variety and new tests of the mind and body.

More, Reese is never static in his approach. After more than 50 years in the sport, he is constantly learning and applying new methodologies in his practices. In recent years, Reese has placed an enhanced emphasis on the dolphin kick, knowing a team superb at kicking can gain an advantage on the opposition.

"A lot of people look for the easy way to do anything," Reese said. "In swimming, there is no easy way. To succeed in any sport there are two keys—after the obvious need of a certain amount of ability and hard work. These keys are self-image and enjoyment. It's something you have to work on every day, day-in and day-out. Everybody knows how to work people hard. The key is to work them hard and protect the mind."

Beyond the college stage, Reese has also flourished internationally, serving as a Team USA coach in seven Olympiads, highlighted by three stints as the head coach (1992, 2004, 2008). He has coached more than 30 Olympians who have combined to win 44 gold medals, 16 silver medals, and eight bronze medals. Not surprising, he has been honored as the American Swim Coaches Association Coach of the Year four times.

Reese is a regular presenter at clinics throughout the United States, happy to share his knowledge and allow veteran and young coaches to pick his brain for ideas that can benefit a range of swimmers. Inducted into the International Swimming Hall of Fame in 2002, Reese continues to make an impact.

"Eddie is constantly teaching," said Kris Kubik, a former longtime assistant coach under Reese. "He does a lot of talking about life, as much as he talks about swimming. He talks about how to apply what you learn in swimming to life. It's very important to him that his swimmers enjoy what they are doing. Eddie has designed a program that is totally unpredictable. I don't think there is a harder working team in the country."

MARK SCHUBERT

He's always had a brusque demeanor, a my-way-is-the-only-way approach that easily ruffles feathers. If a swimmer or parent doesn't like his style, they can take their swimsuit and goggles elsewhere. Under his watch, athletes are put through grinding workouts that test them physically and weed out the mentally weak.

Those characteristics have certainly made Mark Schubert a polarizing figure in the sport, but they've also accounted for another identity: winner.

Since the early 1970s, when he took command of the Mission Viejo Nadadores, Schubert has been regarded as one of the best coaches in the world. He has masterfully succeeded at every major level—club, collegiate, and international. That across-the-board excellence was rewarded in 1997 with induction into the International Swimming Hall of Fame.

Schubert was a fresh-faced 22-year-old when he was named head coach at Mission Viejo in 1972, seeking to build what was a summer-league program into a powerhouse. His dream came to fruition. Between 1972 and 1985, Schubert churned out team and individual champions with regularity, and to the point where Mission Viejo became the most successful club in USA Swimming history with 44 national team titles.

En route to establishing a championship identity at the Southern California club, Schubert instituted a demanding culture. His swimmers logged massive amounts of yardage during workouts and were held to strict standards. If an athlete was a minute or two late for a workout, it was not uncommon for Schubert to lock him or her out of practice. More, parents were banned from the deck.

The demanding style of Mark Schubert led him to vast success at the club, collegiate, and international levels. Peter H. Bick.

Due to Schubert's approach, Mission Viejo wasn't for everyone. Additionally, his style and philosophy didn't endear him with other coaches. Fellow Hall of Fame coach Dick Jochums once claimed that Schubert did not bring enough variety to his program, and that his pupils would burn out. Even some of his swimmers have acknowledged his not-for-everyone personality.

"When Mark came here, nobody in the club liked him," said two-time Olympic champion Brian Goodell. "He was always yelling, but he kind of grows on you. Besides, he got the best out of us. Mark runs the toughest program in the country, and sometimes I ask myself if it's worth it. But I like to win, and that's what it takes."

After building Mission Viejo into the finest club in the world, Schubert was offered the head-coaching position—and a lucrative salary—with the Mission Bay Makos Swim Team in 1985. Schubert found success at that Florida stop, too, but in 1988 took over the women's program at the University of Texas, which he led to a pair of NCAA titles. In 1992, Schubert moved again, this time replacing Peter Daland as the head coach at the University of Southern California, where he led the women to one NCAA crown and stayed until USA Swimming came calling in 2006.

In his early years at Mission Viejo, Schubert made it a point to study the coaches around him, looking to pick up ideas to incorporate into his program. He also studied the work ethic of the East German women's swimming machine, which was producing Olympic champions and world-record holders in assembly line fashion. While it was eventually proven that East Germany's success was due to a systematic doping program, Schubert embraced the hard-working culture and weightlifting program that was in place in the European nation.

Meanwhile, Schubert was innovative in his own right. Rather than watch his swimmers, especially in the distance events, slow down during the back half of races, Schubert encouraged negative-splitting and closing strong. He also included lactic-acid testing in his program, using the information from blood tests to understand how and when his swimmers tired during practices and races.

"Swimming isn't rocket science. It's hard work," Schubert said. "You have to pay attention to not only things you are doing in the pool, but what you're doing outside of the pool, like rest and nutrition. Once a month [at Mission Viejo], I'd travel to other teams, and learn from them. It helped me out and it was a great way to learn."

Schubert was named to his first Olympic staff in 1980, but he did not get the opportunity to coach at the Moscow Games due to the U.S.

boycott instituted by President Jimmy Carter. However, Schubert was an American coach at the next seven Olympics, highlighted by head-coaching duties in 1992, 2000, and 2004.

In 2006, USA Swimming hired Schubert as its National Team director and general manager, handing the veteran coach oversight of the American swim scene. Schubert was charged with working with the nation's elite coaches to continue production of U.S. excellence on the international stage. One of Schubert's successes in his role with USA Swimming was creating Centers for Excellence, where professional swimmers could train under the direction of some of the best coaches in the country.

The role seemed appropriate for a man who had coached a slew of Olympic champions and medalists, including Goodell, Shirley Babashoff, Mary T. Meagher, Janet Evans, Cynthia Woodhead, Tiffany Cohen, and Lenny Krayzelburg, among others. For Schubert, the opportunity was deeply satisfying.

"Having the honor to help the nation's best coaches cultivate the nation's best talent is huge," Schubert said. "Anything I can do to help them win Olympic medals and give our athletes the best possible Olympic experience will be my goal."

Schubert enjoyed considerable success while in his USA Swimming role. The United States topped the medals table at the three global competitions that he presided over, with the Americans dominating at the 2007 World Championships and 2008 Olympics Games. But there were plenty of rocky moments, too.

In November of 2010, USA Swimming fired Schubert from his role as National Team director and general manager. It was known that Schubert had a frosty relationship with the organization's executive director, Chuck Wielgus, as the two butted heads over a financial-incentive program for top-tier athletes, and over Schubert's gruff personality. Still, the firing was a surprise.

In the months and years that followed, it was revealed that USA Swimming had covered up sexual assaults by coaches of athletes. Schubert was specifically accused of helping to conceal two cases of sexual assault, one while he was the National Team director and one while he was the head coach of the Golden West Swim Club. With USA Swimming, Schubert was said to know of a relationship between coach Sean Hutchison and athlete Ariana Kukors but did not have USA Swimming investigate the situation aggressively enough, or seek to punish Hutchison.

At Golden West, assistant coach Dia Rianda, a former close friend of Schubert, allegedly told the coach about inappropriate relationships between another assistant coach, Bill Jewell, and Golden West swimmers, only to have Schubert ignore her allegations. Eventually, Schubert fired Rianda, who subsequently filed a wrongful termination lawsuit against Schubert.

"Mark Schubert was in a position of power at one time, and he turned his back on victims and, worse, allowed his friends and coaching peers to continue to commit crimes against children," Rianda said. "It is disgusting and tragic that he is still coaching and leading coaches."

However, Schubert also received support during the tumultuous years following his firing by USA Swimming.

"I would defend Mark Schubert to the gills," said Dara Torres, a five-time Olympian who once trained under Schubert. "He's not only a great coach, but he's a wonderful human being, a man of integrity."

Schubert eventually left Golden West and his career came full circle when he returned to Mission Viejo after 30-plus years. In his second stop with the club, Schubert has worked with a variety of age groups, seeking to spark the same kind of run he had in the 1970s and 1980s.

Now in the twilight of his career, it is uncertain if Schubert will develop another Olympian or national champion. What is unquestioned is his status as one of the greatest coaches in swimming history.

"He has such a commitment to the swimmer and the sport," Goodell once said. "He is a class coach. He knew how to push you and how to get everything out of you. Everything I learned from him, I carried over into my everyday life. I have a lot to thank him for."

DON TALBOT

It's never a positive development when a coach faces a potential revolt by his athletes. But in 1990, less than a year after he took the reins as the head coach of the Australian National Team, Don Talbot was in the crosshairs. More than half of the Dolphins, the nickname given for National Team members, had signed a letter of complaint against Talbot, a drill-sergeant type who didn't spare feelings.

Twelve years later, Talbot was still in control.

Success tends to shift perceptions, leading to forgetfulness and a willingness to lower that previously aimed firearm. This scenario is exactly what unfolded around Talbot. If his biting commentaries, high expectations, and my-way demands were not easily digestible at the start of his tenure, the improvement he generated made his style palatable.

When Talbot was put in charge of the Australian National Team, the country was coming off several subpar Olympic performances. At the 1984 Games in Los Angeles, Australia won just one gold medal and 12 overall medals, a poor showing considering the boycott of several Eastern Bloc nations. Four years later in Seoul, Australia put forth a dismal showing, collecting one medal of each color. Given the rich tradition of Aussie swimming, these performances were unacceptable, and led to the tabbing of Talbot for a resurrection.

"We want to build the component of team support that the Americans have, which others criticize but secretly envy," he said. "We're an island nation of 18 million, 95 percent (who live) within 10 minutes of the sea. We should have the best swimmers."

Talbot made his name known through the work he did with John and Ilsa Konrads, freestyle aces for Australia in the 1950s and the 1960s. With Talbot guiding their careers, the Konrads siblings each set world records in the 400 freestyle, 800 freestyle, and 1,500 freestyle, with John adding a global standard in the 200 freestyle and three medals at the 1960 Olympics in Rome. At the same time, he developed Kevin Berry, who made his first Olympic squad as a 14-year-old in 1960 and won gold in the 200 butterfly in 1964.

Thanks to the success he had with the Konrads Kids and Berry, Talbot was named the head coach of the Australian men's team at the 1964 Games and held that role at the next two Olympiads. During that stretch, Talbot led Ian O'Brien, Bob Windle, Beverley Whitfield, and Gail Neall to Olympic gold medals. However, a lack of support from Australian Swimming led to Talbot taking more lucrative jobs elsewhere.

He first left his homeland for Canada, where he served a stint as that country's National Team coach and followed by taking the head job at the Nashville Aquatic Club, where he coached Tracy Caulkins. A role at the Australian Institute for Sport brought him home in 1980, but Talbot left again for Canada a few years later. During his second stop as Canada's National Team coach, he prepared the nation to produce some of its best Olympic performances in 1984 and 1988, although he was let go from his position just before the 1988 Games. Between 1984 and 1988, Canada collected 12 medals, including four gold.

Based on his track record and Australia's need to escape its struggles, Talbot was given the chance to lead the Land of Oz back to elite status. Initially, his hard-nosed and demanding tactics were a rude awakening for members of the National Team. Even political figures got involved in the rift between Talbot and the Aussie athletes, and Talbot was referred to by one media outlet as a tyrant in the form of Ming the Merciless, a character from the science fiction television show *Flash Gordon*.

"We need a head coach who is going to encourage our swimmers, not use Rambo tactics to retaliate when his oversized ego is threatened," stated Labor Party member Con Sciacca during a session of Parliament.

Eventually, Talbot's grip took hold and the clamor for his removal died down. Why? The answer is simple: Australia started to produce results reminiscent of its glory days, when the likes of Dawn Fraser and Murray Rose stood atop the sport. By the 1992 Olympics, Australia was up to nine medals, with that number moving to 12 at the 1996 Games. More, stars were starting to surface, such as Kieren Perkins, Susie O'Neill, and Petria Thomas.

At the 2000 Olympics, Australia was up to 18 medals, second to the United States, and Ian Thorpe and Grant Hackett had become superstars. At the 2001 World Championships, Talbot realized his greatest achievement when Australia won the most gold medals with 13, ahead of the United States' nine. Instead of remaining at the helm, Talbot resigned.

During his career, Talbot was an outspoken critic of performance-enhancing drug use and was among the most vocal opponents of the sudden rise of China in the 1990s. His stance against drug use, however, was called into question in 2007 when Talbot suggested all swimmers be able to use steroids or another form of illegal assistance.

"I still believe that there should be no drug use in any sport," Talbot said. "But we should bring into the light the things many talk about in the shadows. And the fundamental question for me is, how do we ensure that the true champion gets justly rewarded in the way he or she deserves? I have yet to hear a solution that is better than legalizing steroids. I'm waiting to hear it and it will only come through open debate."

Talbot's words received harsh criticism, but his commentary was largely designed and intended to bring focus to one of the biggest problems in swimming: doping.

Additional controversy courted Talbot when he vehemently defended Thorpe as the greatest swimmer in the world and, perhaps, as the greatest of all time. Those remarks came at a time when Michael Phelps was rapidly rising, but Talbot didn't want to hear comparisons. Phelps' coach, Bob Bowman, made his protégé aware of Talbot's comments, allowing them to serve as motivation.

"He's accomplished nothing in the world," Talbot said of Phelps before the 2003 World Championships. "People trying to say (Phelps) is a greater swimmer than Ian is absolute nonsense. The promise with Phelps is there, but for people saying he's going to outdo Thorpey, I live to see that day."

At the 2003 World Championships, Phelps won individual titles in the 200 butterfly, 200 individual medley, and 400 individual medley—all in world-record time. More, the 200 medley win arrived over Thorpe. While Thorpe delivered an illustrious career, Talbot missed the mark on his assessment that he would go down as a bigger legend than Phelps, who won a record 28 Olympic medals.

For his part, Thorpe has recognized the significance of Talbot in Australian swimming.

"You hear about him and his (gruff) exterior," Thorpe said. "But you get to know him, and he only wants to see you do your best."

He sure knew how to produce it.

BIBLIOGRAPHY

BOOKS AND ARTICLES

Alexander, Amy. "Mark Spitz's Will to Win and Work Led to Golden Years." *Investor's Business Daily* (5 May 2015). https://www.investors.com/news/mana gement/leaders-and-success/mark-spitz-swam-to-olympic-glory/.

Amdur, Neil. "The DeMont Case Isn't Closed." *New York Times* (15 October 1972). https://www.nytimes.com/1972/10/15/archives/the-de-mont-case-isnt -closed-the-demont-case-isnt-closed.html.

Anderson, Dave. "America's Best Swimmer." *New York Times* (3 August 1984). https://www.nytimes.com/1984/08/03/sports/sports-of-the-times-america-s -best-swimmer.html.

Anderson, Kelli. "Richard Quick: 1943-2009." *Sports Illustrated* (22 June 2009). https://vault.si.com/vault/2009/06/22/richard-quick-19432009.

Atkin, Ross. "Stroke of a Different Swimmer: Gold for Janet Evans." *Christian Science Monitor* (20 September 1988). https://www.csmonitor.com/1988/0920 /r1swim.html.

Attard, Monica. "Dawn Fraser: Still Kicking." *Australian Broadcasting Company* (15 April 2007). http://www.abc.net.au/sundayprofile/stories/s1897086.htm.

Auerbach, Nicole. "As Katie Ledecky Approaches Her Record, Debbie Meyer is Thrilled to Watch." *USA Today* (11 August 2016). https://www.usatoday .com/story/sports/olympics/rio-2016/2016/08/11/katie-ledecky-approaches -her-record-debbie-meyer-thrilled-watch/88556616/.

———. "Cullen Jones Blown Away By Simone Manuel's Iconic Moment." *USA Today* (12 August 2016). https://www.usatoday.com/story/sports/olympics/rio -2016/2016/08/12/cullen-jones-simone-biles-gold-medal/88636630/.

———. "Anthony Ervin Becomes Oldest Male Individual Swimming Champion." *USA Today* (12 August 2016). https://www.freep.com/story/sports/olympics/ rio-2016/2016/08/12/nathan-adrian-anthony-ervin-swimming-mens-50-freest yle-final-results/88647072/.

"Australia's Thorpedo Swimming for Gold." *ESPN* (24 August 2000). http://www.espn.com/oly/summer00/swimming/s/2000/0816/688228.html.

"Authorities Had Long History of Difficulty in Getting de Bruin to Comply with Dope-Testing Procedures." *Irish Times* (7 August 1998). https://www.irishtimes.com/news/authorities-had-long-history-of-difficulty-in-getting-de-bruin-to-comply-with-dope-testing-procedures-1.180601.

Banks, Leo. "Gold Medal Lockdown." *Tucson Weekly* (20 November 2008). https://www.tucsonweekly.com/tucson/gold-medal-lockdown/Content?oid=1093265.

Barnard, Bill. "U.S. Pins Olympic Hopes on 16-Year-Old Janet Evans." *Associated Press* (21 August 1988). https://apnews.com/dbf1d843d6e3816f1fe0e770a14550fc.

Bedics, Mark. "The Best Ever – Maybe Forever." *NCAA Champion Magazine* (22 January 2019). http://www.ncaa.org/champion/best-ever-maybe-forever.

Bednall, Jai. "Michael Phelps Has Ian Thorpe to Thank for Turning Him Into the Swimmer He is Today." *News.com* (5 August 2016). https://www.news.com.au/sport/olympics/michael-phelps-has-ian-thorpe-to-thank-for-turning-him-into-the-swimmer-he-is-today/news-story/45b37f082b9d4061009d282e20a4f1e1.

Benjamin, Philip. "Then and Now." *New York Times* (6 August 1961). https://timesmachine.nytimes.com/timesmachine/1961/08/06/118047517.pdf?pdf_redirect=true&ip=0.

Berlin, Peter. "Tie in 50-Meter Freestyle is Only the Second in the History of the Games: Ervin and Hall Strike Gold Together." *New York Times* (23 September 2000). https://www.nytimes.com/2000/09/23/sports/IHT-tie-in-50meter-freestyle-is-only-the-2d-in-the-history-of-the.html.

Biondi, Matt. "Diary of a Champion." *Sports Illustrated* (3 October 1988). http://sportsillustrated.cnn.com/vault/article/magazine/MAG1067810/index.htm.

Boateng, Grace. "It's Time to Dive In: Texas Native and Gold Medalist Simone Manuel Continues to Dominate as a Swimming Phenomenon." *Houston Forward Times* (7 August 2019). http://forwardtimes.com/its-time-to-dive-in-texas-native-and-gold-medalist-simone-manuel-continues-to-dominate-as-a-swimming-phenomenon/.

"Bob Bowman Pulls Michael Phelps From International Competition; Ban Shiny Suits." *Swimming World Magazine* (28 July 2009). https://www.swimmingworldmagazine.com/news/bob-bowman-pulls-michael-phelps-from-international-competition/.

Bowers, Peter. "Armstrong Catches a Wave to Gold." *Sydney Morning Herald* (20 September 1988). https://www.smh.com.au/sport/swimming/from-the-archives-armstrong-catches-a-wave-to-gold-20190903-p52nlp.html

Braithwaite, Alyssa. "A Look at Olympic Doping Scandals Through the Decades." *Dateline* (8 April 2016). https://www.sbs.com.au/news/dateline/a-look-at-olympic-doping-scandals-through-the-decades.

Brown, Doug. "Thompson Continues to Make Splash." *Baltimore Sun* (30 July 1997). https://www.baltimoresun.com/news/bs-xpm-1997-07-30-1997211004-story.html.

Cahill, Tim. "Mark and the Seven Wisemen: Everybody Needs Milking." *Rolling Stone* (26 April 1973). https://www.rollingstone.com/culture/culture-news/mark-and-the-seven-wisemen-everybody-needs-milking-162738/.

Carlile Swimming. "How Forbes Carlile Became One of Sport's Most Influential and Innovative Leaders." *Carlile Swimming* (8 February 2019). https://www.carlile.com.au/how-forbes-carlile-became-one-of-sports-most-influential-and-innovative-leaders/.

Cart, Julie. "Smith Hardly Able to Bask in Spotlight." *Los Angeles Times* (23 July 1996). https://www.latimes.com/archives/la-xpm-1996-07-23-ss-27205-story.html%20.

Cazeneuve, Brian. "Question II: Will Ian Thorpe and the Rest of the Aussies Rule the Pool?" *Sports Illustrated* (11 September 2000). https://vault.si.com/vault/2000/09/11/question-2-will-ian-thorpe-and-the-rest-of-the-aussies-rule-the-pool.

Cazeneuve, Brian. "World Beater Teenage Sensation Michael Phelps Dominated the World Championships." *Sports Illustrated* (4 August 2004). https://vault.si.com/vault/2003/08/04/world-beater-teenage-sensation-michael-phelps-dominated-the-world-championships.

Chapin, Kim. "Old and New Pool Their Talent." *Sports Illustrated* (21 August 1967). https://vault.si.com/vault/1967/08/21/old-and-new-pool-their-talent.

"Chinese Doping Chronology." *Reuters* (28 July 2008). https://www.reuters.com/article/us-olympics-doping-china-chronology/chinese-doping-chronology-idUSL761329820080729.

Clarey, Christopher. "Chinese Swimmers Win with Drugs, U.S. Team Leader Charges." *New York Times* (9 September 1994). https://www.nytimes.com/1994/09/09/sports/swimming-chinese-swimmers-win-with-drugs-us-team-leader-charges.html.

———. "A Dolphin Swimming with the Sharks." *New York Times* (14 July 1996). https://archive.nytimes.com/www.nytimes.com/specials/olympics/cntdown/0714oly-swm-popov.html.

———. "Popov Has Returned to Barcelona, the Scene of Past and Present Gold-Medal Glories." *New York Times* (25 July 2003). https://www.nytimes.com/2003/07/25/sports/swimming-popov-has-returned-barcelona-scene-past-present-gold-medal-glories.html.

———. "Coach for Two Countries Gives Swimming His Undivided Attention." *New York Times* (8 March 2012). https://www.nytimes.com/2012/03/09/sports/olympics/09iht-swim09.html.

Colvin, Mark. "Shane Gould Reflects on Former Coach Forbes Carlile." *ABC* (2 August 2016). https://www.abc.net.au/radio/programs/pm/shane-gould-reflects-on-former-coach-forbes-carlile/7683730.

Colwin, Cecil. "Coach George Haines, Swim Maestro: A Remembrance." *Santa Clara Swim Club* (1 May 2006). http://www.santaclaraswimclub.org/alumni/tribute.html.

Corrigan, Maureen. "In Ederle Bio, a Channel-Crosser's Defiant Spirit." *NPR* (23 July 2009). https://www.npr.org/templates/story/story.php?storyId=106857551.

Cowley, Michael. "Hackett Believes His Thorpe Rivalry May Be Over." *The Age* (23 November 2005). https://www.theage.com.au/sport/hackett-believes-his-thorpe-rivalry-may-be-over-20051123-ge1al2.html.

———. "Klim Relives the Night We Smashed Them Like Guitars." *Sydney Morning Herald* (8 September 2010). https://www.smh.com.au/sport/swimming/klim-relives-the-night-we-smashed-them-like-guitars-20100907-14zms.html.

Crouse, Karen. "Phelps Wins Seventh Gold with 0.01 to Spare." *New York Times* (15 August 2008). https://www.nytimes.com/2008/08/16/sports/olympics/16swim.html?_r=1&oref=slogin.

———. "Swimming Bans High-Tech Suits, Ending an Era." *New York Times* (24 July 2009). https://www.nytimes.com/2009/07/25/sports/25swim.html.

———. "Phelps Loses, and a Debate Boils Over." *New York Times* (28 July 2009). https://www.nytimes.com/2009/07/29/sports/29swim.html.

Crumpacker, John. "USOC Honors DeMont." *San Francisco Chronicle* (1 February 2012). https://www.sfgate.com/sports/article/USOC-honors-DeMont-2925147.php.

Davis, Scott. "Ryan Lochte Gave a Brutally Honest Quote About His Underappreciated Career Compared to Michael Phelps." *Business Insider* (11 August 2016). https://www.businessinsider.com/ryan-lochte-quote-being-in-michael-phelps-shadow-2016-8.

"De Bruin Banned." *BBC News* (6 August 1998). http://news.bbc.co.uk/2/hi/sport/146638.stm.

"DeMont Sues USOC Over Lost Gold Medal." *Associated Press* (4 June 1996). https://apnews.com/7c50dfec940a5de82dfd0afbc5a1f14e.

Denman, Elliott. "A Pioneer Looks Back on Her Unforgettable Feat." *New York Times* (30 April 2001). https://www.nytimes.com/2001/04/30/sports/swimming-a-pioneer-looks-back-on-her-unforgettable-feat.html.

Dichter, Myles. "How China's Sun Yang Became Swimming's Most Controversial Figure." *CBC* (25 July 2019). https://www.cbc.ca/sports/olympics/summer/aquatics/world-aquatics-sun-yang-timeline-1.5224721.

Dillman, Lisa. "James Counsilman, 83; U.S. Olympic and Indiana University Swim Coach, Author." *Los Angeles Times* (5 January 2004). https://www.latimes.com/archives/la-xpm-2004-jan-05-me-counsilman5-story.html.

Donnelly, Marea. "Controversy Threatened to Sink Heart-Throb and Swimmer John Devitt's Rome Olympics Gold Medal." *Daily Telegraph* (4 February 2017). https://www.dailytelegraph.com.au/news/today-in-history/controversy-threatened-to-sink-heartthrob-and-swimmer-john-devitts-rome-olympics-gold-medal/news-story/8a4464a971b7d9be9b67ef841d02679b.

"Fanny Durack: World Champion's Career." *Sydney Morning Herald* (25 March 1914). http://trove.nla.gov.au/ndp/del/article/15467185.

Faller, Mary Beth. "Bob Bowman Uses Michael Phelps to Explain How to Achieve Excellence." *Sun Devil Life* (30 January 2017). https://asunow.asu.edu/20170130-sun-devil-life-bob-bowman-uses-michael-phelps-explain-how-achieve-excellence.

Faraudo, Jeff. "Hall Churns Up Water to Grab Gold." *East Bay Times* (21 August 2004). https://www.eastbaytimes.com/2004/08/21/hall-churns-up-water-to-grab-gold/.

"Four Chinese Swimmers Suspended for Drugs." *Los Angeles Times* (15 January 1998). https://www.latimes.com/archives/la-xpm-1998-jan-15-sp-8667-story.html.

Fowler, Scott. "Depression. Drugs. Alcohol. Tourette's. And at 35, Another Olympics." *Charlotte Observer* (23 July 2016). https://www.charlotteobserver.com/sports/spt-columns-blogs/scott-fowler/article91388447.html.

Gallagher, Brendan. "Inspired Wilkie Left the World in His Wake." *The Telegraph* (24 July 2006). https://www.telegraph.co.uk/sport/olympics/swimming/2341390/Inspired-Wilkie-left-the-world-in-his-wake.html.

Ginsburg, David. "Michael Phelps Honored for Honesty on Mental Health, Helping Others." *Arizona Republic* (21 May 2019). https://www.azcentral.com/story/sports/2019/05/21/michael-phelps-honored-honesty-mental-health-helping-others/3760802002/.

Glock, Allison. "Do You Really Still Hate Ryan Lochte?" *ESPN The Magazine* (6 June 2017). http://www.espn.com/espn/feature/story/_/id/19506033/will-hate-ryan-lochte-end-story.

Gordos, Phil. "Thorpe Steals Phelps' Thunder." *BBC Sport* (17 August 2004). http://news.bbc.co.uk/sport2/hi/olympics_2004/swimming/3571978.stm.

Gould, Shane. "Dancing with the Shane Gould Legend." *University of Tasmania Magazine* (June 2012). https://www.utas.edu.au/__data/assets/pdf_file/0010/262648/3188_Alumni_Mag_June_2012_forweb.pdf.

Hall, Mia. "Cullen Jones, Simone Manuel and the Impact of Blacks in Swimming." *NBC News* (13 August 2016). https://www.nbcnews.com/news/nbcblk/cullen-jones-simone-manuel-impact-blacks-swimming-n629601.

Harris, Beth. "Thorpe Sets World Mark, Thompson Wins Sixth Gold." *ABC News* (7 January 2006). https://abcnews.go.com/Sports/story?id=100551&page=1.

Healy, Michelle. "Breaststroker Designs Future." *The Crimson* (8 April 1981). https://www.thecrimson.com/article/1981/4/8/breaststroker-designs-future-pbreaststrokers-beware-the/.

Hersh, Philip. "Just Janet Just Wants to Be a Star." *Chicago Tribune* (28 August 1988). https://www.chicagotribune.com/news/ct-xpm-1988-08-28-8801260190-story.html.

———. "Red Flag Raised Over Smith's Great Waves." *Chicago Tribune.* (23 July 1996). https://www.chicagotribune.com/news/ct-xpm-1996-07-23-9607230067-story.html.

———. "Phelps, Lochte Going At Each Other Again in Their Sport's Greatest Rivalry." *Team USA* (30 June 2016). https://www.teamusa.org/News/2016/June/30/Phelps-Lochte-Going-At-Each-Other-Again-In-Their-Sports-Greatest-Rivalry.

———. "For Olympic Swimmer Anthony Ervin, Voyage of Self-Discovery is a Long, Strange Trip." *Team USA* (1 August 2016). https://www.teamusa.org/News/2016/August/01/For-Olympic-Swimmer-Anthony-Ervin-Voyage-Of-Self-Discovery-Is-A-Long-Strange-Trip.

———. "Chasing Katie Ledecky." *ESPNW* (4 August 2016). http://www.espn .com/espn/feature/story/_/page/espnw-ledecky160804/what-makes-olympic-swimmer-katie-ledecky-remarkable.

Heusner, William. "Swimming Officiating – Science or Art?" *Journal of Health, Physical Education, Recreation* (May–June 1961). https://shapeamerica.tandfonline .com/doi/abs/10.1080/00221473.1961.10611510?needAccess=true&journalC ode=ujrd18#.XmhMJqhKjZs.

"Ian Thorpe Fails to Qualify for London 2012 at Trials." *BBC Sport* (18 March 2012). https://www.bbc.com/sport/swimming/17419436.

Isaacson, Melissa. "The Final Bows: Doc and the Shoe Say So Long." *Chicago Tribune* (4 February 1990). https://www.chicagotribune.com/news/ct-xpm-19 90-02-04-9001100842-story.html.

"It's Your Race, Ian, at $325 a Metre." *Sydney Morning Herald* (27 April 2004). https://www.smh.com.au/sport/its-your-race-ian-at-325-a-metre-20040427 -gditd9.html.

Jacobs, Jeff. "Hall and Popov: Below the Surface." *Hartford Courant* (19 July 1996). https://www.courant.com/news/connecticut/hc-xpm-1996-07-19-960719 0435-story.html.

Johnson, Holly. "Matt Biondi's Next Challenge: Teaching." *The Chronicle Magazine* (Summer 2000). https://www.lclark.edu/live/news/21077-matt-b iondis-next-challenge-teaching.

Kahn, E.J. "Harmony and Progress." *New Yorker* (12 December 1988). https://ww w.newyorker.com/magazine/1988/12/19/harmony-and-progress.

Kevles, Daniel. "Coach Kiphuth Biography." *Yale University Athletics* (2019). https ://yalebulldogs.com/sports/2019/7/19/coach-kiphuth-biography.aspx?id=887.

Kepner, Tyler. "Sacrifice of Another Lifts Thorpe to Gold." *New York Times* (15 August 2004). https://www.nytimes.com/2004/08/15/sports/olympics/sacr ifice-of-another-lifts-thorpe-to-gold.html.

Kirshenbaum, Jerry. "Mexico to Munich: Mark Spitz and the Quest for Gold." *Sports Illustrated* (4 September 1972). https://vault.si.com/vault/1972/09/04/me xico-to-munich-mark-spitz-and-the-quest-for-gold.

———. "The Golden Days of Mark the Shark." *Sports Illustrated* (11 September 1972). https://vault.si.com/vault/1972/09/11/the-golden-days-of-mark-the-shark.

———. "A Big Splash by the Mighty Madchen." *Sports Illustrated* (17 September 1973). https://vault.si.com/vault/1973/09/17/a-big-splash-by-the-mighty-mdchen.

———. "A Good Naber Gets Gunned Down." *Sports Illustrated* (5 April 1976). https://vault.si.com/vault/1976/04/05/a-good-naber-gets-gunned-down.

———. "They're Pooling Their Talent." *Sports Illustrated* (10 July 1978). https:// vault.si.com/vault/1978/07/10/theyre-pooling-their-talent-in-the-past-five-ye ars-members-of-californias-mission-viejo-swim-club-have-won-48-national-tit les-their-mission-nuevo-for-the-next-two-years-is-moscow.

———. "The Golden Moment." *Sports Illustrated* (20 August 1979). https://vault.s i.com/vault/1979/08/20/the-golden-moment-swimmer-rick-demont-left-with -bronze-medalist-steve-genter-exulted-after-winning-at-the-72-olympics-but-his-medal-was-taken-away-and-his-life-was-never-the-same.

Kiss, Laszlo. "Krisztina Egerszegi: The Development of a World Champion Backstroker." American Swimming Magazine, June 2008, 32–34.

Knapp, Gwen. "Olympic Champion Popov Jumps Back Into Pool." *San Francisco Examiner* (29 June 1997). https://www.sfgate.com/sports/article/Olympic-champion-Popov-jumps-back-into-pool-3111743.php.

Layden, Tim. "After Rehabilitation, the Best of Michael Phelps May Lie Ahead." *Sports Illustrated* (9 November 2015). https://www.si.com/olympics/2015/11/09/michael-phelps-rehabilitation-rio-2016.

"Lezak Runs Down French to Win Relay Gold for U.S." *ESPN* (10 August 2008). https://www.espn.com/olympics/summer08/swimming/news/story?id=3528865.

Linden, Julian. "Egerszegi Joins Exclusive Swim Club." *United Press International* (25 July 1996). https://www.upi.com/Archives/1996/07/25/Egerszegi-joins-exclusive-swim-club/3055838267200/.

Little, Becky. "The First Woman to Swim the English Channel Beat the Men's Record by Two Hours." *History* (3 August 2018). https://www.history.com/news/gertrude-ederle-first-woman-swim-english-channel.

Litsky, Frank. "Sieben Upsets Gross." *New York Times* (4 August 1984). https://www.nytimes.com/1984/08/04/sports/swimming-sieben-upsets-gross.html.

———. "Gold Medal Consoles Biondi." *New York Times* (22 September 1988). https://www.nytimes.com/1988/09/22/sports/the-seoul-olympics-swimming-gold-medal-consoles-biondi.html.

———. "New Accusations Aimed at Chinese Swimmers." *New York Times* (9 January 1998). https://www.nytimes.com/1998/01/09/sports/swimming-new-accusations-aimed-at-chinese-swimmers.html.

———. "George Haines, Coach of Elite Swimmers, Dies at 82." *New York Times* (3 May 2006). https://www.nytimes.com/2006/05/03/sports/othersports/03haines.html.

———. "Peter Daland, Who Coaches Swimming Champions, Is Dead at 93." *New York Times* (20 October 2014). https://www.nytimes.com/2014/10/21/sports/peter-daland-coached-swim-champions-is-dead-at-93.html.

———. "Forbes Carlile, Innovative Coach Who Studied Science of Swimming, Dies at 95." *New York Times* (2 August 2016). https://www.nytimes.com/2016/08/03/sports/olympics/forbes-carlile-olympic-swimming-coach-for-australia-dies-at-95.html.

"Lochte Fires Up Phelps with World Title and Record in Shanghai." *CNN* (28 July 2011). http://edition.cnn.com/2011/SPORT/07/28/swimming.phelps.lochte.china/index.html.

Lohn, John. "Hansen, Kitajima Trade Verbal Rat Tails." *Delaware County Daily Times* (7 July 2008). https://www.delcotimes.com/news/hansen-kitajima-trade-verbal-rat-tails/article_d840855f-987a-5e46-9617-18c376fc37bf.html.

———. "Bronze Finish Makes Hansen's Comeback Even Sweeter." *Delaware County Daily Times* (30 July 2012). http://www.delcotimes.com/articles/2012/07/30/sports/doc50160781e44c9923657945.txt.

———. *The Most Memorable Moments in Olympic Swimming.* Lanham, Md.: Rowman & Littlefield, 2014.

———. "Sixteen Years Later, Anthony Ervin Writes Another Golden Chapter in 50 Freestyle." *SwimVortex* (12 August 2016). http://www.swimvortex.com /sixteen-years-later-anthony-ervin-writes-another-golden-chapter-in-50-free style/.

———. *The 100 Greatest Swimmers in History.* Lanham, Md.: Rowman & Littlefield, 2018.

———. "They Were Young; They Were Talented; They Defined an Era." *Swimming World Magazine* (19 November 2019). https://www.swimmingworld magazine.com/news/the-sydney-six-they-were-young-they-were-talented-they -defined-an-era/.

Longman, Jere. "Swimmer, 28, Finds Niche in New Guard." *New York Times* (13 March 1996). https://www.nytimes.com/1996/03/13/sports/swimming-swim mer-28-finds-niche-in-new-guard.html.

———. "Popov Defeats Hall in 100 By Eyelash." *New York Times* (23 July 1996). https://archive.nytimes.com/www.nytimes.com/specials/olympics/0723/oly -swm-popov-hall.html.

———. "After Seven Years Off, Swimmer Returns at 33." *New York Times* (8 August 2000). https://www.nytimes.com/2000/08/08/sports/olympics-the- road-to-sydney-after-7-years-off-swimmer-returns-at-33.html.

———. "Big Feet, Bigger Splash for Australia." *New York Times* (11 September 2000). https://www.nytimes.com/2000/09/11/sports/2000-sydney-games-big -feet-bigger-splash-for-australian.html.

———. "Australia Aglow as Young Star Gets Two Golds." *New York Times* (17 September 2000). https://www.nytimes.com/2000/09/17/sports/sydney-2000 -swimming-australia-aglow-as-young-star-gets-two-golds.html.

Lord, Craig. "Michelle Smith: Busted!" *Swimming World Magazine* (28 April 1998). https://www.swimmingworldmagazine.com/news/michelle-smith-busted/.

———. "Compensation But No Closure for GDR Doping Victims." *Swim News* (14 December 2006). http://swimnews.com/News/view/4961.

———. "Phelps Takes a Peek at the Pantheon." *Swim News* (27 March 2007). http://www.swimnews.com/News/view/5180.

———. "Schubert: This Was the Greatest Performance Ever." *Swim News* (1 April 2007). http://www.swimnews.com/News/view/5235.

———. "Don Says It Ain't So, But Fans the Flame of Debate." *Swim News* (16 October 2007). http://www.swimnews.com/News/view/5641.

———. "Cavic Pays Price; Oh That Others Had Too." *Swim News* (21 March 2008). http://www.swimnews.com/News/view/5930.

———. "Kornelia Ender Turns 50." *Swim News* (26 October 2008). http://swim-news.com/News/view/6496.

———. "The Divisive Nature of Suit Wars." *Swim News* (21 July 2009). http:// www.swimnews.com/News/view/7056.

———. "World Record Bull Run: The List in Full." *Swim News* (20 December 2009). http://www.swimnews.com/News/view/6723.

———. "Sporting Crime of the Century – 20 Years on." *Swim News* (1 October 2010). http://www.swimnews.com/news/view/8102.

————. "A Waking Nightmare for Women's Sport." *State of Swimming* (5 June 2019). http://www.stateofswimming.com/a-waking-nightmare-for-womens -sport/.

————. "GDR 30 Years On: The Day in 1989 the Berlin Wall Came Tumbling Down on Doping Regime." *Swimming World Magazine* (9 November 2019). https://www.swimmingworldmagazine.com/news/gdr-30-years-on-the-day -in-1989-the-berlin-wall-came-tumbling-down-on-doping-regime/.

————. "Matt Biondi, Living Legend of Olympic Swimming, Returns as Director of Swimmers' Alliance." *Swimming World Magazine* (22 November 2019). https:/ /www.swimmingworldmagazine.com/news/matt-biondi-living-legend-of-oly mpic-swimming-returns-as-director-of-the-swimmers-alliance/.

————. "Ian Thorpe, Part 3: Thorpedo, Thorpey, The Pele of the Pool & Boy with the World at His Flippers for Feet." *Swimming World Magazine* (15 May 2020). https://www.swimmingworldmagazine.com/news/ian-thorpe-thorpedo -thorpey-the-pele-of-the-pool-the-boy-with-the-world-at-his-flippers-for-feet- wr-video/.

————. "The Athlete Voice: Alliance Not Union Aims to Take ISL Model to Multi-Sports Games of Magic." *Swimming World Magazine* (25 January 2020). https://www.swimmingworldmagazine.com/news/2020s-vision-the-athlete -voice-alliance-not-union-aims-to-take-isl-model-to-multi-sports-games-of -magic/.

————. "Sun Yang Says He Will Definitely Appeal 8-Year Ban at Swiss Federal Court." *Swimming World Magazine* (28 February 2020). https://www.swimming worldmagazine.com/news/sun-yang-says-he-will-definitely-appeal-8-year-ban -at-swiss-federal-court/.

————. "Sun Yang Lawyer Accuses WADA & CAS of Evil Lies; Will Fight to Race At Tokyo 2020 & Sue Testing Agent." *Swimming World Magazine* (29 February 2020). https://www.swimmingworldmagazine.com/news/sun-yang -lawyer-accuses-wada-will-fight-to-race-at-tokyo-2020-sue-testing-agent/.

Lutton, Phil. "Mack Horton Tears Into Sun Yang at Rio Olympics." *Sydney Morning Herald* (7 August 2016). https://www.smh.com.au/sport/i-dont-have -time-or-respect-for-drug-cheats-mack-horton-tears-into-sun-yang-20160807 -gqmptz.html.

Lydon, Susan. "A Second Look...At Mark Spitz." *New York Times* (11 March 1973). https://www.nytimes.com/1973/03/11/archives/all-that-gold-waiting -to-glitter-a-second-look-at-mark-spitz-mark.html.

"Mack Horton Lauded by Fell Swimmers After Protesting Sun Yang's Win." *The Guardian* (21 July 2019). https://www.theguardian.com/sport/2019/jul/22 /mack-horton-accused-of-disrespecting-china-after-protesting-sun-yangs-win.

Martinelli, Michelle. "Olympic Legend Debbie Meyer on Katie Ledecky's Quest to Join Her Exclusive Freestyle Club." *Vice* (12 August 2016). https://www.vic e.com/en_us/article/53x9p5/olympic-legend-debbie-meyer-on-katie-ledeckys -quest-to-join-her-exclusive-freestyle-club.

————. "Cullen Jones on Simone Manuel and the Future of African-Americans in Swimming." *Vice* (17 August 2016). https://www.vice.com/en_us/article/

gvayx4/cullen-jones-on-simone-manuel-and-the-future-of-african-americans
-in-swimming.

McCallum, Jack. "Unflagging." *Sports Illustrated* (14 August 2000). https://ww
w.si.com/vault/2000/08/14/286566/unflagging-five-time-gold-medalist-jenny
-thompson-27-plans-to-undress-her-younger-rivals-in-sydney-and-become-the
-most-decorated-us-woman-olympian-ever.

McMullen, Paul. "Growth of Bowman on a Par with Star's." *Baltimore Sun* (20
August 2003). https://www.baltimoresun.com/bal-sp.bowman20aug20-story
.html.

McMullen, Paul. "A Reluctant Prodigy." *Baltimore Sun* (8 August 2004). https://
www.baltimoresun.com/sports/olympics/bal-te.phelps08aug08-story.html.

"Michael Phelps Blows Away Competition in 200-Meter I.M. for 22nd Gold
Medal." *CBS News* (11 August 2016). https://www.cbsnews.com/news/michae
l-phelps-blows-away-competitors-in-200-meter-i-m-for-22nd-gold-medal/.

Mitchell, Kevin. "Dismantling of an Irish Legend." *The Age* (17 April 2004). https:/
/www.theage.com.au/sport/dismantling-of-an-irish-legend-20040417-gdxoyv
.html.

Montville, Leigh. "Australia's 17-Year-Old Hero, Ian Thorpe, Was the Hit of a
Record-Smashing Pool Party in Sydney, Until Others, Including a Bunch of
Americans, Began Horning in on the Fun." *Sports Illustrated* (25 September 2000).
https://www.si.com/vault/2000/09/25/288505/fast-lanes-australias-17-year-ol
d-hero-ian-thorpe-was-the-hit-of-a-record-smashing-pool-party-in-sydney-unt
il-others-including-a-bunch-of-americans-began-horning-in-on-the.fun.

Morgan, Mark. "When World Records Improved 1.8% in 22 Months." *Swim News*
(24 February 2010). http://www.swimnews.com/News/view/7469.

Morrissey, Rick. "Tarnished Golden Girl." *Chicago Tribune* (6 August 2000). https:/
/www.chicagotribune.com/news/ct-xpm-2000-08-06-0008060427-story.html.

———. "Pool Rivals Happy to be Teammates." *Chicago Tribune* (11 August
2000). https://www.chicagotribune.com/news/ct-xpm-2000-08-11-000811
0285-story.html.

Mortimer, Gavin. "Gertrude Ederle: The First Woman to Swim the English
Channel). *History Extra* (4 March 2020). https://www.historyextra.com/period
/20th-century/gertrude-ederle-first-woman-swim-swam-english-channel-ma
tthew-webb-american/.

Munoz, Theresa. "USC's Daland Retires as Coach at 71." *Los Angeles Times* (22
April 1992). https://www.latimes.com/archives/la-xpm-1992-04-22-sp-471-st
ory.html.

Neff, Craig. "Swim Six, Win Six." *Sports Illustrated* (3 October 1988). https://va
ult.si.com/vault/1988/10/03/swimming-swim-six-win-six-kristin-otto-of-east-
germany-got-gold-after-gold-after.

Newsweek Staff. "Swimming Wars." *Newsweek* (7 August 2000). https://www
.newsweek.com/swimming-wars-158961.

O'Connell, Chris. "How Eddie Reese Turned Texas Men's Swimming and
Diving Into the Best Program in the Nation." *The Alcalde* (1 January 2018). https
://medium.com/the-alcalde/stroke-of-genius-176cdcae50ee.

"Once Again, It's Thompson vs. Torres." *ESPN* (25 September 2000). https://ww
w.espn.com/oly/summer00/swimming/s/2000/0921/765132.html.

Park, Alice. "Rivalries." *Time* (19 July 2012). https://olympics.time.com/2012/07
/19/ryan-lochte-michael-phelps-rivalry/.

Pearson, Alexander. "Systematic Doping of Chinese Athletes in Olympic Games
Revealed by Former Doctor." *DW News* (21 October 2017). https://www.dw.
com/en/systematic-doping-of-chinese-athletes-in-olympic-games-revealed-by-f
ormer-doctor/a-41065227.

Pentony, Luke. "Mack Horton Wins Australia's First Swimming Medal, Winning
400-Metres Freestyle." *ABC* (6 August 2016). https://www.abc.net.au/news/20
16-08-07/rio-2016-mack-horton-wins-400m-freestyle-gold/7698338.

Peters, Keith. "There's Just No Quit in Jenny Thompson." *Palo Alto Online* (3
July 1996). https://www.paloaltoonline.com/weekly/morgue/sports/1996_Jul
_3.THOMPSON.html.

"Phelps Won't Break Spitz's Gold Record: Thorpe." *China Daily* (29 January
2008). http://www.chinadaily.com.cn/olympics/2008-01/29/content_642
7997.htm.

Phinizy, Coles. "The Best in Any Tank, By George." *Sports Illustrated* (22 July
1968). https://vault.si.com/vault/1968/07/22/the-best-in-any-tank-by-george.

Phinizy, Coles. "High Priest of the High Rev." *Sports Illustrated* (17 February 1975).
https://vault.si.com/vault/1975/02/17/high-priest-of-the-high-rev.

Plaschke, Bill. "Thrills and Chills." *Los Angeles Times* (22 September 2000). https:/
/www.latimes.com/archives/la-xpm-2000-sep-22-ss-25071-story.html.

Pleasants, Julian. "Interview with Tracy Caulkins." *University of Florida George A. Smathers
Libraries* (19 September 1997). https://ufdc.ufl.edu/UF00006251/00001/1x.

Poirier-Leroy, Olivier. "Jon Sieben and the Power of Rocking the Underdog
Mindset." *Swim Swam* (4 February 2020). https://swimswam.com/jon-sieben
-underdog/.

Potts, Andrew. "How Gold Coast Coach Laurie Lawrence Helped Duncan
Armstrong Win at Seoul 1988." *Gold Coast Bulletin* (7 August 2016). https:/
/www.goldcoastbulletin.com.au/flashback-how-gold-coast-coach-laurie-lawre
nce-helped-duncan-armstrong-win-at-seoul-1988/news-story/0412131125cb5
a2768a9ac553e008977.

Pretot, Julien. "New Bodysuits Trigger Controversy in France." *Reuters* (25 April
2009). https://www.reuters.com/article/us-swimming-suits/new-bodysuits-t
rigger-controversy-in-france-idUSTRE53O23U20090425.

Rasmussen, Frederick. "From the Pool to Hollywood Stardom." *Baltimore Sun* (17
August 2008). https://www.baltimoresun.com/news/bs-xpm-2008-08-17-080
8160072-story.html.

Reed, William. "Swimming Isn't Everything, Winning Is." *Sports Illustrated* (9
March 1970). https://vault.si.com/vault/1970/03/09/swimming-isnt-everythi
ng-winning-is.

Reid, Scott. "This Time, Evans Takes Time to Smell the Roses." *Orange County
Register* (9 June 2012). https://www.ocregister.com/2012/06/09/this-time-ev
ans-takes-time-to-smell-the-roses/.

Reid, Scott. "Mark Schubert is a Legend for Making U.S. Swimmers Champions, But Did He Fail When They Need Him Most." *Orange County Register* (20 December 2018). https://www.ocregister.com/2018/06/11/mark-schubert-is-a-legend-for-making-us-swimmers-champions-but-did-he-fail-when-they-needed-him-most/.

Rieder, David. "Simone Manuel Collecting Medals and Making a Difference." *Swimming World Magazine* (14 February 2020). https://www.swimming worldmagazine.com/news/simone-manuel-collecting-medals-and-making-a-difference/.

Robb, Sharon. "New Mission: Schubert Attempts to Bring Success From Viejo to Bay Sharks." *Sun-Sentinel* (3 December 1985). https://www.sun-sentinel.com/news/fl-xpm-1985-12-03-8502240779-story.html.

———. "Biondi Stepping in as the Next Spitz." *Sun Sentinel* (26 July 1987). https://www.sun-sentinel.com/news/fl-xpm-1987-07-26-8703020563-story.html.

———. "Biondi, Jager Battle, But for Second and Third." *Sun-Sentinel* (31 July 1992). https://www.sun-sentinel.com/news/fl-xpm-1992-07-31-9202220619-story.html.

Rosen, Karen. "The Greatest Split Ever: Jason Lezak Recalls His Iconix 4x100 Free Leg 10 Years Later." *Team USA* (6 March 2018). https://www.teamusa.org/News/2018/March/06/The-Greatest-Split-Ever-Jason-Lezak-Recalls-His-Iconic-4x100-Free-Leg-10-Years-Later.

Rosen, Mikael. "Barred From the 1976 Olympics, These Swimmers Still Beat Olympic Records." *Literary Hub* (25 July 2019). https://lithub.com/barred-from-the-1976-olympics-these-swimmers-still-beat-olympic-records/.

Rosewater, Amy. "For Tracy Caulkins, 1984 Games Were Well Worth the Wait." *Team USA* (29 July 2014). https://www.teamusa.org/News/2014/July/29/For-Tracy-Caulkins-LA-Games-In-1984-Were-Well-Worth-The-Wait.

Ross, Andy. "World Championships Throwback: When Michael Phelps Passed Ian Thorpe as the Greatest Swimmer of All-Time in 2007." *Swimming World Magazine* (24 May 2019). https://www.swimmingworldmagazine.com/news/world-championships-throwback-when-michael-phelps-passed-ian-thorpe-as-the-greatest-swimmer-of-all-time-in-2007/.

Rutemiller, Brent. "Shirley Babashoff Breaks 30-Year Silence on East Germany's Systematic Doping of Olympians." *Swimming World Magazine* (5 February 2016). https://www.swimmingworldmagazine.com/news/exclusive-shirley-babashoff-breaks-30-year-silence-on-east-germanys-systematic-doping-of-olympians/.

———. "Rare Audio Reliving USA Women's 400 Free Relay Last Gold Victory Over East Germans." *Swimming World Magazine* (16 June 2016). https://www.swimmingworldmagazine.com/news/1976-us400-free-relay-last-gold-victory-over-eaa-womens-st-germans/.

Schardy, Arlie. "13 Records in a Watery Grave." *Sports Illustrated* (11 April 1960). https://vault.si.com/vault/1960/04/11/13-records-in-a-watery-grave.

"Serbs Fail in Protest Over Phelps Win." *Reuters* (15 August 2008). https://www.reuters.com/article/us-olympics-swimming-butterfly-protest/serbs-fail-in-protest-over-phelps-win-idUSSP21997420080816.

Severo, Richard. "Gertrude Ederle, the First Woman to Swim Across the English Channel, Dies at 98." *New York Times* (1 December 2003). https://www.nyt imes.com/2003/12/01/sports/gertrude-ederle-the-first-woman-to-swim-across -the-english-channel-dies-at-98.html.

Sheinin, Dave. "Birth of a Legend." *Washington Post* (2 August 2016). https://ww w.washingtonpost.com/sf/sports/wp/2016/08/02/birth-of-a-legend/?utm_te rm=.5e528a45217f.

Sherman, Joel. "Damn the Thorpedo! Ian Sinks: Dutchman Upsets Aussie in the 200-Meter Freestyle." *New York Post* (19 September 2000). https://nypost.com /2000/09/19/damn-the-thorpedo-ian-sinks-dutchman-upsets-aussie-in-the-20 0-meter-freestyle/.

Shinn, Peggy. "Simone Manuel is Making a Splash – With Spreading a Message of Diversity and Teaching Kids to Swim." *Team USA* (5 June 2019). https://www .teamusa.org/News/2019/June/05/Simone-Manuel-Is-Making-A-Splash-with-Spreading-A-Message-Of-Diversity-And-Teaching-Kids-To-Swim.

Silverman, Audra. "Speedo Unveils Revolutionary Elite Speed Suit: The LZR Racer." *Business Wire* (12 February 2008). https://www.businesswire.com/n ews/home/20080212006580/en/SPEEDO-Unveils-Revolutionary-Elite-Speed -Suit-LZR.

Slater, Jim. "Matt Biondi Chased a Legend at the Seoul Games." *United Press International* (25 September 1988). https://www.upi.com/Archives/1988/09 /25/Matt-Biondi-chased-a-legend-at-the-Seoul-Games/6613591163200/.

Smith, Gary. "The Man with the Golden Feet." *Sports Illustrated* (22 November 1999). https://www.si.com/vault/1999/11/22/8112487/the-man-with-the -golden-feet-australian-swimming-sensation-ian-thorpewho-figures-to-be-a-ho usehold-name-everywhere-by-the-end-of-the-2000-olympicsowes-his-worldr ecord-speed-partly-to-his-size17-dogs-but-even-more-to-the-inspira.

Sports Illustrated Staff. "Outsider in the Mainstream." *Sports Illustrated* (24 March 1975). https://vault.si.com/vault/1975/03/24/outsider-in-the-mainstream.

Stathoplos, Demmie. "She Pooled Her Talents." *Sports Illustrated* (20 April 1981). https://vault.si.com/vault/1981/04/20/she-pooled-her-talents-the-short-cour se-championships-were-a-showcase-for-versatile-tracy-caulkins.

———. "Afloat, He's a Quick Study." *Sports Illustrated* (23 June 1986). https://va ult.si.com/vault/1986/06/23/afloat-hes-a-quick-study.

Swift, E.M. "Tracy Caulkins: 'I Could Be Over the Hill in 1984." *Sports Illustrated* (21 July 1980). https://vault.si.com/vault/1980/07/21/tracy-caulkins-i-could -be-over-the-hill-in-1984.

"Swim Officials withhold Images of Finish." *New York Times* (16 August 2008). https://www.nytimes.com/2008/08/17/sports/olympics/17fina.html.

"Swimmer Still Mistrusted: Smith Not Home When Drug Testers Comes; Another Miss Could Lead to a Suspension." *Associated Press* (18 February 1997). https:// www.spokesman.com/stories/1997/feb/18/swimmer-still-mistrusted-smith-not -home-when-drug/.

Talese, Gay. "Memories Are Still Golden for Gertrude Ederle." *New York Times* (6 August 1958). https://timesmachine.nytimes.com/timesmachine/1958/08/0 6/79446161.pdf?pdf_redirect=true&ip=0.

Texas Sports Information. "Eddie Reese." *University of Texas* (30 March 2020). https://texassports.com/sports/mens-swimming-and-diving/roster/coaches/eddie-reese/1720.

Thomazeau, Francois. "I'm Favorite and We'll Smash U.S.: Bernard." *Reuters* (7 August 2008). https://www.reuters.com/article/us-olympics-swimming-bernard/im-favorite-and-well-smash-u-s-bernard-idUSSP28868620080807.

"Thorpedo Announces Retirement." *The Guardian* (21 November 2006). https://www.theguardian.com/sport/2006/nov/21/australia.swimming.

"Two Former East German Swimmers Accuse Otto of Doping at '88 Olympics." *Winnipeg Free Press* (1 June 2007). https://www.winnipegfreepress.com/historic/32258029.html.

Van Valkenburg, Kevin. "Phelps on Staying with His Swimsuit: What Handicap?" *Baltimore Sun* (7 July 2009). https://www.baltimoresun.com/sports/bal-sp.phelps07jul07-story.html.

Walker, Childs. "A Grown-Up Michael Phelps Looks Back on the Beijing Olympics, 10 Years Later." *Baltimore Sun* (10 August 2018). https://www.baltimoresun.com/sports/olympics/bs-sp-michael-phelps-beijing-anniversary-0812-htmlstory.html.

Warner, Chuck. "How World War II Impacted Yale Great Bob Kiphuth." *Swimming World Magazine* (27 May 2019). https://www.swimmingworldmagazine.com/news/memorial-day-rewind-how-world-war-ii-impacted-yale-great-bob-kiphuth/.

Watson, Stephanie. "Gary Hall's Toughest Competitor: Diabetes." *WebMD Magazine* (15 April 2012). https://www.webmd.com/diabetes/features/gary-hall-toughest-competitor-diabetes#1.

"What Chinese Doping Scandal? Official Says." *Deseret News* (17 December 1994). https://www.deseret.com/1994/12/17/19148420/what-chinese-doping-scandal-official-says.

"When Tarzan Struck Gold at the Games: The Legend of Johnny Weissmuller." *International Olympic Committee* (20 July 2019). https://www.olympic.org/news/when-tarzan-struck-gold-at-the-games-the-legend-of-johnny-weissmuller.

Whitten, Phillip. "Why Are People Saying All Those Nasty Things About a Nice Irish Girl Like Michelle Smith?" *Swimming World Magazine* (January 1997).

———. "USOC Set to Clear '72 Olympian, Rick DeMont." *Swimming World Magazine* (31 January 2001). https://www.swimmingworldmagazine.com/news/usoc-set-to-clear-72-olympian-rick-demont/.

Wigo, Bruce. "Black Swimming History: Celebrating Enith Brigitha." *Swimming World Magazine* (1 February 2018). https://www.swimmingworldmagazine.com/news/ishof-celebrates-black-swimming-history-month/.

Wilstein, Steve. "Janet Evans Takes Last Laps." *Washington Post* (26 July 1996). https://www.washingtonpost.com/wp-srv/sports/olympics/daily/swimming/july/31/byejanet.htm.

Woods, David. "Doc's Boys: The Story of Dominant U.S. Swim Team From 1976." *Indianapolis Star* (31 July 2016). https://www.indystar.com/story/sports/2016/07/31/docs-boys-story-dominant-us-swim-team-1976/87614856/.

Wright, Alfred. "Yale Churns on at the Waterworks." *Sports Illustrated* (23 January 1956). https://vault.si.com/vault/1956/01/23/yale-churns-on-at-the-water works.

Zaccardi, Nick. "With 78 Days Till London, Phelps-Lochte Rivalry is Just Heating Up." *Sports Illustrated* (10 May 2012). https://www.si.com/more-sports/2012 /05/11/michael-phelps-ryan-lochte-charlotte.

———. "Five Olympic Questions with Pieter van den Hoogenband." *NBC Sports* (26 June 2015). https://olympics.nbcsports.com/2015/06/26/pieter-van-den -hoogenband-swimming-olympics-michael-phelps/.

———. "Shane Gould Sees a Bit of Herself in Katie Ledecky." *NBC Sports* (21 March 2016). https://olympics.nbcsports.com/2016/03/21/shane-gould-katie- ledecky-swimming-olympics/.

———. "Jason Lezak's Memories of Beijing Olympic Relay." *NBC Sports* (9 August 2018). https://olympics.nbcsports.com/2018/08/09/jason-lezak-beijing -olympic-relay-swimming/.

———. "Katie Ledecky's Competition is Near, Far for Best U.S. Female Swimmer Ever." *NBC Sports* (21 December 2018). https://olympics.nbcsports.com/2018 /12/21/tracy-caulkins-katie-ledecky-swimming/.

WEBSITES

www.fina.org: The official website of the Federation Internationale de Natation, the international governing body for the five aquatic sports: swimming, diving, open-water swimming, water polo, and synchronized swimming.

www.ishof.org: The official website of the International Swimming Hall of Fame. Includes biographies of individuals inducted into the Hall of Fame.

www.olympic.org: The official website of the International Olympic Committee. The website includes lists of all Olympic medal winners, biographical information on numerous athletes, and details of the Olympic movement.

www.swimming.org.au: The official website of Swimming Australia, the governing body of the sport in that country. The website includes archived results of national and international competition and biographical information of Australian athletes.

www.swimmingworldmagazine.com: Website of *Swimming World Magazine*. The website includes archived articles from magazine issues from 1960 to the present.

www.usaswimming.org: The official website of USA Swimming, the governing body of the sport in that country. The website includes archived results of national and international competition and biographical information of U.S. athletes.

INDEX

ABOUT THE AUTHOR

John Lohn is associate editor-in-chief of *Swimming World Magazine* and swimmingworldmagazine.com. He has covered the sport of swimming at the international level for two decades, including stints as Swimming World's Senior Writer and as the American correspondent for SwimVortex, a European-based website. During his career, Lohn has covered the 2008, 2012, and 2016 Olympics Games, during which time he chronicled the record-breaking accomplishments of Michael Phelps. He has covered every United States Olympic Trials since 2000 and has regularly provided coverage of other major competitions, including the World Championships, Pan Pacific Championships, United States Nationals, and NCAA Championships. Through the years, he has been a guest analyst on several networks, including ESPN and the BBC, and has been cited by numerous national and international newspapers, magazines, and websites, including *USA Today*, CNN, and *The Washington Post*, along with outlets in Japan, Australia, China, Brazil, and Europe. He previously authored *The Historical Dictionary of Competitive Swimming*, *The Most Memorable Moments in Olympic Swimming*, and *The 100 Greatest Swimmers in History*, also published by Rowman & Littlefield. He also contributed multiple chapters to *Swimmers: Courage and Triumph*. A Pennsylvania native and graduate of La Salle University, Lohn resides in New Jersey with his wife, Dana, and daughters, twins Taylor and Tiernan, and Tenley. He currently works as a media specialist and enjoys vacationing and fitness training.